E.C.G.
MYSTERY SOLVED

by

Pulak Sahay

MB BS (Honours), MD, MRCP
Consultant Physician
Pontefract General Infirmary
Pontefract, UK

PUBLISHING INITIATIVES
BOOKS

Doral House • 2(b) Manor Road • Beckenham
Kent • BR3 5LE

A NOTE ABOUT THE AUTHOR

Pulak Sahay graduated with honours in 1978 and came to the UK soon after doing his MD in India. He did his entire postgraduate training in the UK where, after getting his membership, he worked with a cardiologist and his fascination for electrocardiography was rekindled. The present book is the result of many years of hard work. Dr Sahay is now a Consultant Physician at Pontefract General Infirmary in Yorkshire.

DEDICATION

To my mother
Professor (Dr) Usha Sahay
who perceived my love for ECGs and spurred me on
to write a book on the subject.

First published 1996

ISBN
1 873839 23 5

Printed and bound by Biddles of Guildford and King's Lynn.

Further copies of *ECG Mystery Solved* may be obtained from Pi books, a division of Publishing Initiatives (Europe) Ltd, This publication reflects the view and experience of the author and not necessarily those of Publishing Initiatives (Europe) Ltd.

FOREWORD

Electrocardiography is one of the mystical areas of cardiology. None of us fully understand the various factors and forces which are expressed on the body surface as tiny electrical signals, and which are filtered and amplified to become a 12-lead ECG. From primitive beginnings in the not too distant past, modern day technology has provided us with a robust clinical tool that has proved invaluable and indispensable for the diagnosis and management of almost every cardiac condition. Yet few of us are confident of our interpretative abilities. As knowledge expands, new approaches to teaching electrocardiography become necessary. As technology progresses, better and better examples are available for publication. Dr Pulak Sahay offers us a distillation of the important electrocardiographic patterns. The text is hard hitting and to the point. The examples are classics in their own right. There is enough here to satisfy basic needs, enough to use as a platform for teaching and more than enough to encourage the interested to take matters a little further and to get to grips with difficult concepts. Dr Pulak Sahay has produced an ECG primer to be proud of. I hope that you enjoy it as much as I did.

Professor R W F Campbell

Head of Department, Academic Unit of Cardiology

Freeman Hospital, Newcastle upon Tyne.

CONTENTS

GLOSSARY

AF	atrial fibrillation
AIVR	accelerated idioventricular rhythm
APB	atrial premature beats
AVNRT	AV nodal re-entrant tachycardia
BBB	bundle branch block
Cor P	cor pulmonale
ECG	electrocardiogram
EMD	Electromechanical dissociation
ECM	external cardiac massage
HOCM	hypertrophic obstructive cardiomyopathy
LAD	left axis deviation
LAH	left anterior hemiblock
LGL	Lown-Ganong-Levine syndrome
LPH	left posterior hemiblock
LVH	left ventricular hypertrophy
MI	myocardial infarction
PSVT	paroxysmal supraventricular tachycardia
RAD	right axis deviation
RVH	right ventricular hypertrophy
SA	sinoatrial
SR	sinus rhythm
SSS	sick sinus syndrome
VF	ventricular fibrillation
VT	ventricular tachycardia
WPW	Wolff-Parkinson-White syndrome

PREFACE

There are very many books devoted to ECGs, but all have their limitations. This book is different. It is not meant for the academic gymnast. It has been written by a general physician for general physicians.

It is a practical book, which assumes a reasonable amount of background knowledge and is aimed at senior house officers and registrars, although house officers on take and general practitioners in their surgeries will also derive benefit from it. The text is telegrammatic, with ECG figures representative of various conditions and showing a variety of features. The layout is designed to ensure clarity, with the figures and explanatory text on facing pages.

The book is divided into four sections. The first describes various wave forms; the second covers, with examples, numerous common and difficult conditions; the third is on rhythm analysis; and the final section is a management guide for arrhythmias. This format should be of great value to doctors preparing for their membership examinations. The book has been deliberately written in a dogmatic style so that junior doctors can get clear guidelines on how to solve the ECG puzzle before proceeding to treat the patient.

Grateful thanks are due to Professor RWF Campbell who took the trouble of painstakingly going through the whole manuscript and each and every ECG, and gave his comments and made extremely helpful suggestions. He has been a source of great encouragement.

I would also like to thank my wife Geeta and my children Medhya, Parnika and Shashwat, who consciously kept away from my study while continuing to offer unswerving support. They have been towers of strength.

Finally, I would be failing in my duty if I did not thank the editorial staff at Publishing Initiatives, without whose enthusiasm this book would not have seen the light of day.

Pulak Sahay
March 1996

Section I

ANALYSIS OF THE ECG

As soon as you are presented with an ECG, look at it in a systematic fashion. The various components to look at are summarised below. These will be discussed one at a time.

RATE

Count the number of large squares between two consecutive R waves.

Divide 300 by the interval, e.g. 300/2 = rate of 150/min; 300/5 = 60/min, or count small squares between two consecutive R waves and divide 1500 by the interval, e.g. 1500/15 = 100/min.

If the rate is irregular then count number of R waves in 10 seconds (50 large squares) and multiply by six. The accuracy decreases if the number of squares counted are few.

(Eg. 1)

Rate of Eg. 1 = 1500/13 = 115/min (counting small squares)

Rate of Eg. 4 = 300/3 = 100/min (counting large squares)

RHYTHM

1. **Sinus** - P wave before each QRS and upright in all leads except aVR and V1.

(Eg. 2)

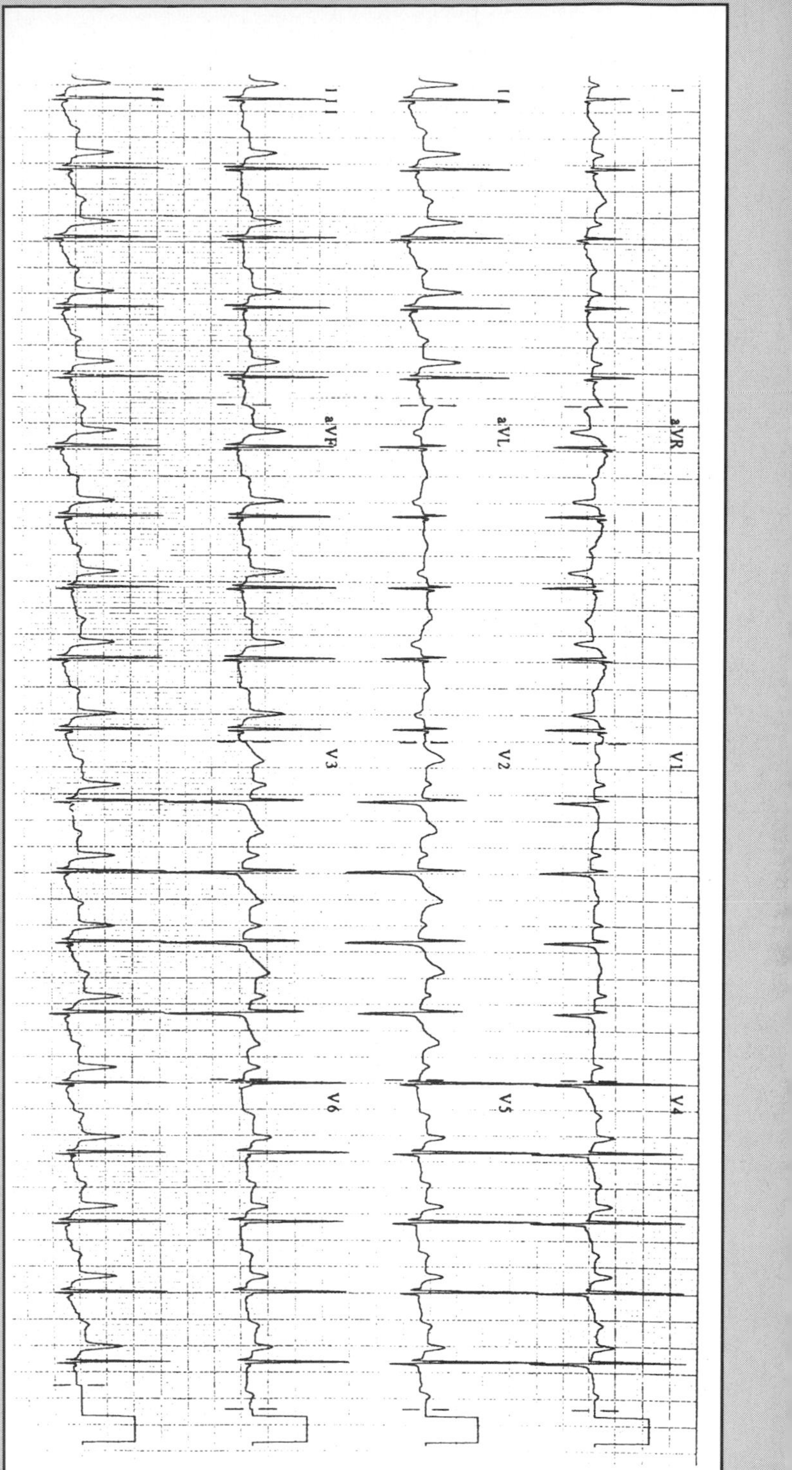

Eg. 1&2

2. **Junctional** - no P wave or inverted P waves before or after QRS.

(Eg. 3)

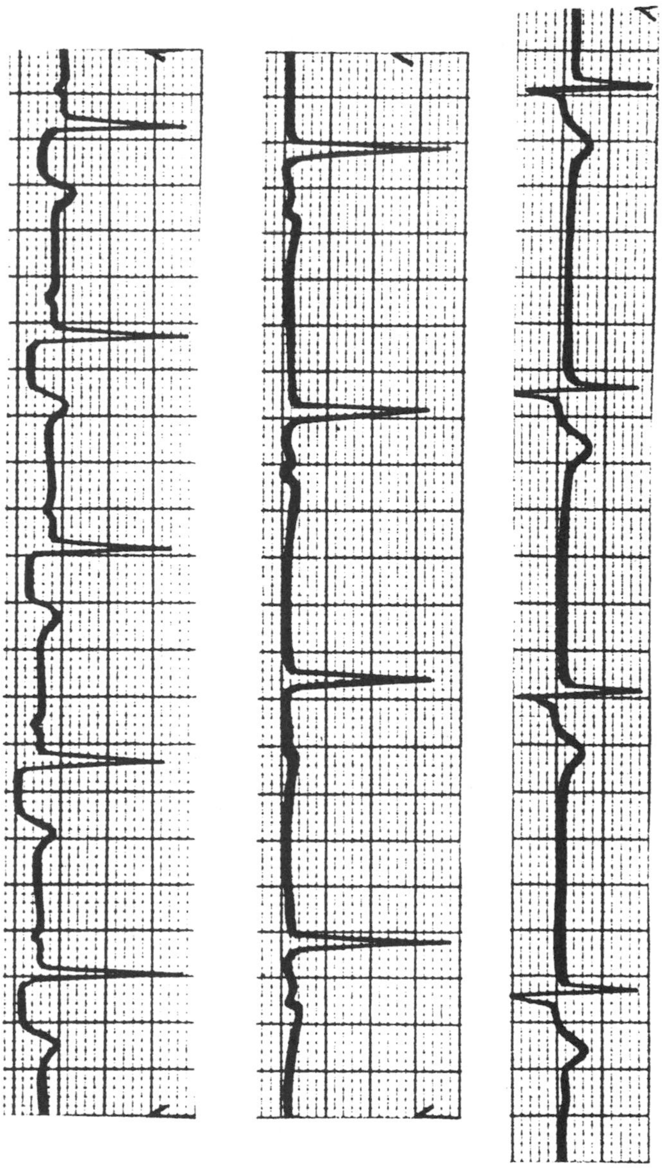

Eg. 3

P WAVE

1. **Broad and bifid** - P mitrale (0.04 sec between the two peaks of the P wave).

   (Eg. 4)

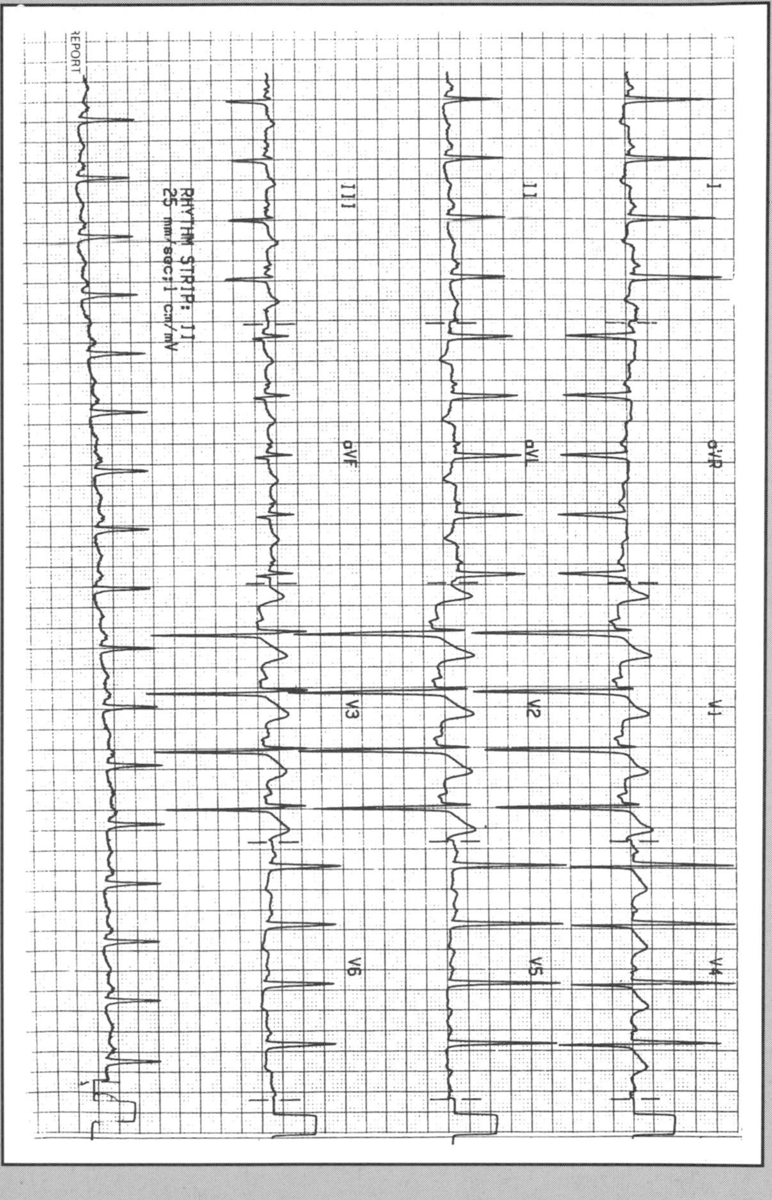

REPORT
I
II
III
aVR
aVL
aVF
V1
V2
V3
V4
V5
V6
RHYTHM STRIP: II
25 mm/sec;1 cm/mV

Eg. 4

2. **Tall and peaked** - P pulmonale (amplitude of P wave > 2.5 mm noted in the inferior leads).

(Eg. 5)

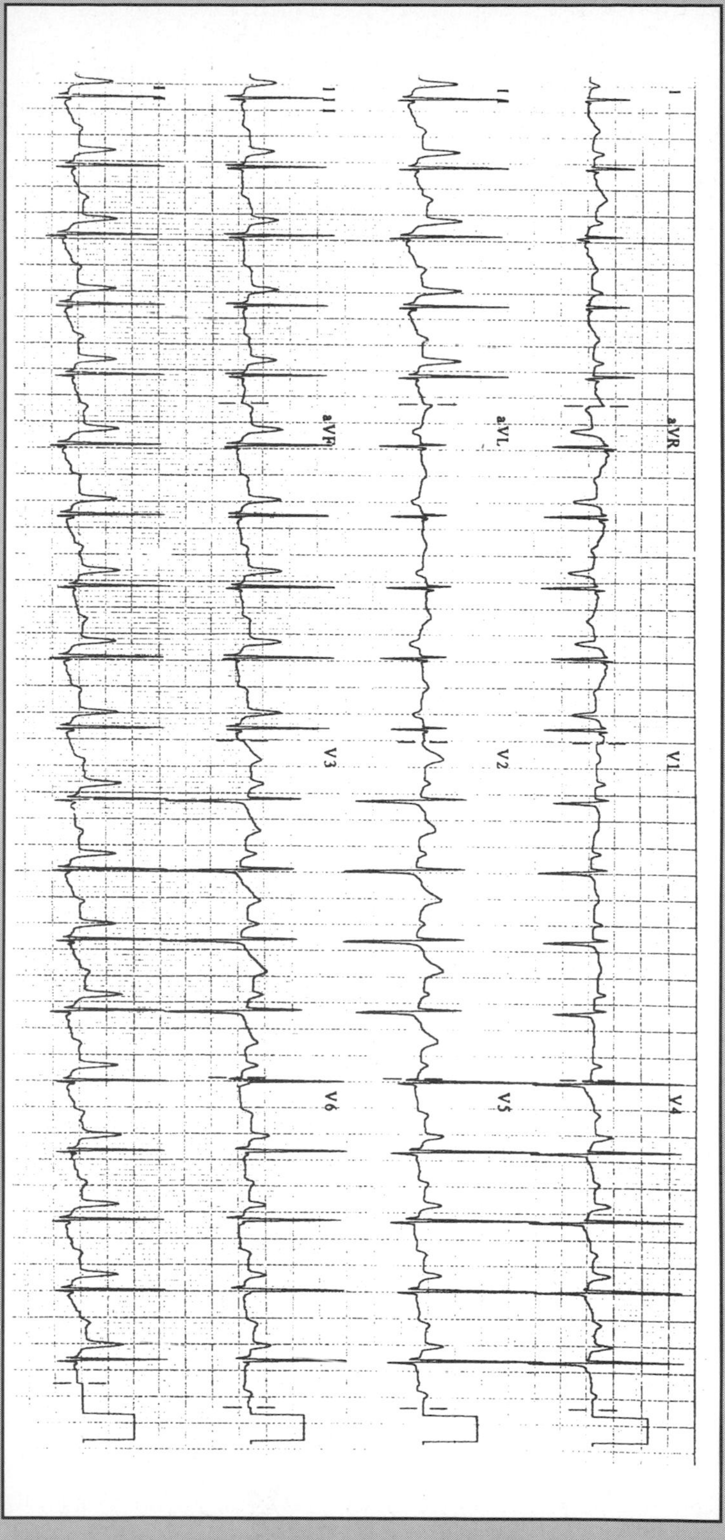

Eg. 5

3. **Biphasic in V1** - left atrial enlargement. The wave is initially positive and then negative. The negative deflection is called P terminal force and should be one small square deep and wide.

(Eg. 6)

PR INTERVAL

1. Prolonged (> 0.20 sec) - indicates first-degree heart block.

(Eg. 7)

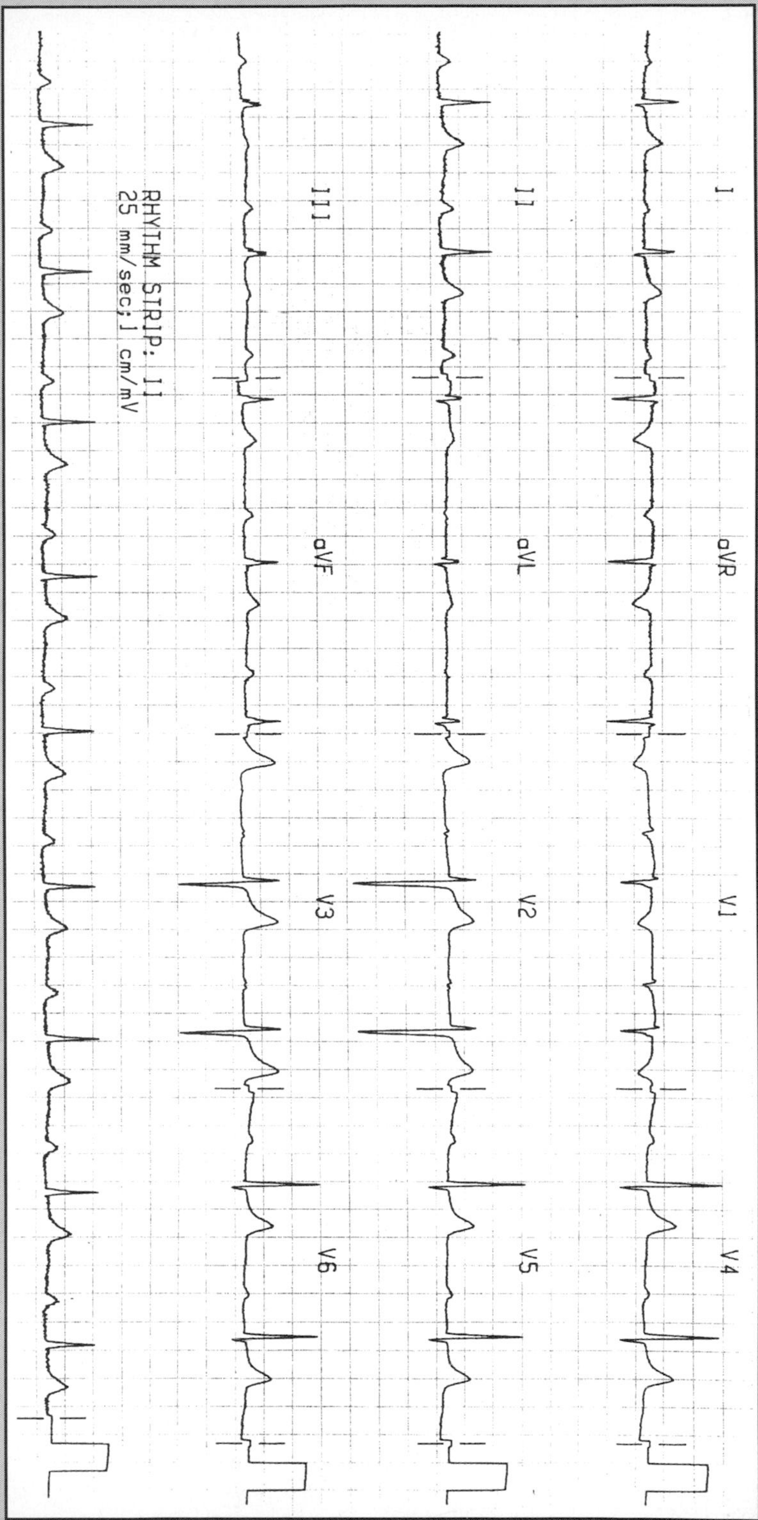
I
aVR
V1
V4
II
aVL
V2
V5
III
aVF
V3
V6
RHYTHM STRIP: II
25 mm/sec;1 cm/mV

Eg. 6&7

2. **Short** (< 0.08 sec) - indicates accessory conducting pathway. Common examples are:

   a) WPW syndrome
      (Eg. 8a)

   b) LGL syndrome
      (Eg. 8b)

   Occasionally, short PR may be present without LGL syndrome.

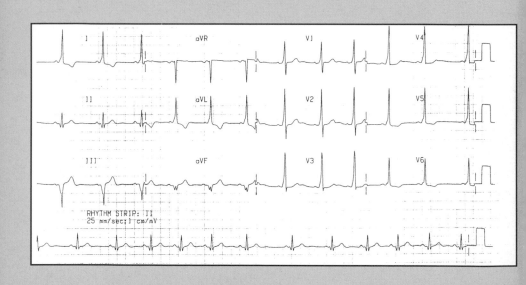

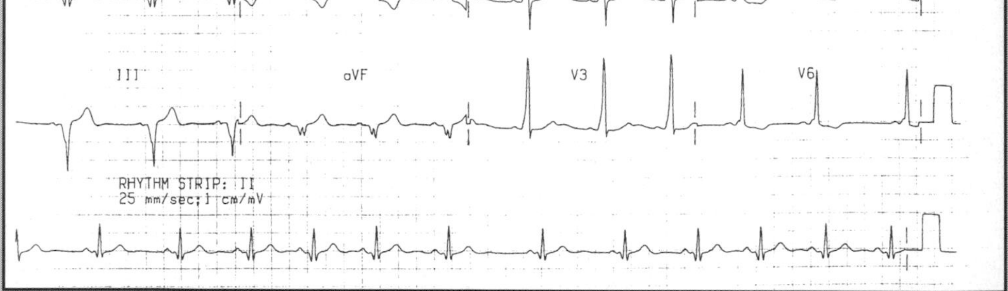

Eg. 8a

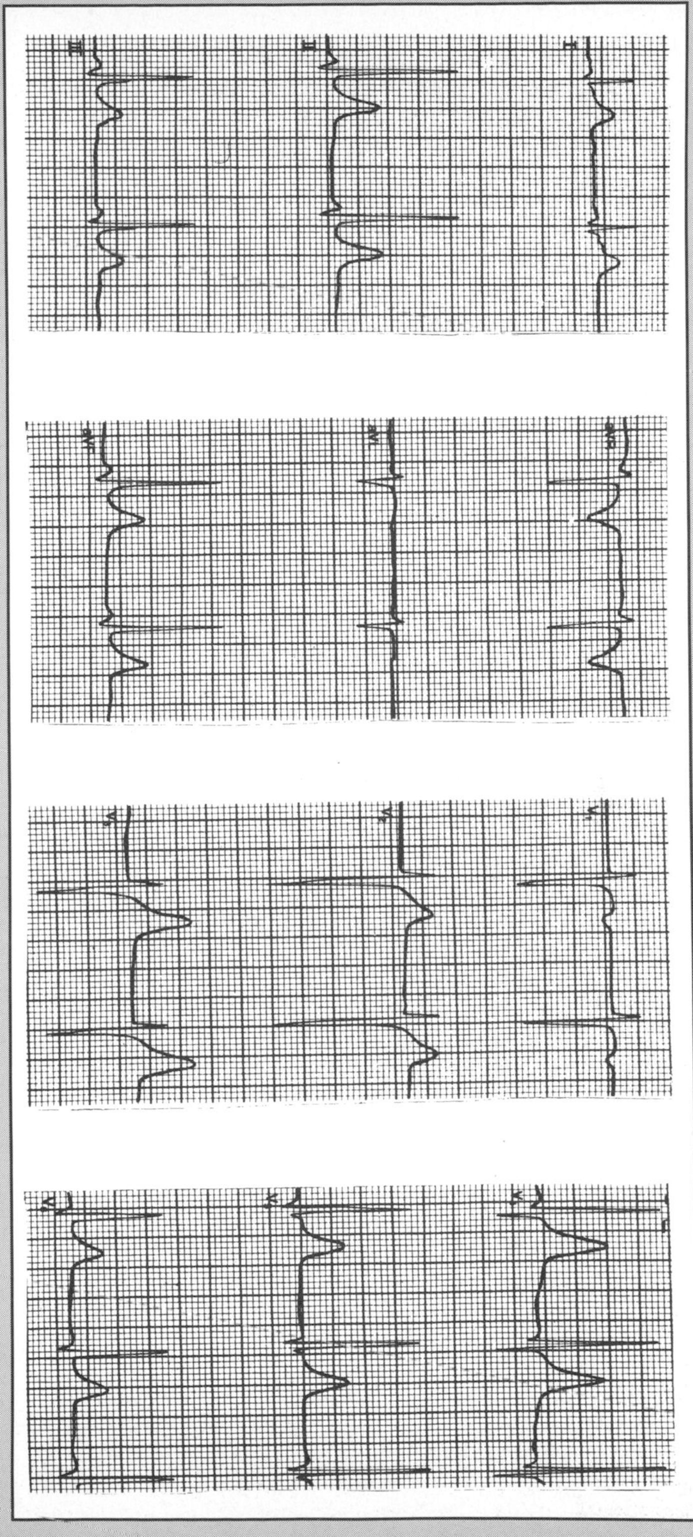

Eg. 8b

QRS

1. **Axis**
   On the hexaxial system the leads perpendicular to each other are F-1; L-2; R-3.

   Normal axis is -30 to +110 degrees.

   Left axis is > -30 degrees. Right axis is > +110 degrees although some consider it > +90 degrees.

   Method:

   a) Identify the lead with the smallest or most equiphasic complex.
   b) Look at the lead perpendicular to it.
   c) Read off the degrees from the positive or negative side of the lead depending on whether the complex is basically positive or negative.

   (Eg. 9)

   Axis of Eg. 6 & 7 is normal at +60°

   Axis of Eg. 10 & 11 is left at -60°

   Axis of Eg. 12 is to the right at > +90°

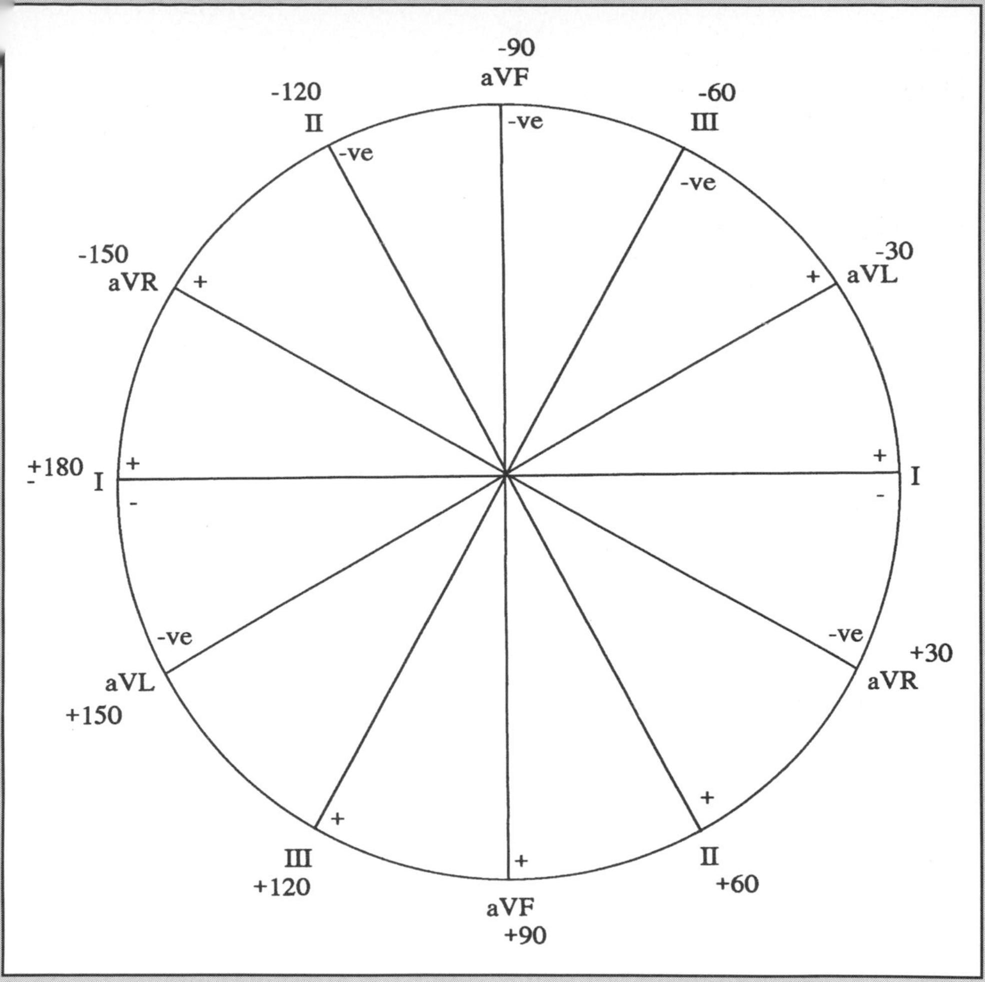
-90
aVF
-ve
-120
II
-ve
-60
III
-ve
-150
aVR
+
-30
+
aVL
+180
-
I
+
-
+
I
-
-ve
aVL
+150
-ve
+30
aVR
+
III
+120
+
aVF
+90
+
II
+60

Eg. 9

2. **Duration**

Normal is up to 0.10 sec with P wave present.

Complete bundle branch block (BBB) is > 0.12 sec.

Incomplete BBB is > 0.10 sec and < 0.12 sec.

A) Right BBB: broad and upright QRS or RSR pattern or qR in V1.

Wide and slurred S wave in V6 and lead 1. **(Eg. 10)**

NOTE: *whenever you see RBBB look for a hemiblock. A hemiblock occurs when one of the two branches of the left bundle is blocked, these two branches being the anterior and the posterior fascicles.*

a) Left axis deviation (LAD) indicates left anterior hemiblock (LAH) - rS present in inferior leads.

(Eg. 11)

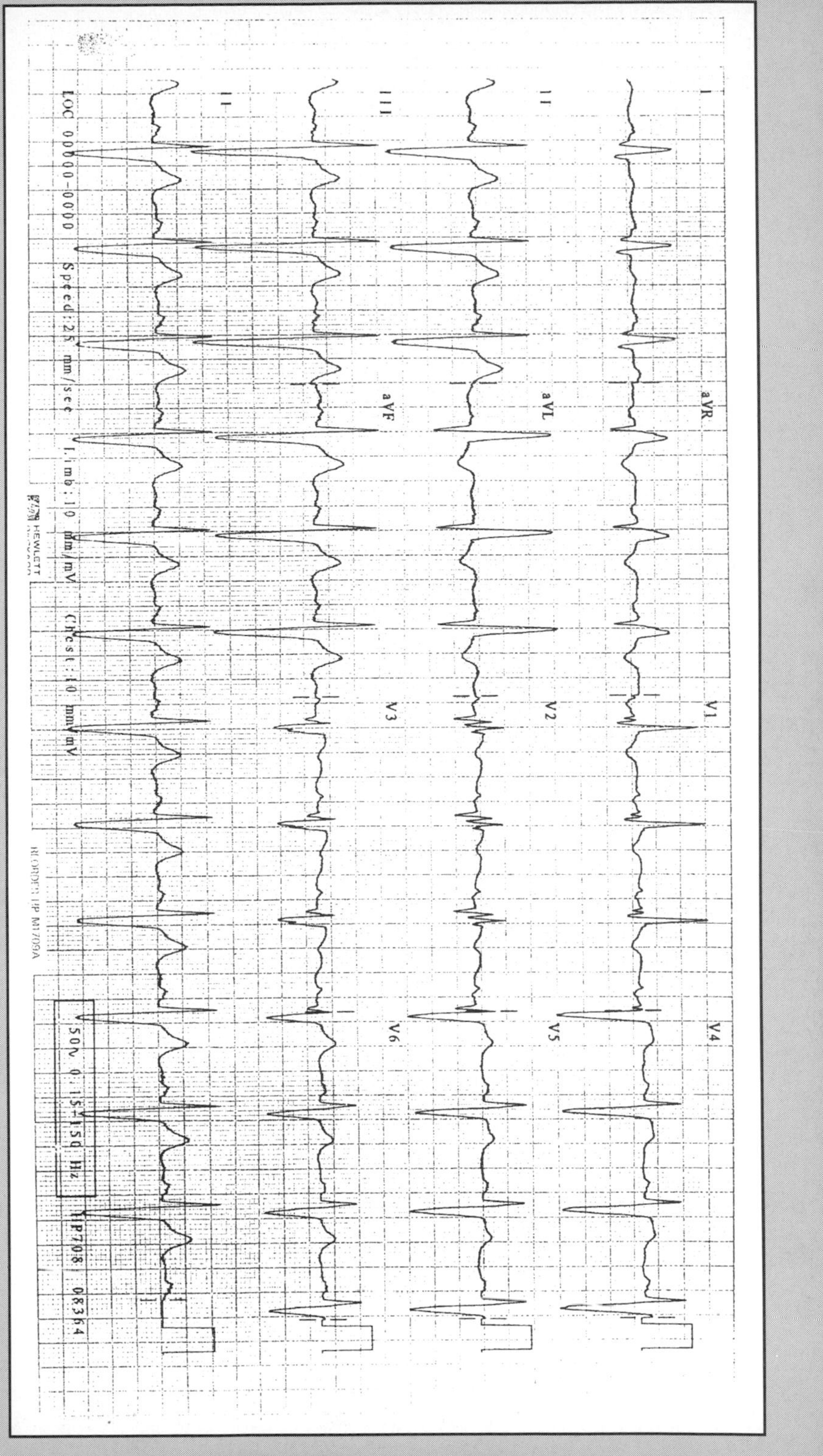
I
aVR
V1
V4
II
aVL
V2
V5
III
aVF
V3
V6
II
LOC 00000-0000 Speed:25 mm/sec Limb:10 mm/mV Chest:10 mm/mV
50~ 0.15-150 Hz
HP708 08364

Eg. 10&11

b) Right axis deviation (RAD) indicates left posterior hemiblock (LPH) - rS present in anterior leads. Provided there is no clinical evidence of right ventricular hypertrophy (RVH) or cor pulmonale (cor P).

(Eg. 12)

NOTE: *whenever you see a prominent R wave in V1 think of four common conditions.*

1. **RBBB**
2. **RVH**
3. **WPW type A**
4. **True posterior myocardial infarction (MI)**

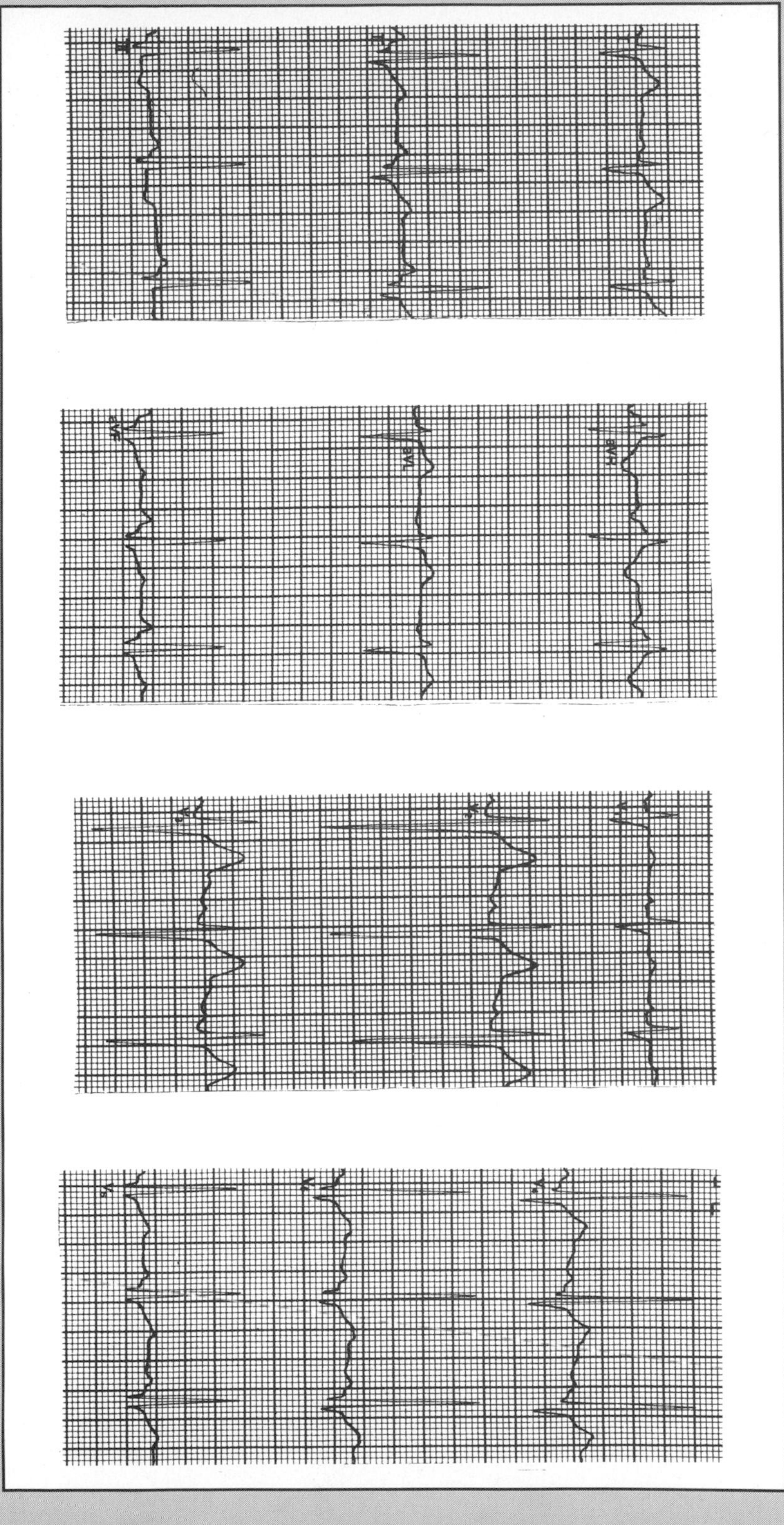

Eg. 12

B) Left BBB: wide S wave in V1 and broad M-shaped or pyramid-shaped R wave in V6 and lead 1.

(Eg. 13)

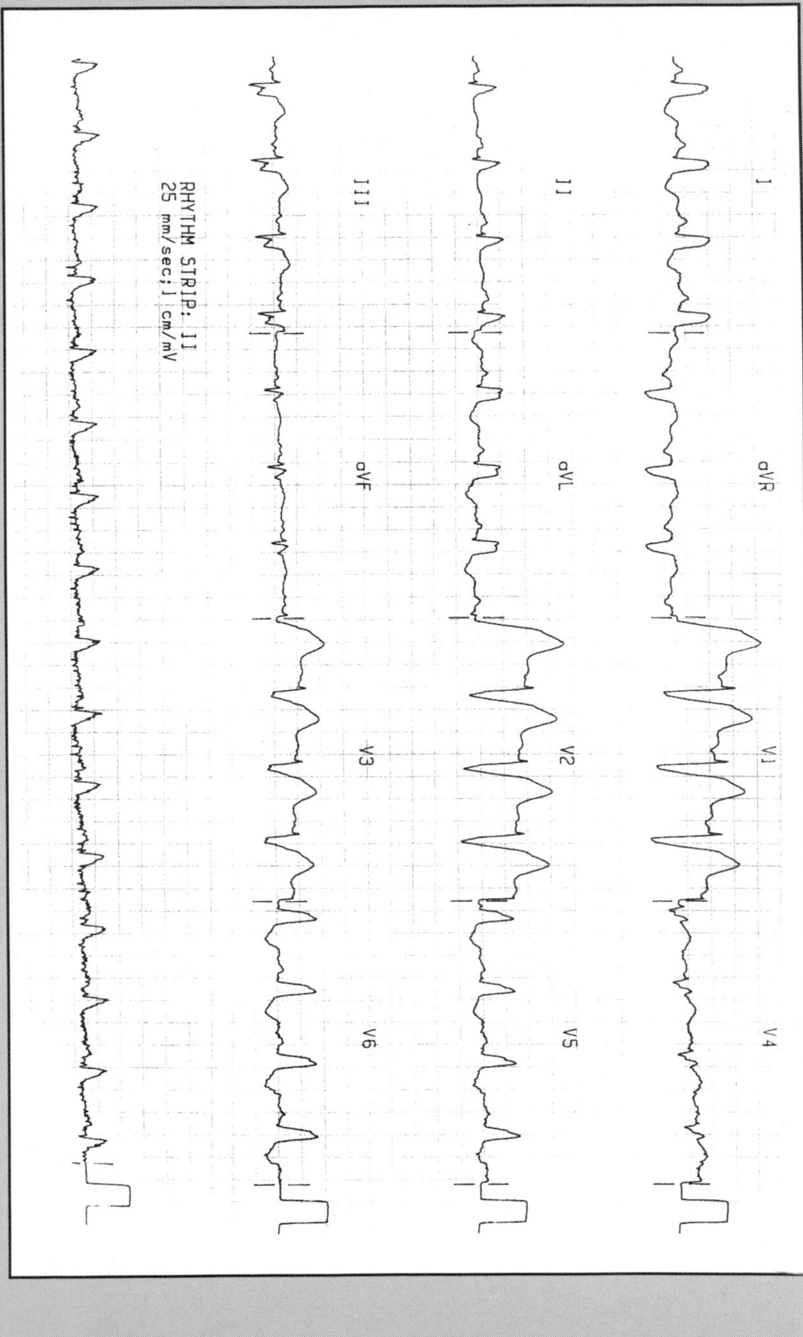
I
aVR
V1
V4
II
aVL
V2
V5
III
aVF
V3
V6
RHYTHM STRIP: II
25 mm/sec;1 cm/mV

Eg. 13

3. **Configuration**

a) Left ventricular hypertrophy (LVH) - S1 + V5 or V6 > 35 mm in patients over the age of 35 years.

(Eg. 14)

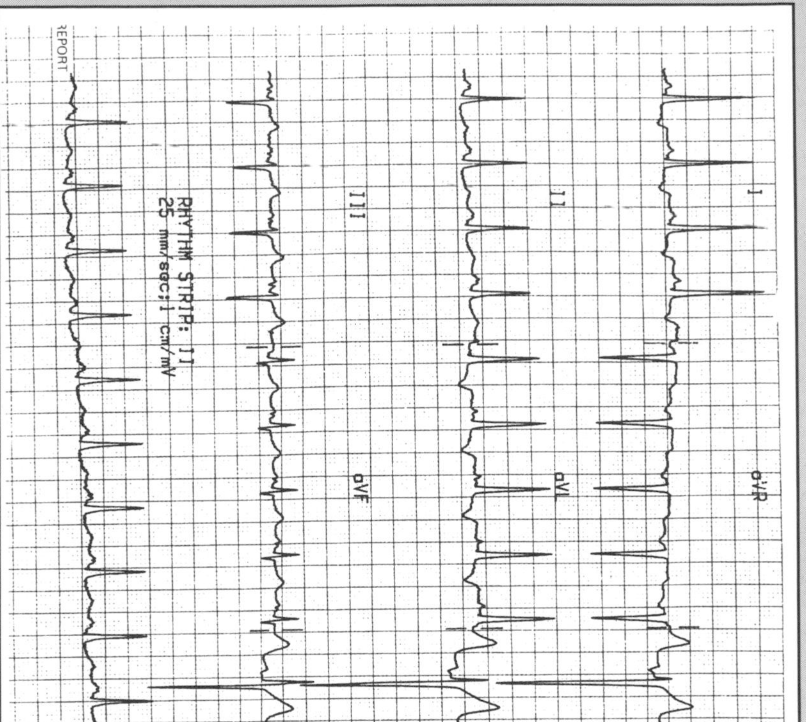
REPORT
I
II
III
aVR
aVL
aVF
V1
V2
V3
V4
V5
V6
RHYTHM STRIP: II
25 mm/sec;1 cm/mV

Eg. 14

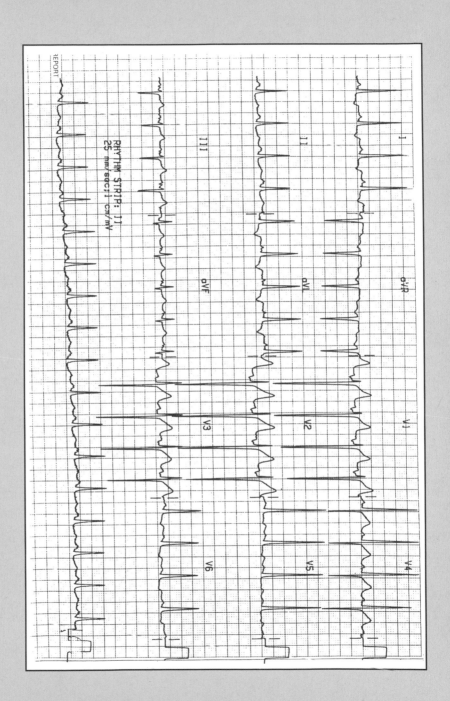

b) RVH - R=S or R>S in V1 without broadening of the QRS complex.

(Eg. 15)

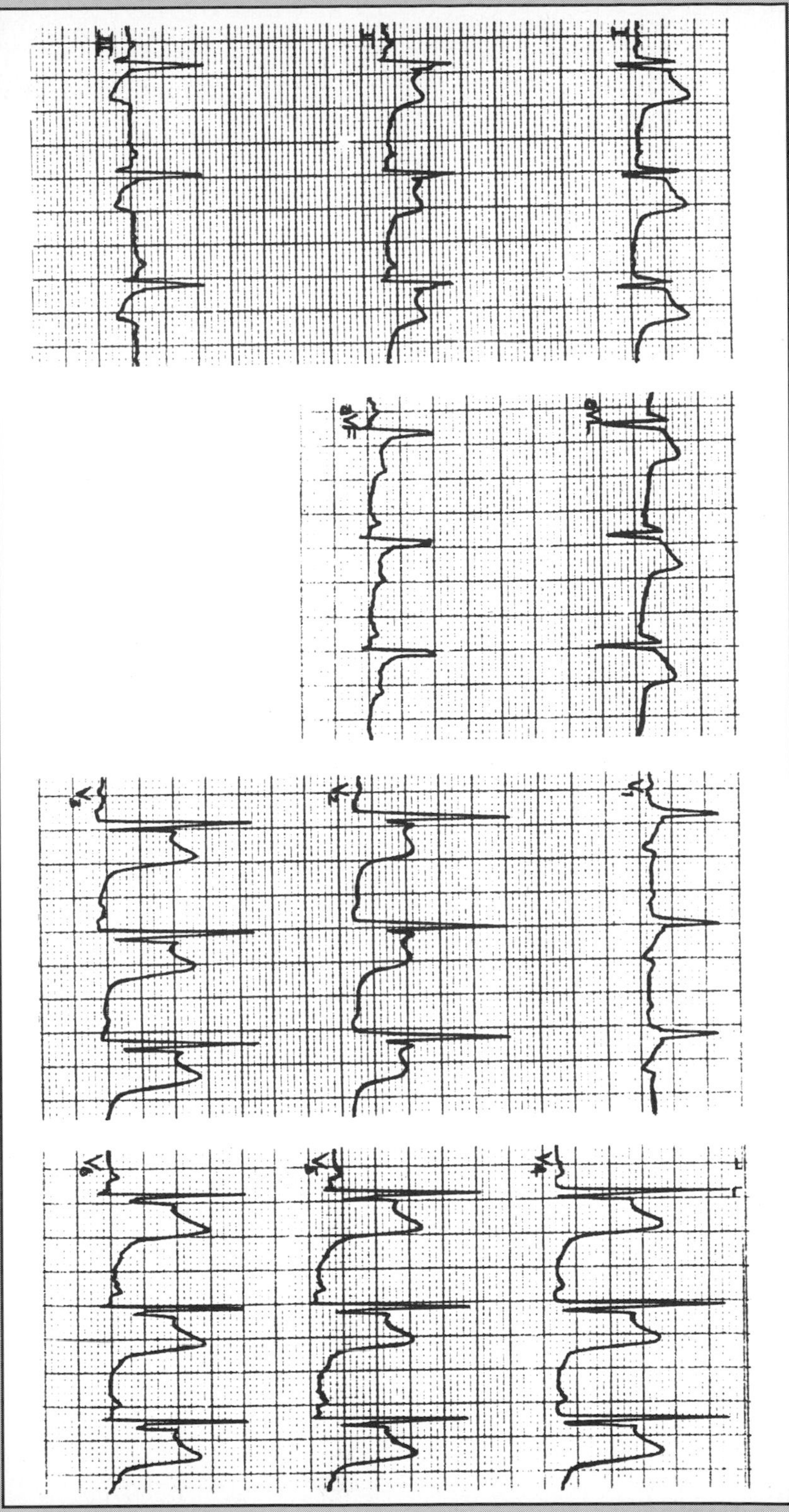

Eg. 15

Q WAVE

Pathological if it is 25% of R wave and/or > 1 small square deep and wide. Found in transmural myocardial infarction (MI) and hypertrophic obstructive cardiomyopathy (HOCM).

If Q wave in L1 then look in AVL and chest leads. If Q wave in L2 or AVF then look in the other inferior leads. Q in L3 alone can be positional and of no significance. This frequently disappears or reduces in size on deep inspiration.

ST SEGMENT

1. **Depression**

   a) Plane depression - when compared to the preceding PR segment is indicative of ischaemia specially if 1 mm or more.

   b) Down sloping - 1 mm or more is ischaemic (very specific but not very sensitive).

   c) Up sloping - sensitive but not very specific.

2. **Elevation**

   a) Convexity upwards: acute MI.

   (Eg. 16)

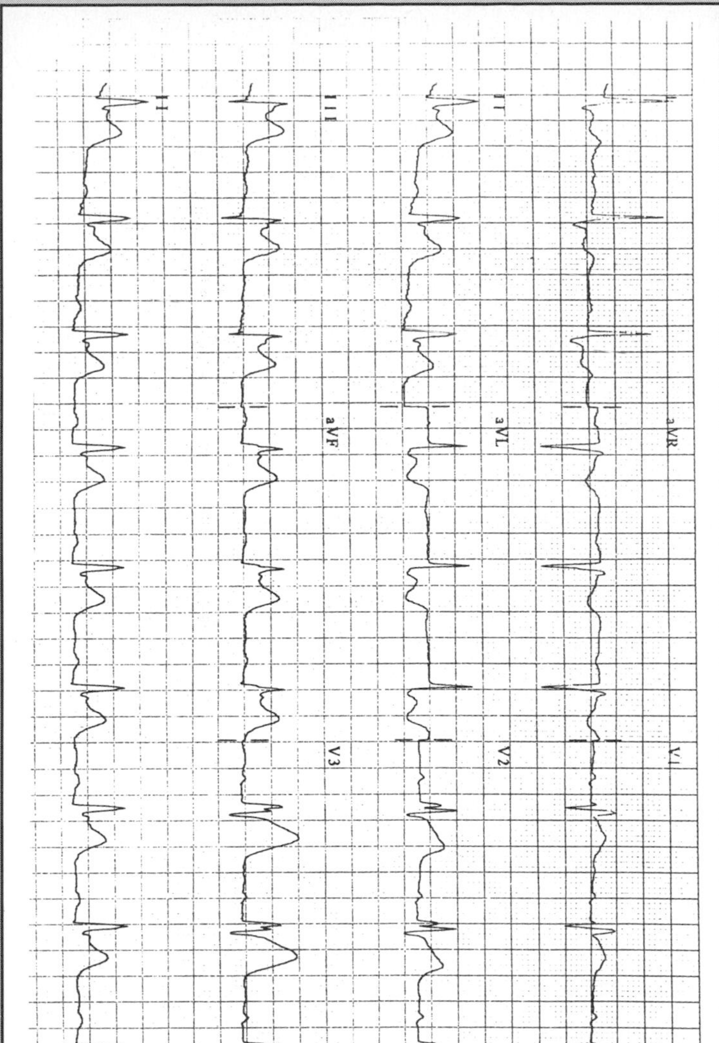

Eg. 16

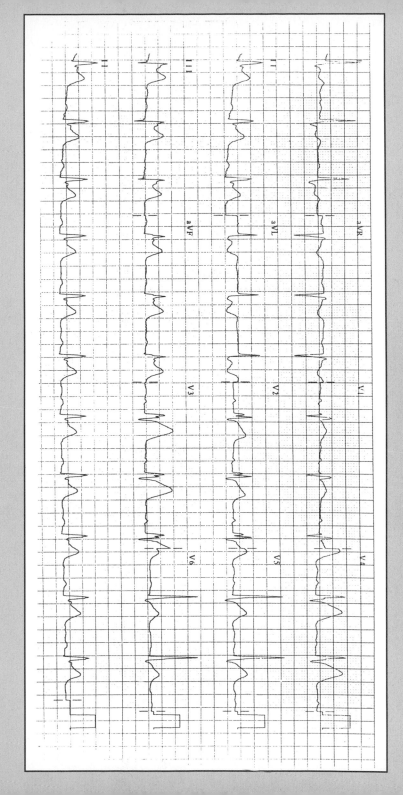

b) Concavity upwards: acute pericarditis.

(Eg. 17)

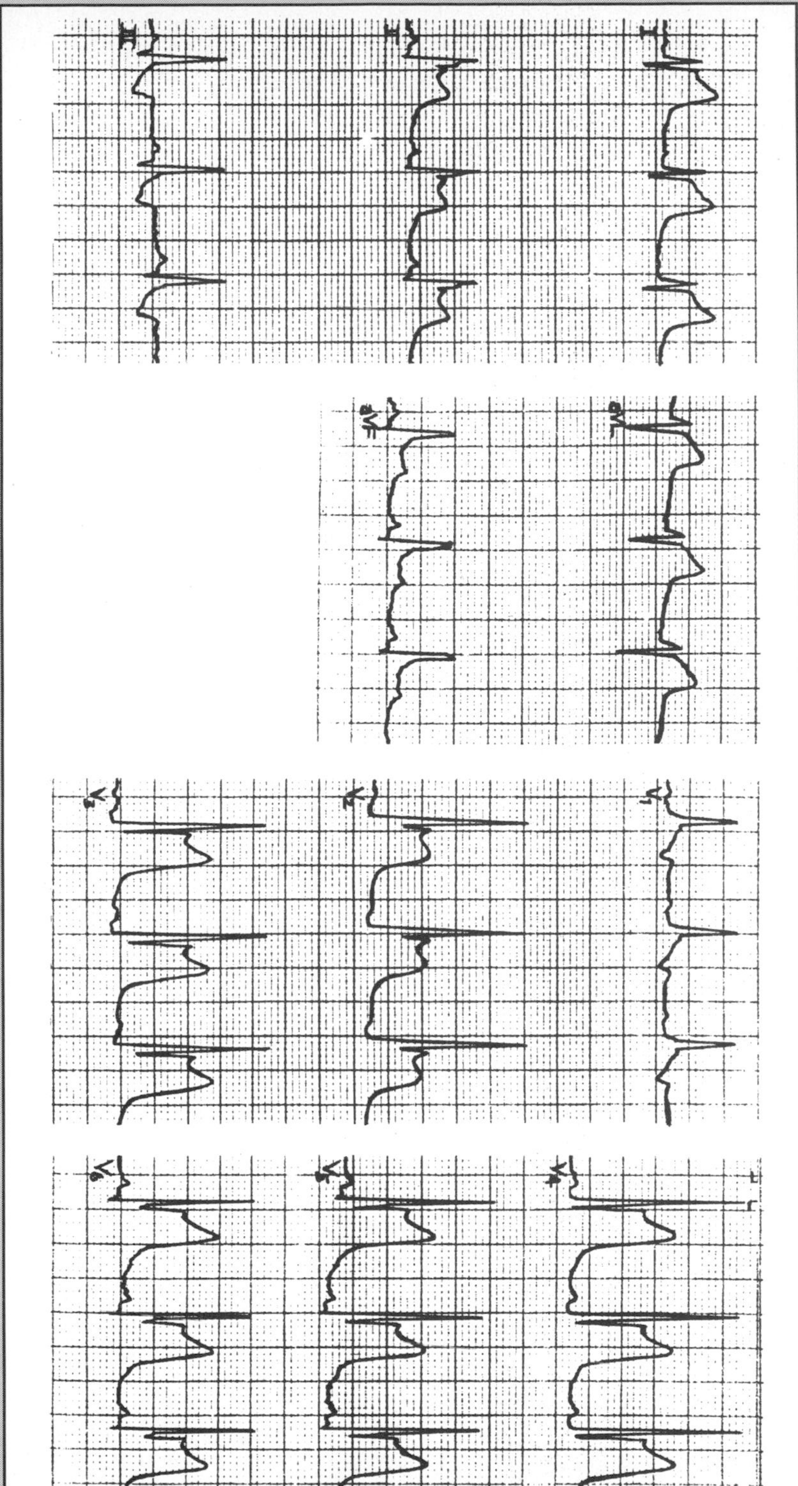

Eg. 17

T WAVE

1. **Flat**- non specific.
2. **Inverted** - may indicate ischaemia.
3. **Arrowhead inversion** - subendocardial MI. **(Eg. 18)**
4. **Very peaked** - may occur in the hyperacute phase of MI.

U WAVE

Usually positive and present in V2 - V4. If prominent it indicates hypokalaemia and if inverted hyperkalaemia.

NOTE: *in both cases check serum potassium.*

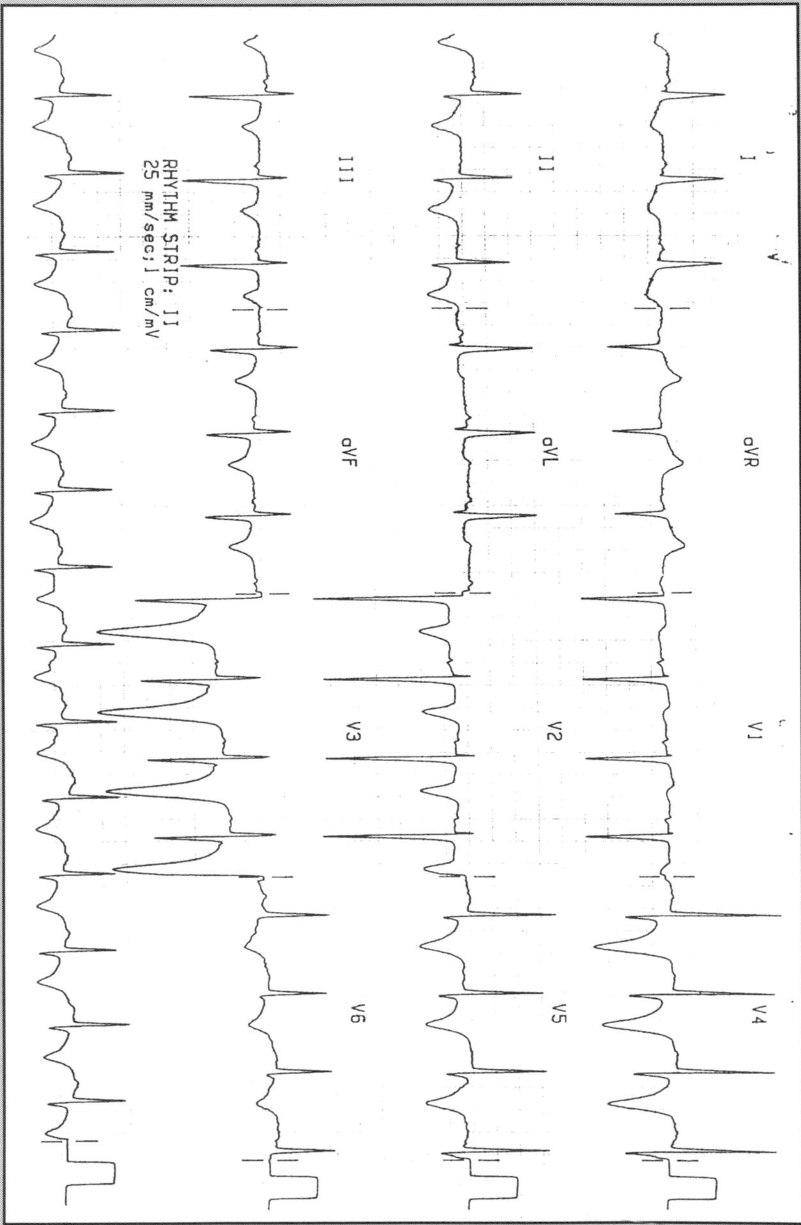
I
aVR
V1
V4
II
aVL
V2
V5
III
aVF
V3
V6
RHYTHM STRIP: II
25 mm/sec;1 cm/mV

Eg. 18

QTc

QT interval is from the beginning of the QRS complex to the end of the T wave. It represents the sum of the total duration of ventricular depolarisation and repolarisation.

Prolonged QTc - congenital long QT syndrome
- hypocalcaemia
- AMI
- hypothermia
- quinidine/procainamide/tricyclic antidepressant (TCA) drugs
- HOCM
- acute myocarditis

QT interval shortens with tachycardia and lengthens with bradycardia. It is therefore important that the QT interval is corrected for the associated heart rate for any meaningful evaluation. This corrected QT interval is called QTc and is calculated by the Bazzett's formula. Normal range of QTc = 0.35 to 0.43. Most serious consequence of a prolonged QTc is torsade de pointes.

Bazett's formula

$$\frac{QT}{\sqrt{RR}}$$

QT and RR interval (measured in seconds)

QTc dispersion

- Calculate the QTc for each of the 12 ECG leads from a standard electrocardiogram.
- Subtract the shortest from the longest interval to get the QTc dispersion.
- QTc dispersion of ≥ 60 ms has a 92% sensitivity and 81% specificity in predicting cardiac death.
- QTc dispersion is a fairly new and simple variable obtained cheaply and non-invasively, and will help to assess the risk of cardiac death in patients with:
  - Chronic heart failure
  - Post myocardial infarction
  - Hypertrophic cardiomyopathy
  - Peripheral vascular disease
  - Long QT syndromes

Section II

SPECIFIC CLINICAL CONDITIONS

INFERIOR MYOCARDIAL INFARCTION

Features of hyperacute, fully evolved and chronic stabilised phase noted in inferior leads.

(Eg. 19)

NOTE: *In patients with inferior MI a V4R lead should be checked preferably within the first 10 hours of the infarct, as an ST segment elevation there will suggest the presence of a right ventricular infarct.*

Criteria

Hyperacute:

a) Increased amplitude of R wave.
b) ST segment slope elevation.
c) Increased VAT.
d) Tall and wide T wave.

Explanation: VAT is ventricular activation time and is the time measured from the onset of the QRS complex to the apex of the R wave. It indicates the time taken for the impulse to travel through the whole thickness of the left ventricular wall.

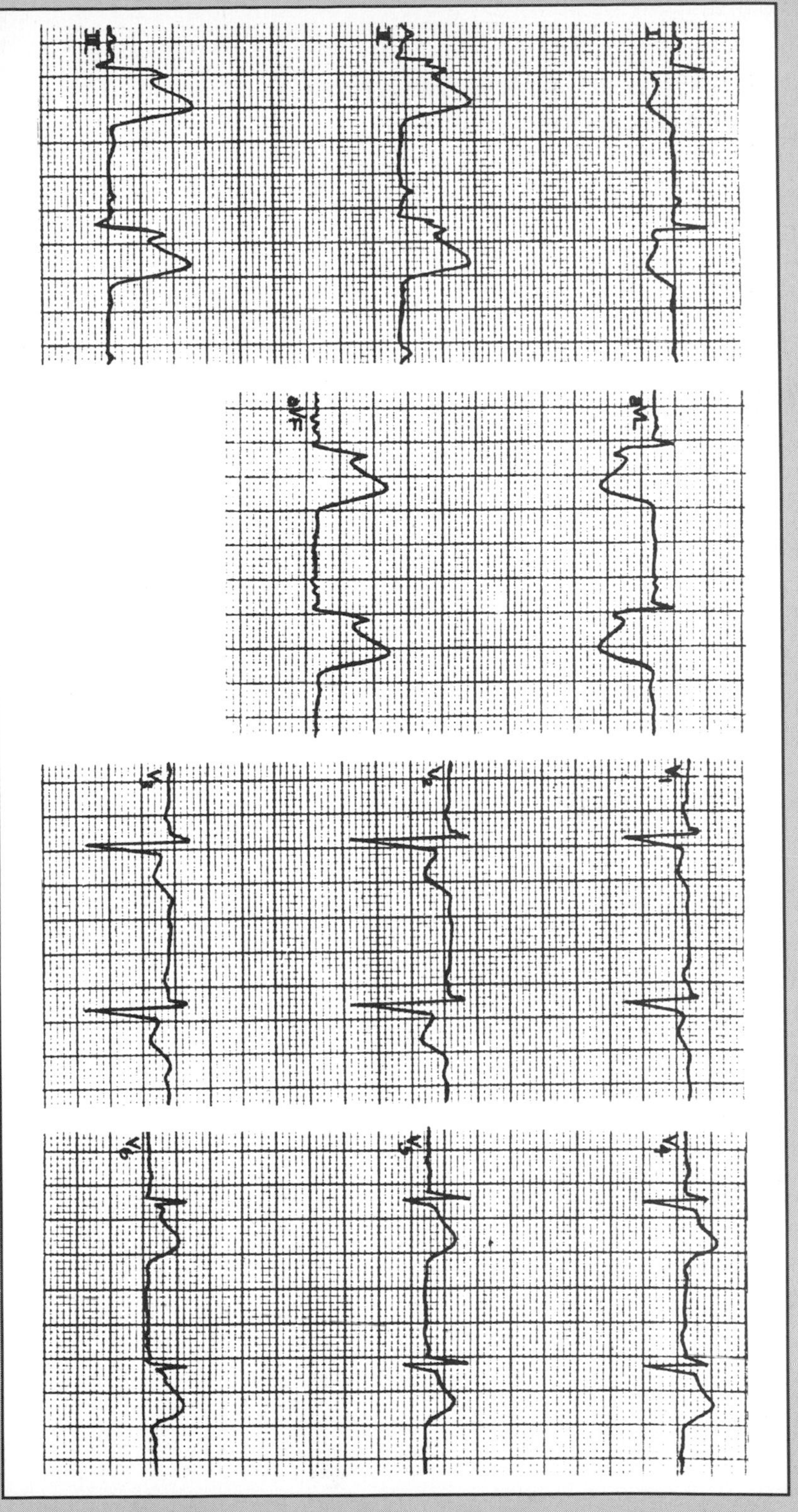

Eg. 19

ANTERIOR MYOCARDIAL INFARCTION

Features of an infarct can be seen:

a) anteroseptal - V1-V4

(Eg. 20a)

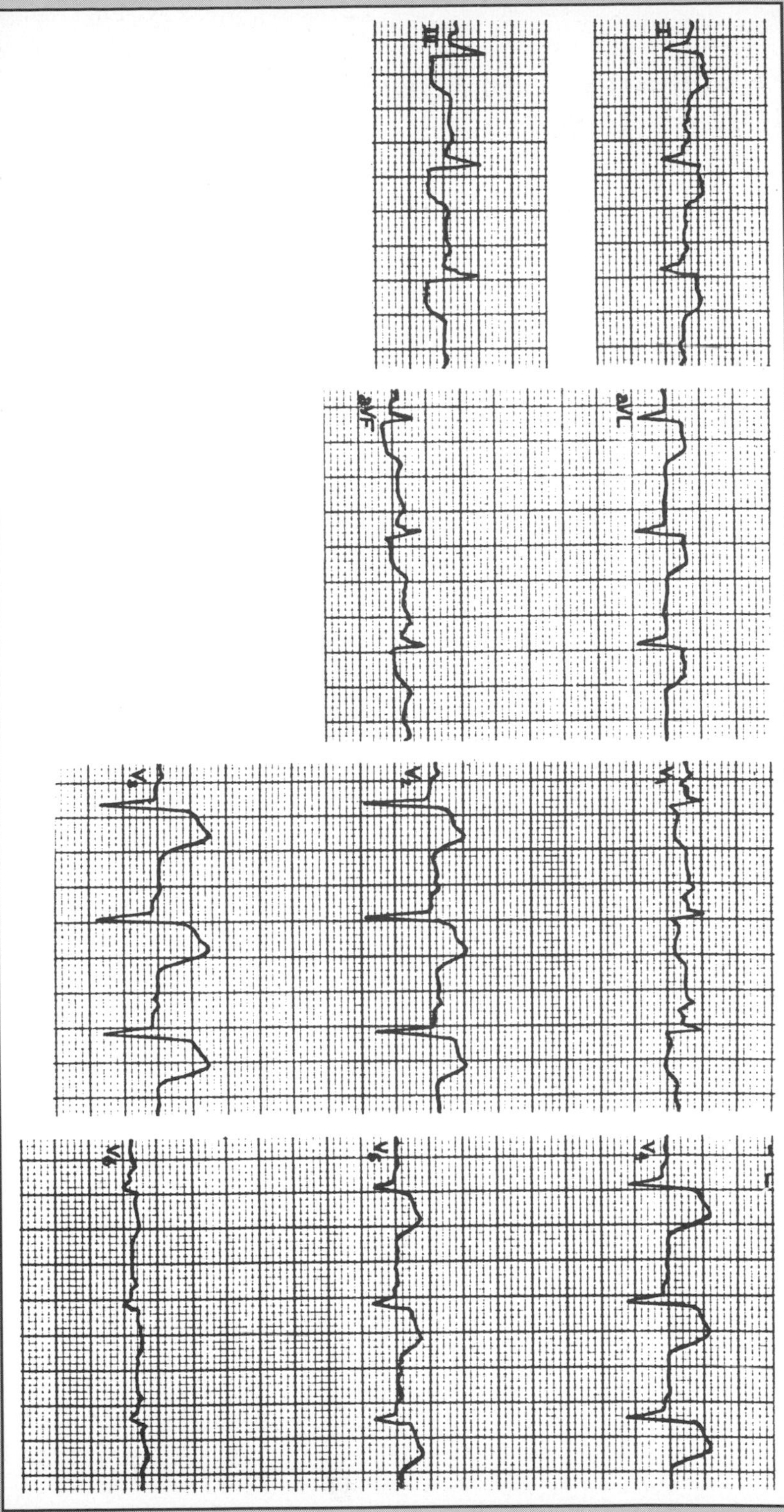

Eg. 20a

b) anterolateral - leads I, AVL, and V4-V6.

(Eg. 20b)

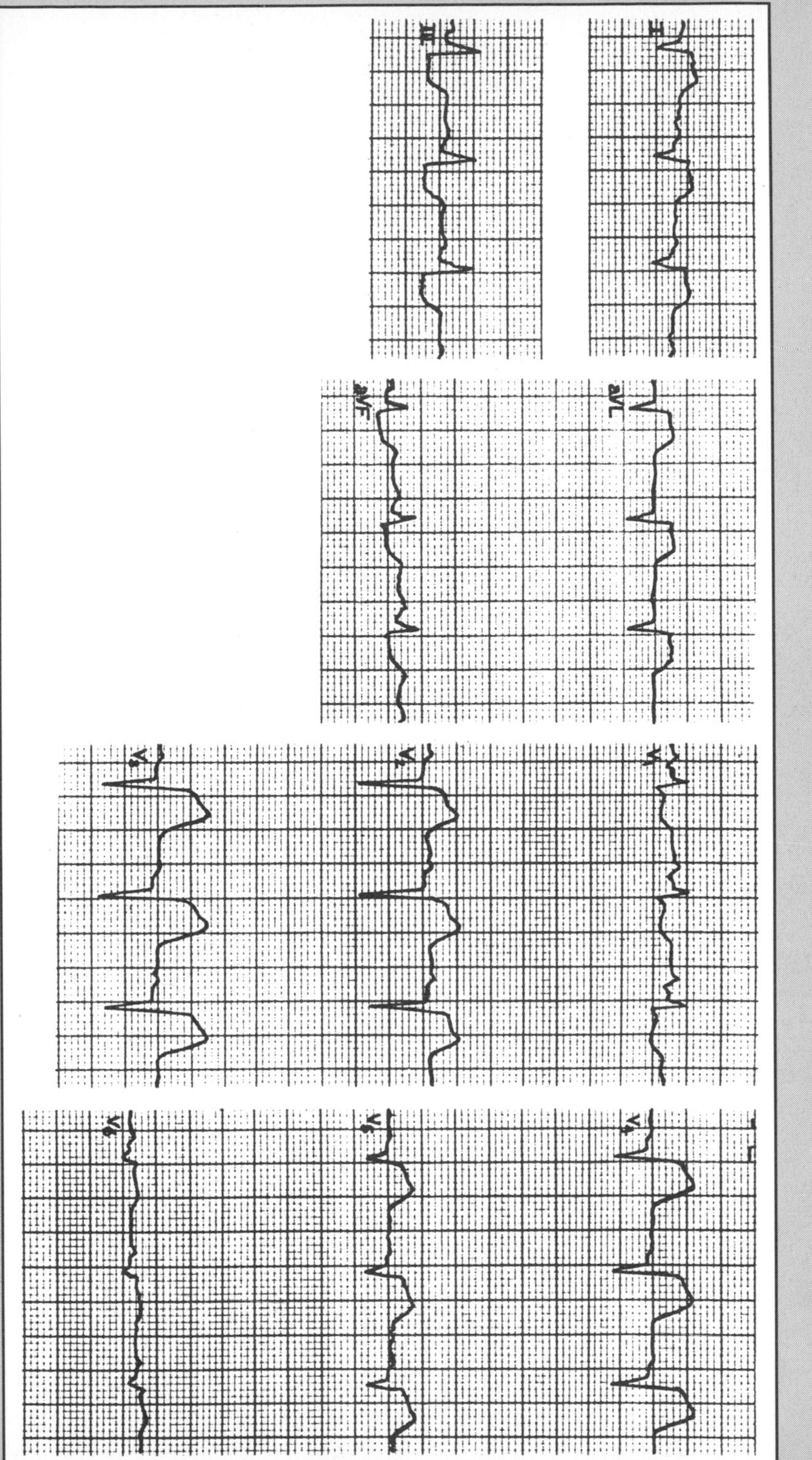

Eg. 20b

TRUE POSTERIOR MYOCARDIAL INFARCTION

Rarely occurs as an isolated phenomenon. Usually associated with inferior or anterolateral MI.

Features

a) Tall R wave in V1
b) Upright and wide T wave in V1

(Eg. 21)

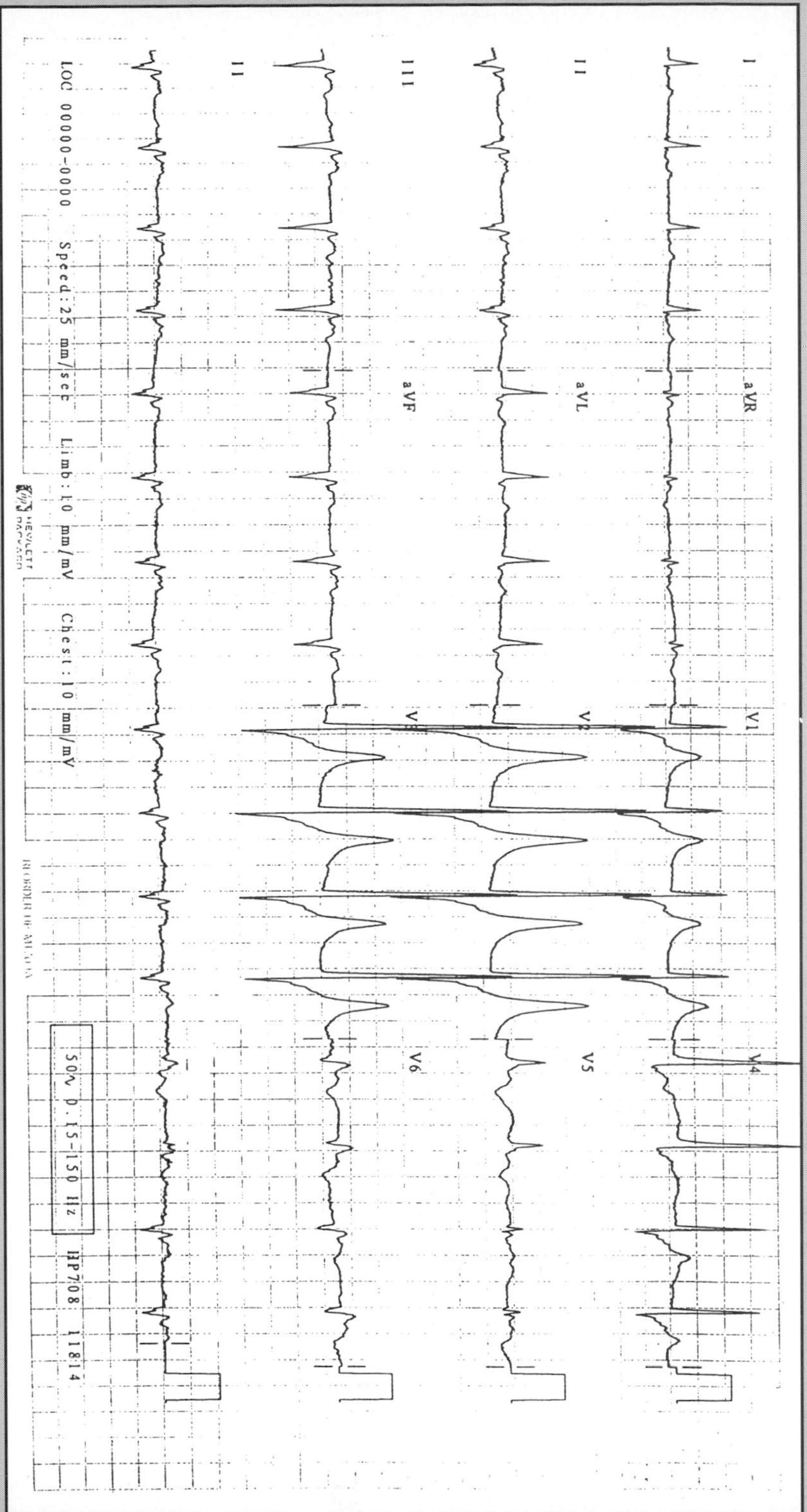
I
aVR
V1
V4
II
aVL
V2
V5
III
aVF
V3
V6
II
LOC 00000-0000 Speed:25 mm/sec Limb:10 mm/mV Chest:10 mm/mV
50∿ 0.15-150 Hz
HP708 11814

Eg. 21

Management

1. Aspirin 150 mg daily.

2. Streptokinase if no contraindications and not given within the past 12 months.

3. Lisinopril or other ACE inhibitors if no contraindications.

4. Standard management, i.e. oxygen/subcutaneous heparin/analgesics etc.

5. I.V. nitrates.

6. ß-blockers within 24-48 hours if no contraindications.

ACUTE PERICARDITIS

1. Sinus tachycardia.

2. Tall, peaked and symmetrical T wave.

3. Concave upwards ST segment.

4. No reciprocal ST segment changes occur.

(Eg. 22)

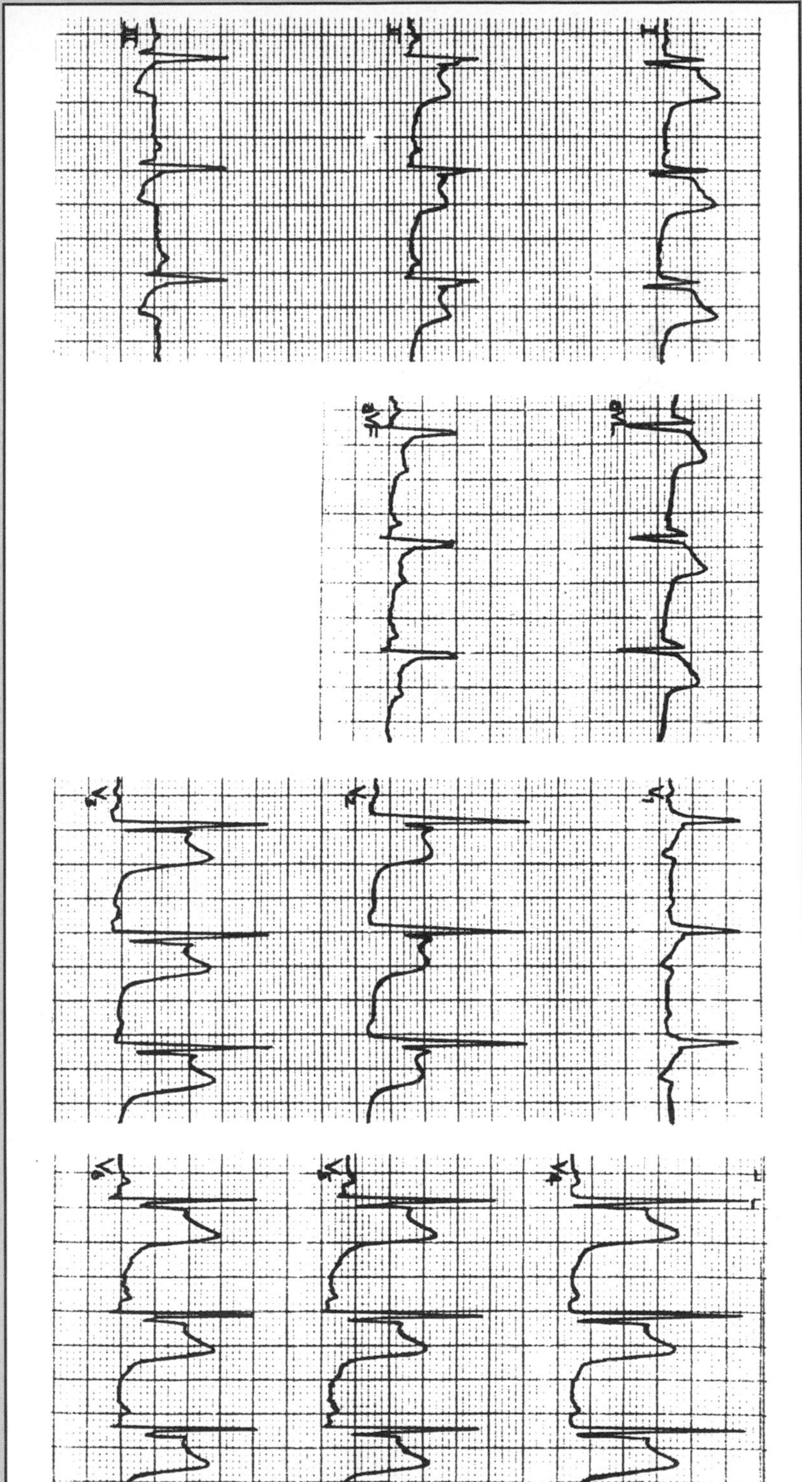

Eg. 22

LEFT VENTRICULAR HYPERTROPHY (LVH)

1. R wave in lead 1 > 15 mm.

2. R wave in AVL > 11 mm.

3. S1 + R5 or R6 > 35 mm.

4. Sum of all the R waves in all the 12 leads > 175 mm.

(Eg. 23)

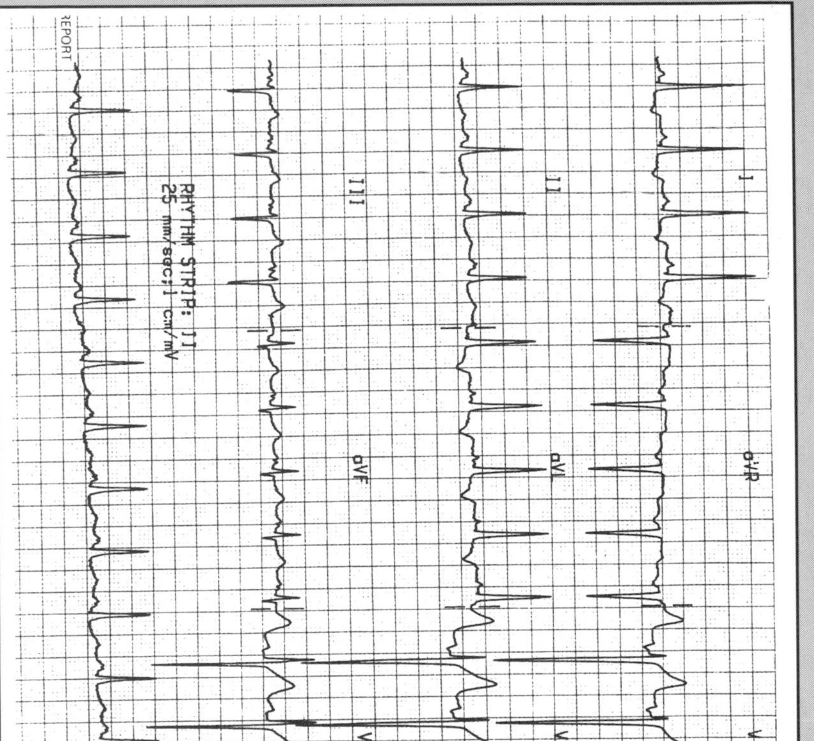
REPORT
I
aVR
V1
V4
II
aVL
V2
V5
III
aVF
V3
V6
RHYTHM STRIP: II
25 mm/sec;1 cm/mV

Eg. 23

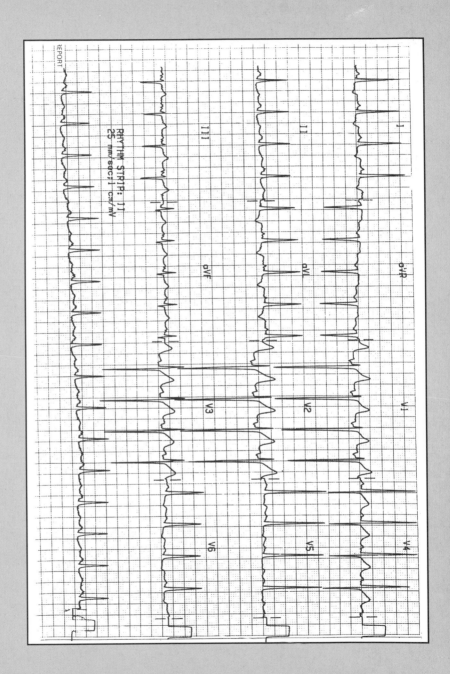

RIGHT VENTRICULAR HYPERTROPHY (RVH)

1. R:S ratio > 1.

2. R wave > 5 mm.

(Eg. 24)

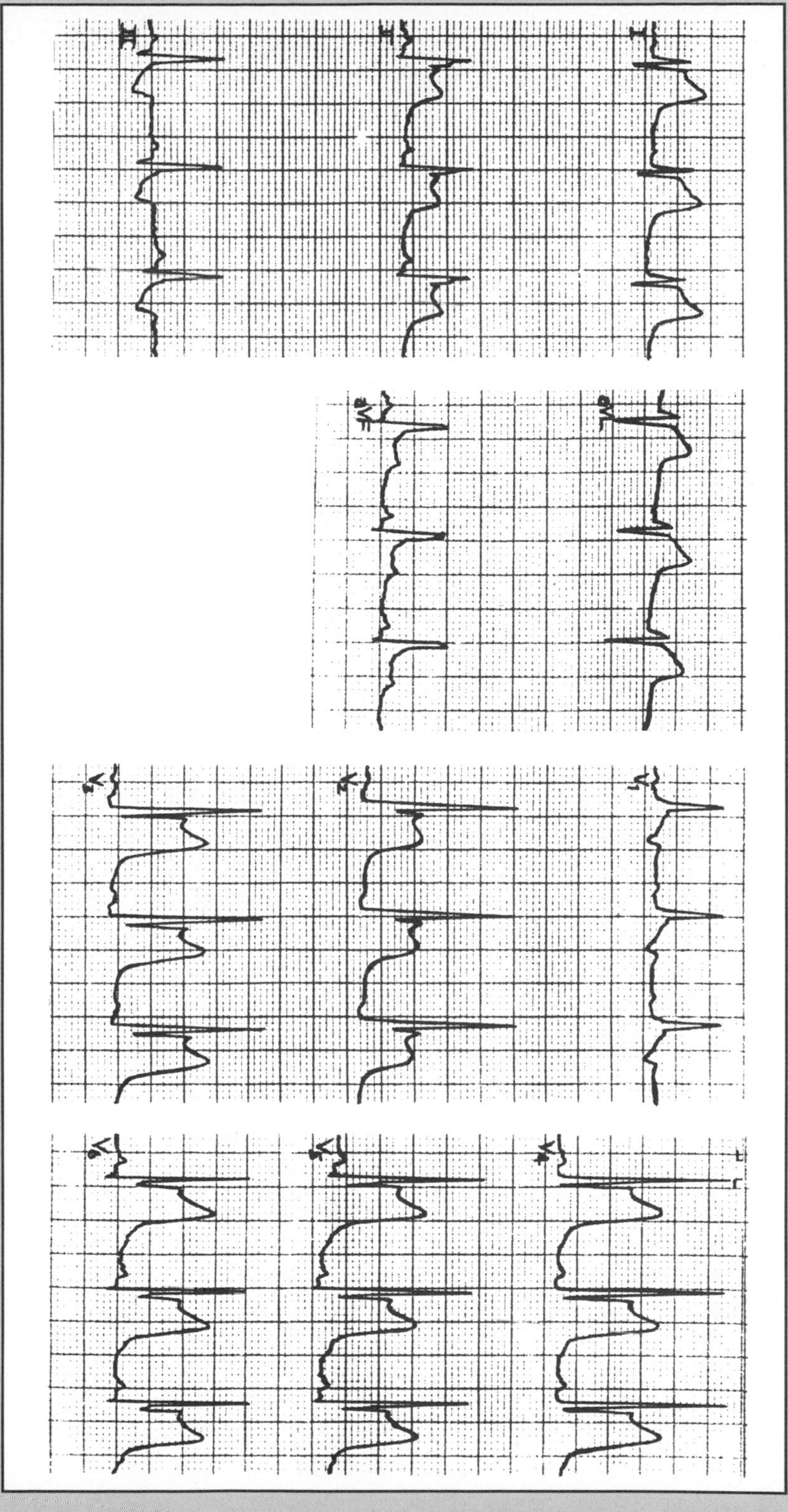

Eg. 24

LEFT ATRIAL ENLARGEMENT

1. Bifid P wave seen especially in lead II.

2. Distance between the two peaks is > 0.04 sec (one small square).

3. Increased duration of P wave > 0.11 sec.

4. P terminal force > 0.03 mm sec.

(Eg. 25)

****Morris index: calculates the P terminal force, e.g. if terminal deflection is 1 mm in depth and 0.04 sec in duration then P terminal force is 0.04 mm sec and is indicative of left atrial enlargement.**

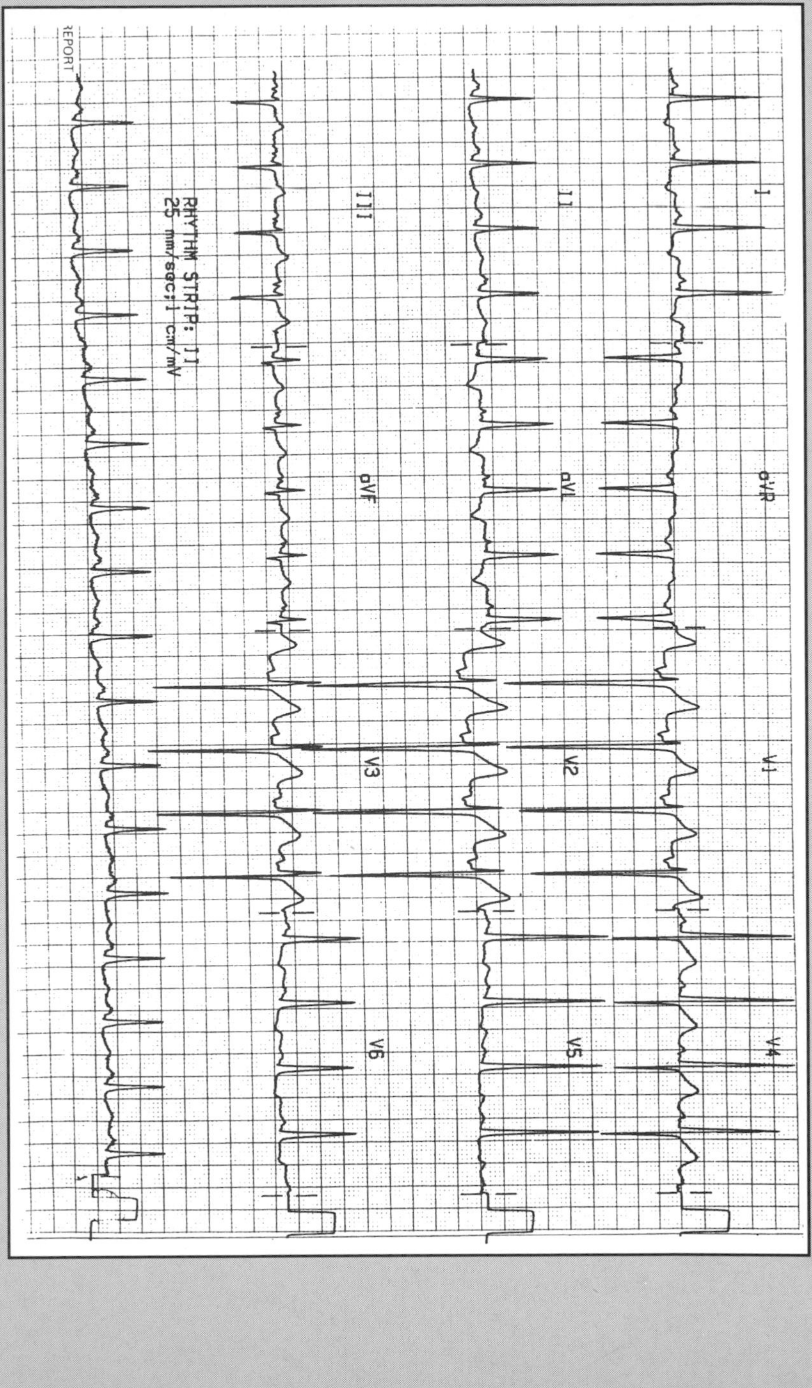

REPORT
I
aVR
V1
V4
II
aVL
V2
V5
III
aVF
V3
V6
RHYTHM STRIP: II
25 mm/sec;1 cm/mV

Eg. 25

RIGHT ATRIAL ENLARGEMENT

P wave amplitude > 2.5 mm - best seen in lead II.

(Eg. 26)

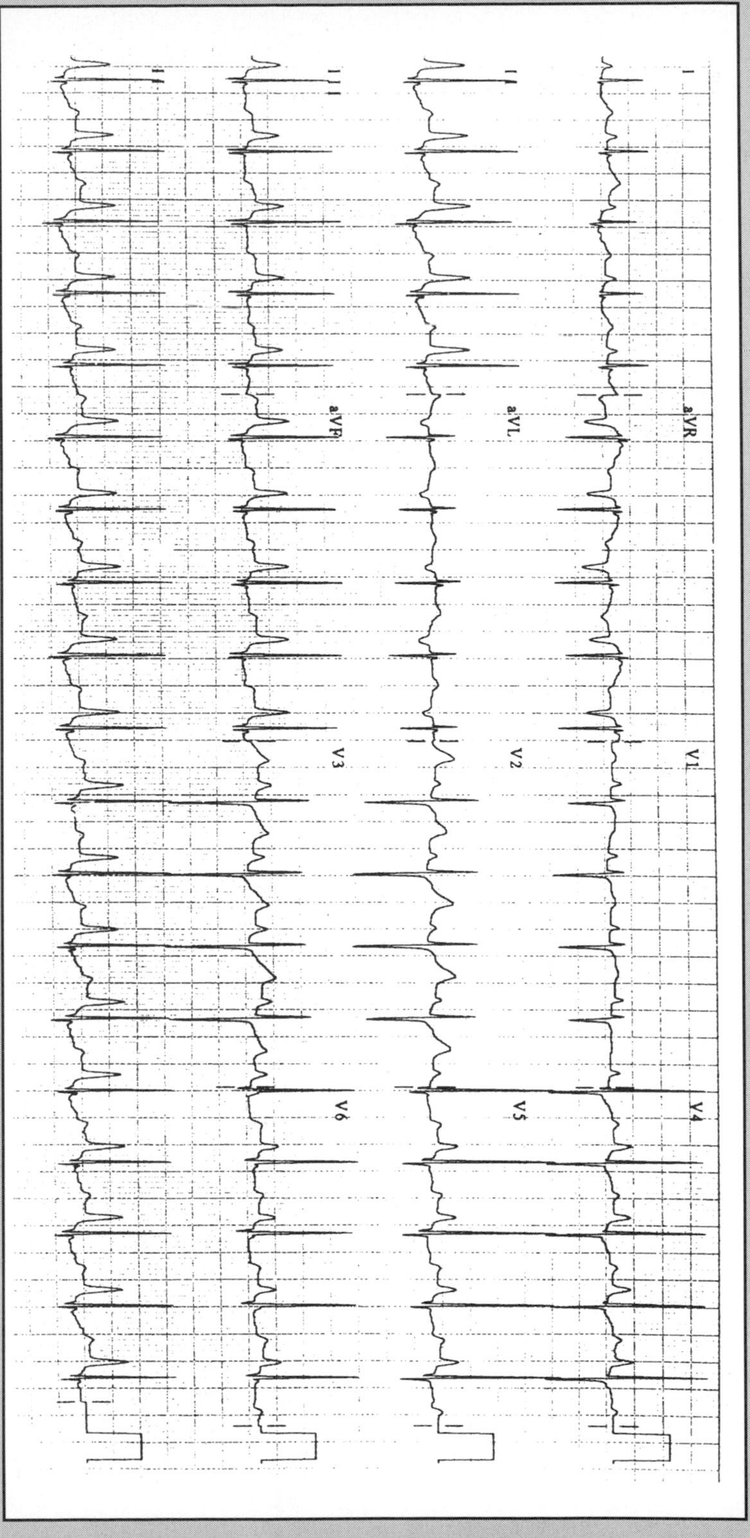

Eg. 26

WPW SYNDROME

Type A

1. Short PR interval.

2. Slurred initial upstroke of QRS - named the delta wave.

3. Slight widening of the QRS complex as a whole.

4. Secondary ST - T wave changes and QRS upright in V1.

(Eg. 27a)

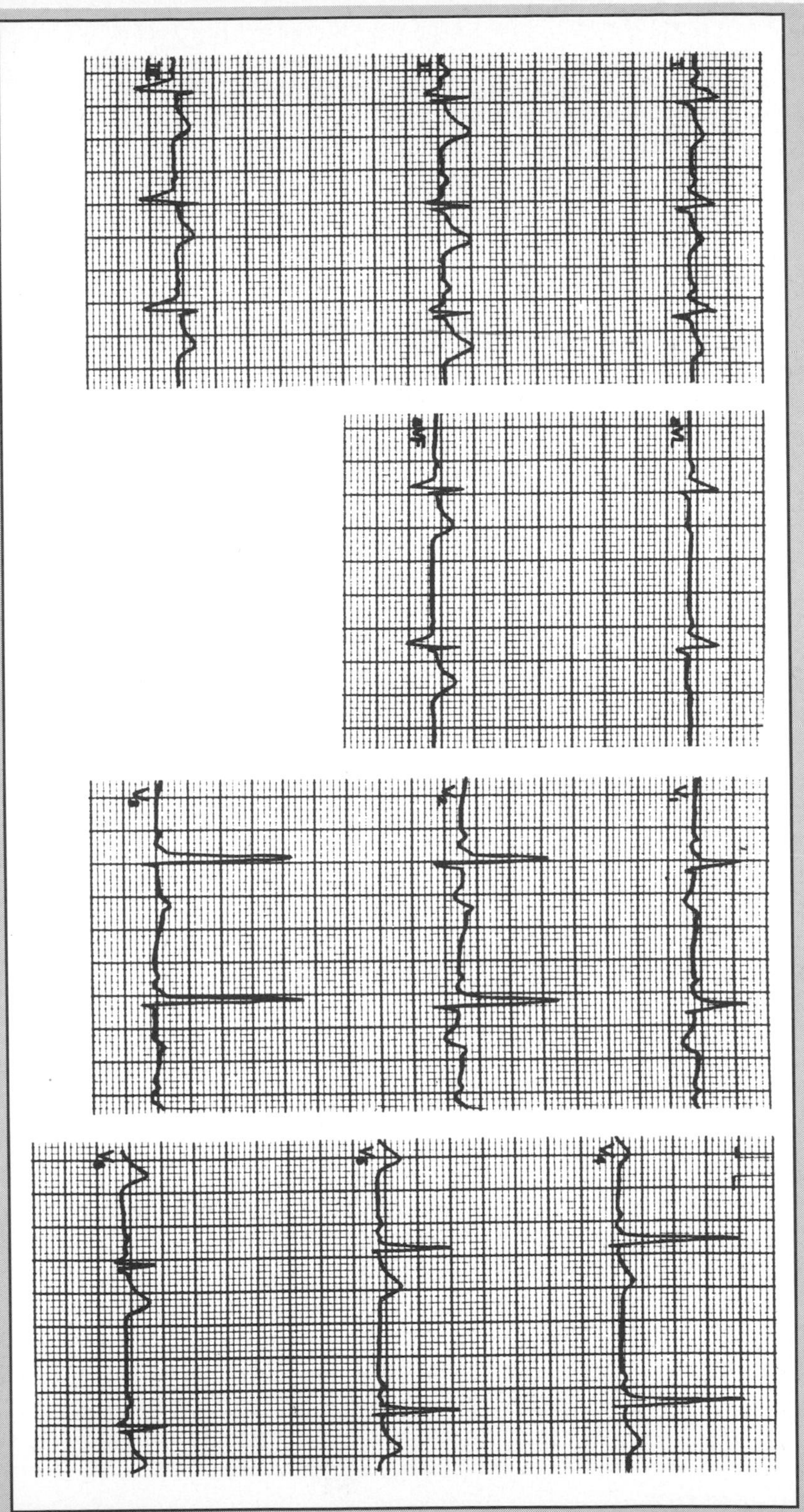

Eg. 27a

Type B

QRS inverted in V1.

(Eg. 27b)

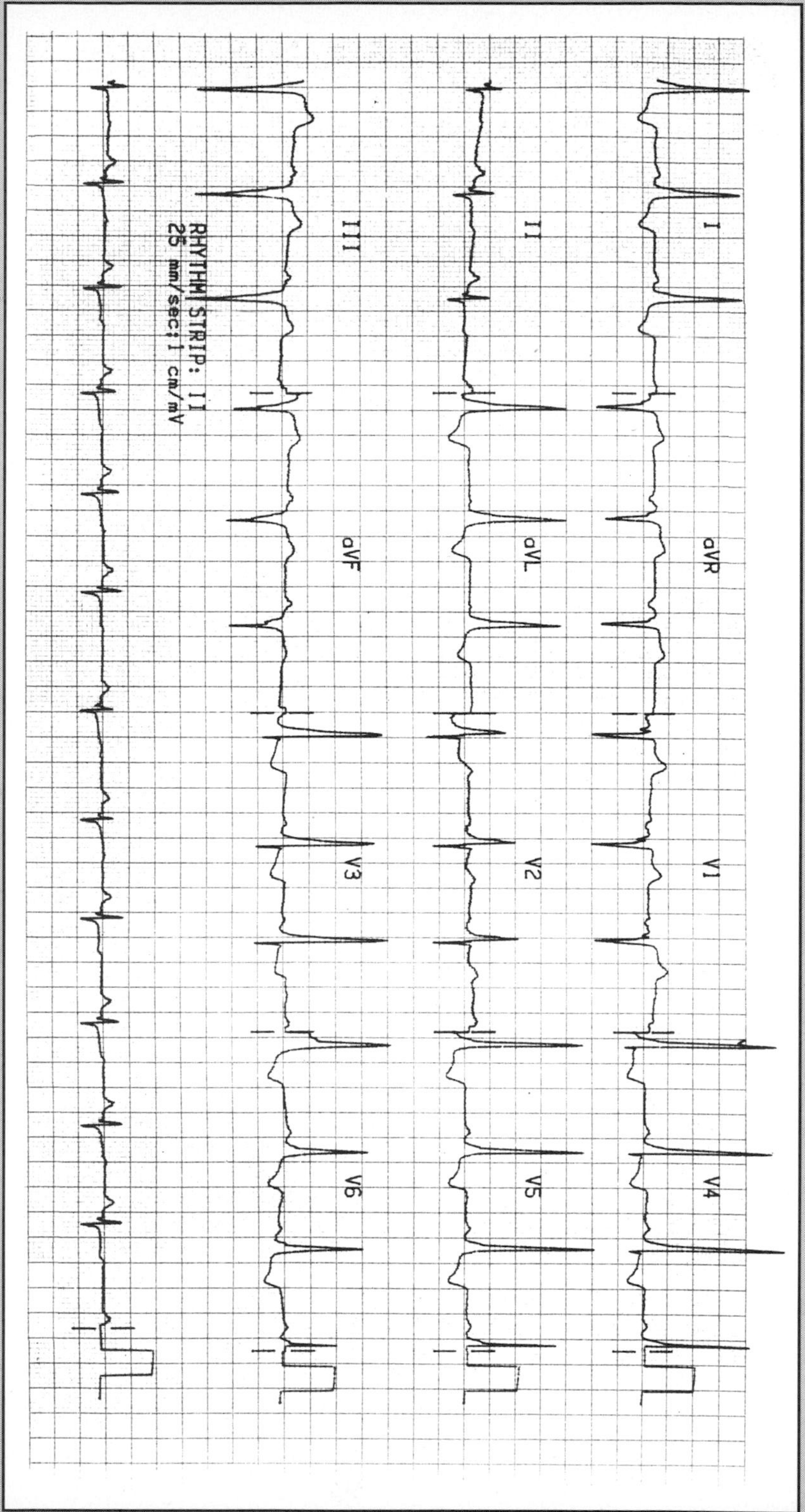
I
aVR
V1
V4
II
aVL
V2
V5
III
aVF
V3
V6
RHYTHM STRIP: II
25 mm/sec:1 cm/mV

Eg. 27b

LGL SYNDROME

1. Short PR interval.

2. No delta wave.

(Eg. 28)

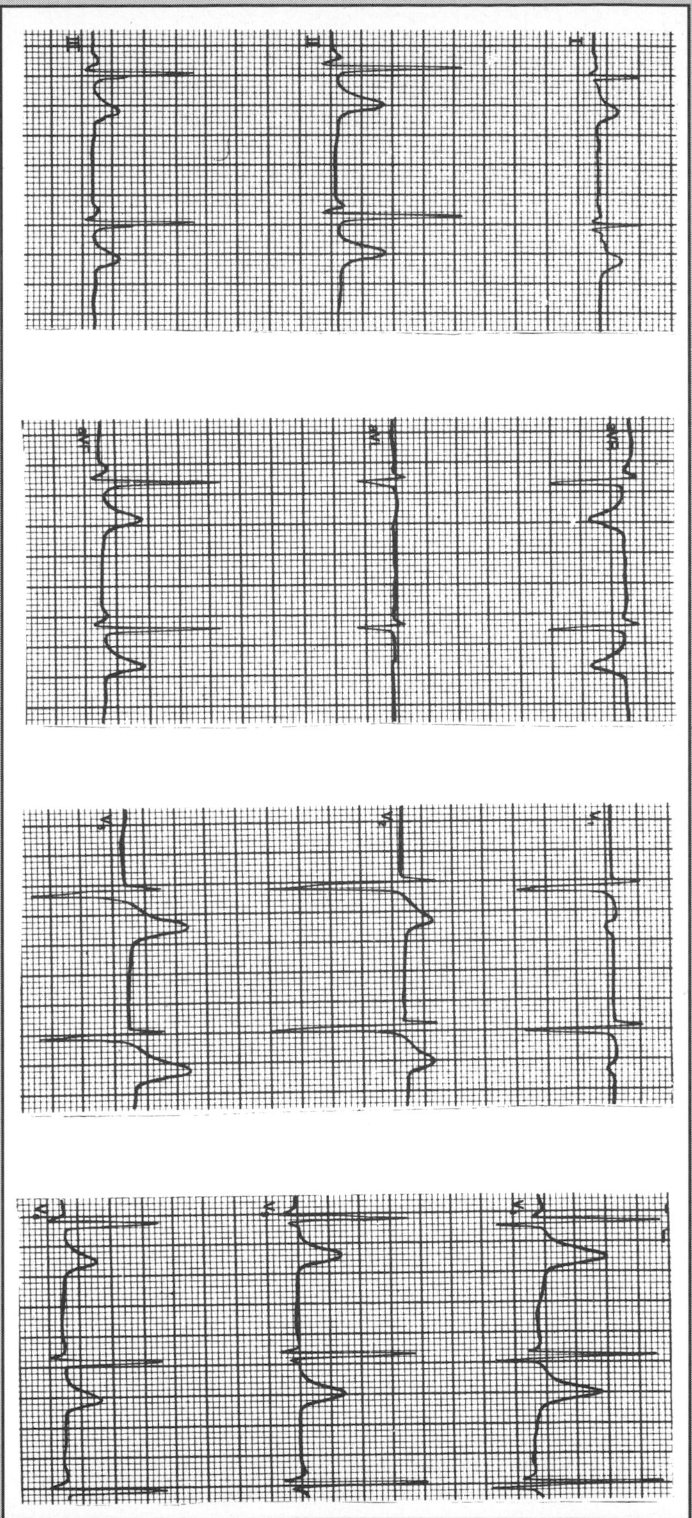

Eg. 28

DEXTROCARDIA

1. Upright P in lead III and AVR.
2. Inverted P in I and AVL.
3. Upright QRS in III, AVF and AVR.
4. QRS negative in I and AVL.
5. Tallest QRS in V1 and decreases progressively up to V6.

(Eg. 29a)

Technical dextrocardia

1. Normal precordial pattern.
2. Limb lead manifestations as in dextrocardia described above.

(Eg. 29b)

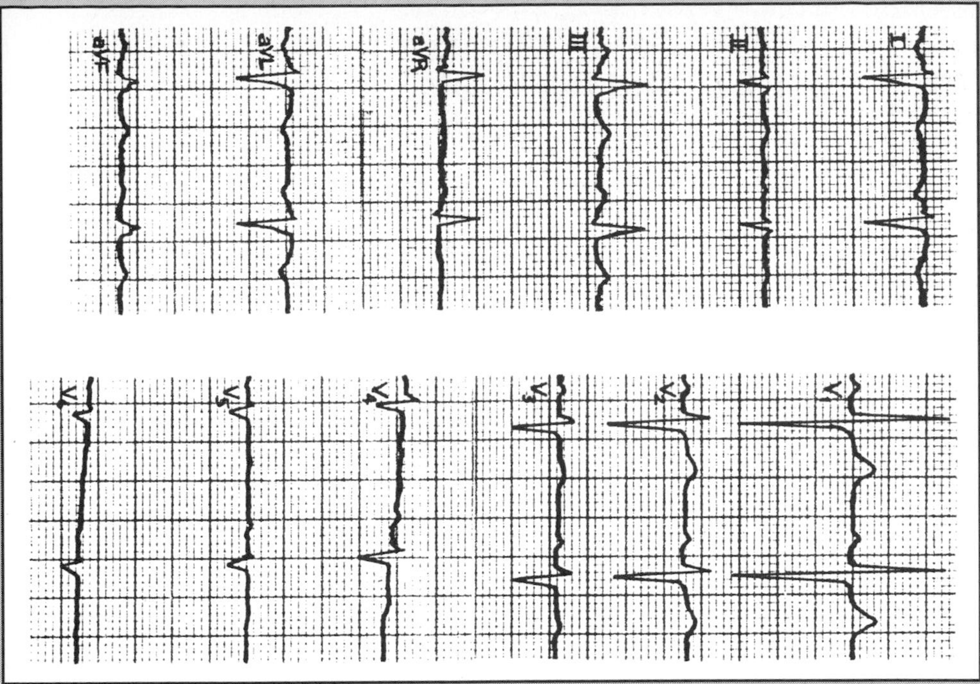

Eg. 29a

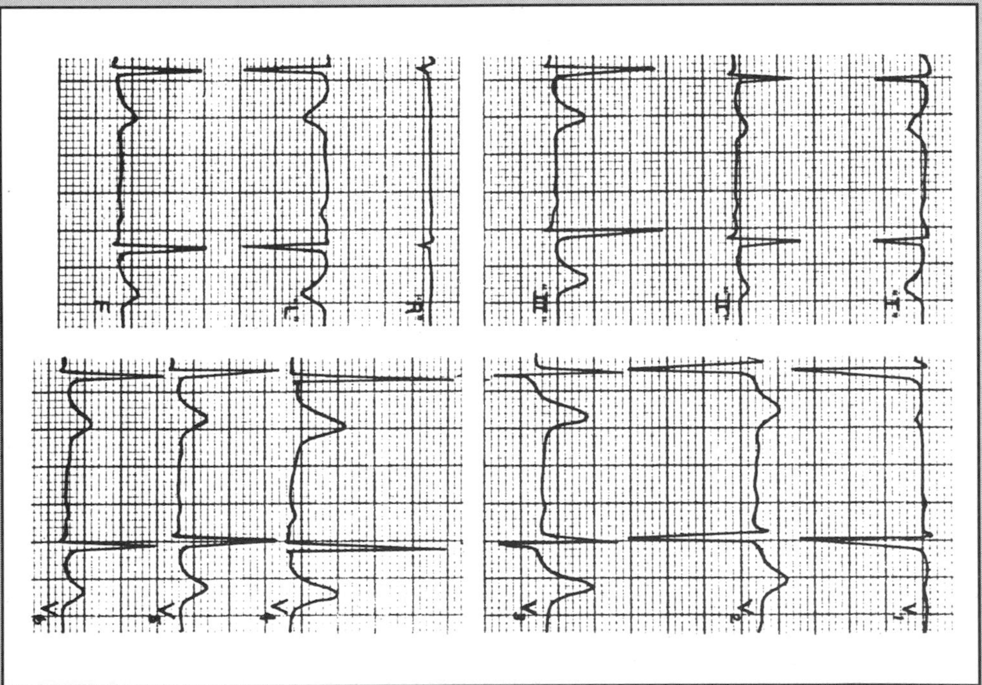

Eg. 29b

PULMONARY EMBOLISM

1. Sinus tachycardia
2. S1, Q3, T3 pattern - prominent S in lead I and prominent Q and inverted T in lead III
3. ST segment depression in leads I and II
4. RAD
5. RBBB
6. Prominent R in AVR
7. Tall peaked P in lead II
8. ST segment elevation in V1-V3 and depression in V5-V6
9. Clockwise rotation - transition zone shifts to the left

(Eg. 30)

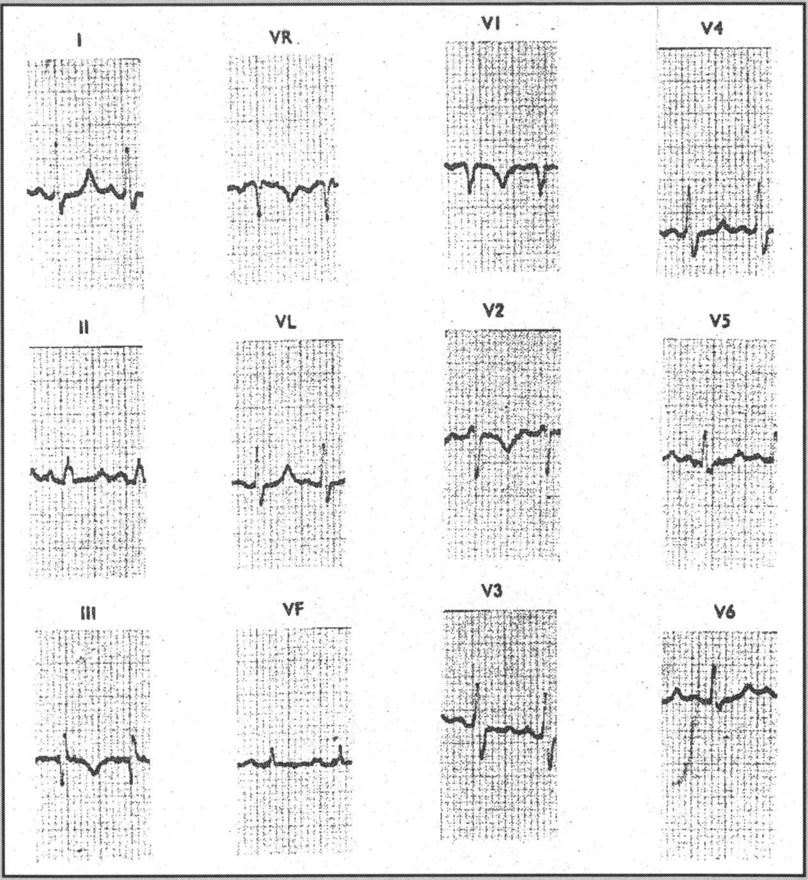

Eg. 30

CARDIOMYOPATHY

Congestive

1. Left or biatrial enlargement
2. First-degree AV block (prolonged PR)
3. LAD
4. LBBB
5. LVH
6. ST segment depression and T wave inversion in left precordial leads and inferior leads
7. QRS - T angle is > 45°
8. Cardiac arrhythmia - atrial and ventricular ectopics and AF

HOCM

1. LAH and LBBB
2. Left atrial enlargement or biatrial enlargement
3. Short PR
4. Ventricular hypertrophy
5. Simulates WPW
6. Prolonged QTc
7. Cardiac arrhythmia - AF, PSVT and VT

(Eg. 31)

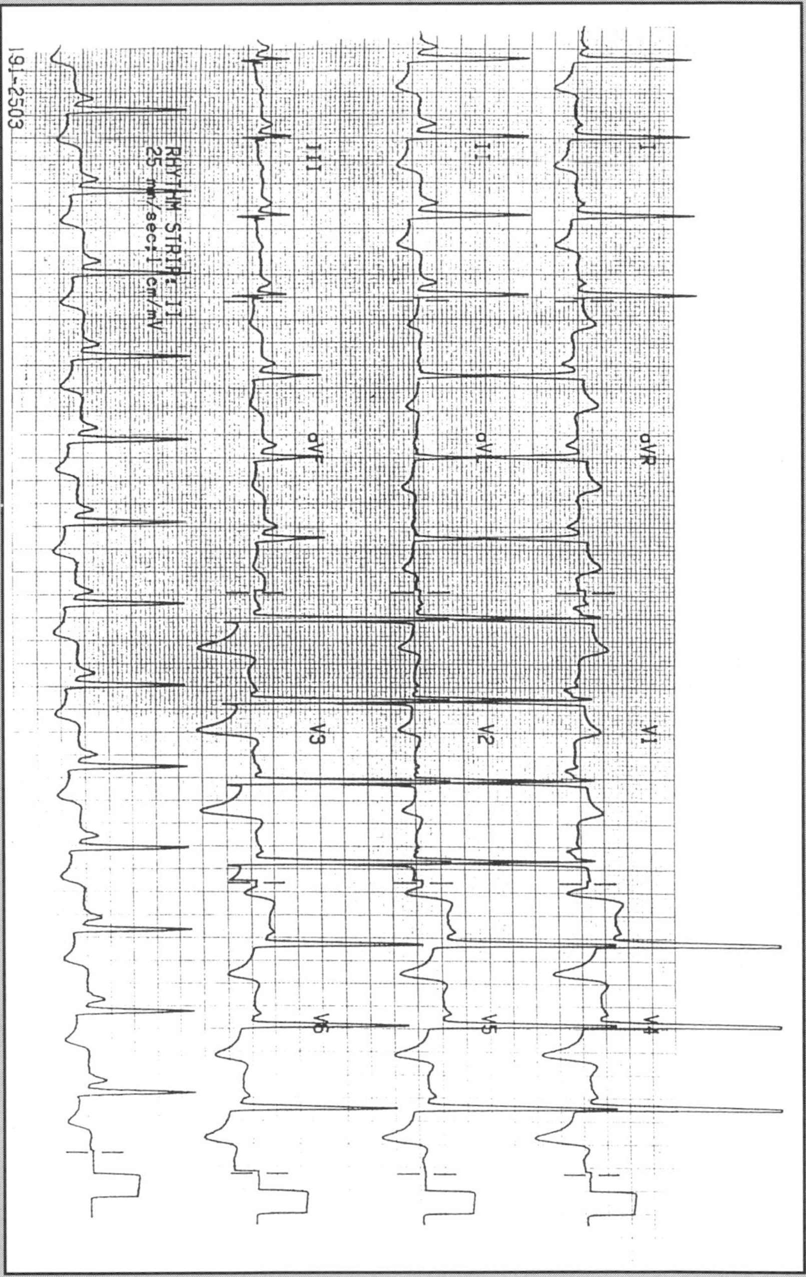
191-2503
I
II
III
aVR
aVL
aVF
V1
V2
V3
V4
V5
V6
RHYTHM STRIP: II
25 mm/sec;1 cm/mV

Eg. 31

Ventricular hypertrophy in cardiomyopathy

1. Septal - deep narrow Q wave in left and inferior leads.
2. Free left wall - deep S in V1-V2 and tall R with inverted T in V5-V6.
3. Apical - tall R in V2-V4 with S-T segment shelf and T wave inversion.
4. RVH

LOW ATRIAL RHYTHM

Inverted P waves in the inferior leads.

(Eg. 32)

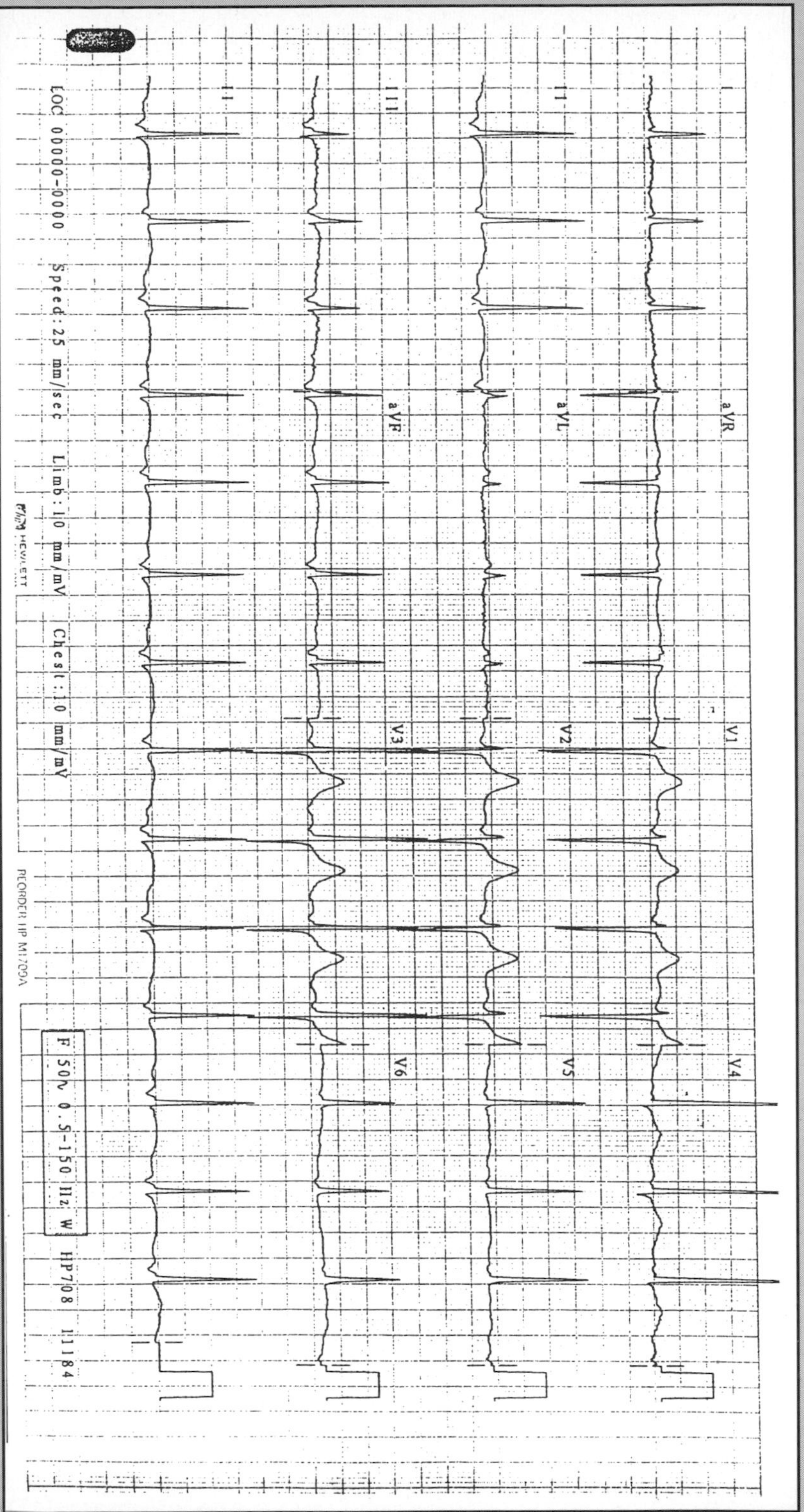
I
II
III
aVR
aVL
aVF
V1
V2
V3
V4
V5
V6
LOC 00000-0000 Speed:25 mm/sec Limb:10 mm/mV Chest:10 mm/mV
F 50~ 0.5-150 Hz W
HP708 11184
HEWLETT
REORDER HP M1709A

Eg. 32

CONDITIONS SIMULATED BY WPW SYNDROME

1. **RVH** - due to tall R waves in V1.

Differentiation - (in RVH)	i) invariably a right axis deviation ii) right atrial enlargement iii) normal PR interval iv) no delta waves

2. **BBB** - due to widening of QRS complex.

Differentiation - (in BBB)	i) PR not short ii) no delta wave

3. **Posterior MI** - due to tall R waves in VI.

Differentiation - (in post MI)	i) tall upright T waves ii) usual association of inferior or lateral wall extension of MI iii) normal PR interval iv) no delta wave

4. **Anterolateral or inferior MI** - due to negative delta wave in I, AVL or inferior leads.

Differentiation - (in MI)	i) presence of ST-T wave changes of MI but these often occur in WPW ii) no delta wave

5. **Primary myocardial disorders** - with secondary ST-T wave changes.

Differentiation - (in myocardial disease)	i) PR interval not short ii) no delta wave

6. **VT** - WPW with AF gives rise to bizarre complexes.

Differentiation - (in VT)	i) only slightly irregular unlike AF ii) no normal QRS seen - can be seen in WPW with AF iii) no WPW fusion beats

Section III

RHYTHM ANALYSIS

Type 2 (fast-slow)

Criteria:

1. Regular fast ventricular rate.
2. Inverted P waves present in front of each QRS complex with R-P' interval exceeding P'-R interval.

(Eg. 35)

b) Concealed AV bypass tract

Criteria:

1. P wave inverted in LI during the PSVT and occurring after QRS with R - P' interval > 0.07 sec.
2. Ventricular rate > 230/min (i.e. - R-R interval < 0.26 sec or 6.5 small squares). Many examples have a slower ventricular rate.

Type 1 (orthodromic)

1. No delta wave.
2. QRS normal (except when rapid atrial rate produces aberrant intraventricular conduction).
3. AV conduction through AV node.

(Eg. 36)

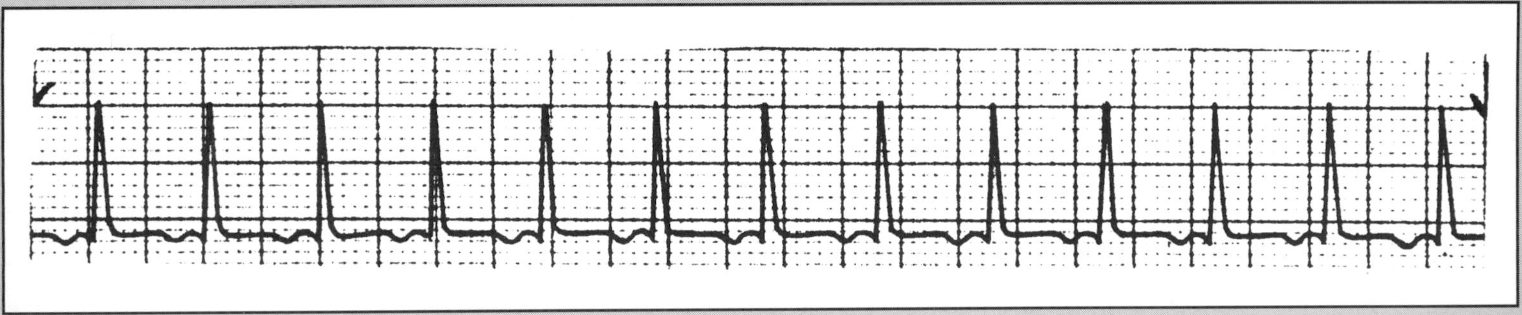

Eg. 35

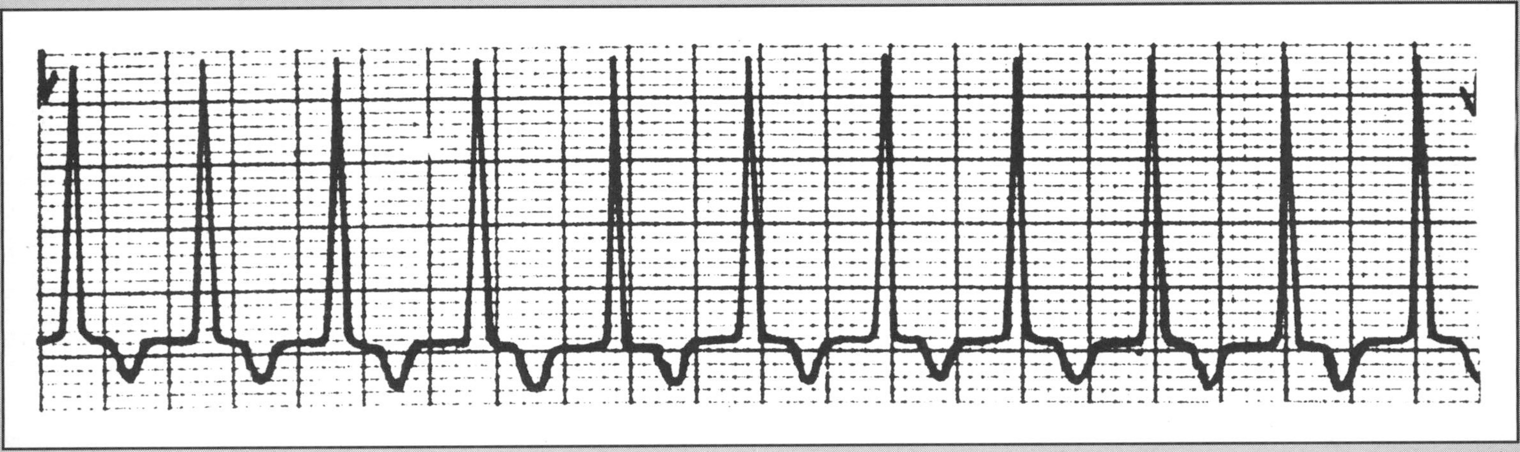

Eg. 36

4. Atrial flutter with fixed block

Criteria:

1. Regular atrial rate of about 300/min.

2. Typical saw tooth pattern may be seen in V1 and inferior leads.

3. Regular QRS complexes with different grades of block may be present.

NOTE: *atrial flutter must be considered in the differential diagnosis of a tachycardia of >150/min even if flutter waves are absent.*

(Eg. 39)

5. Junctional tachycardia

Criteria:

1. P waves may be absent, but if present may be hidden in the QRS complex or may precede or follow the QRS complex.

2. QRS is regular and rapid.

(Eg. 40)

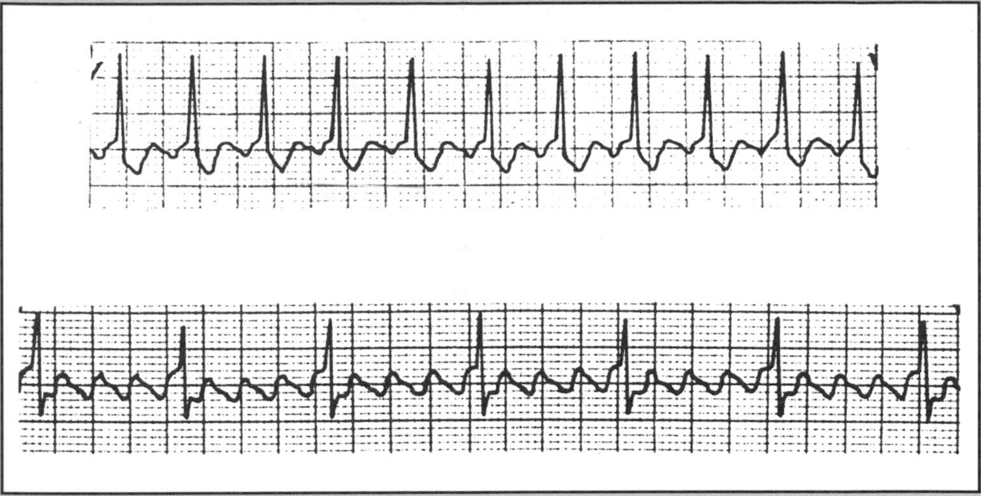

Eg. 39

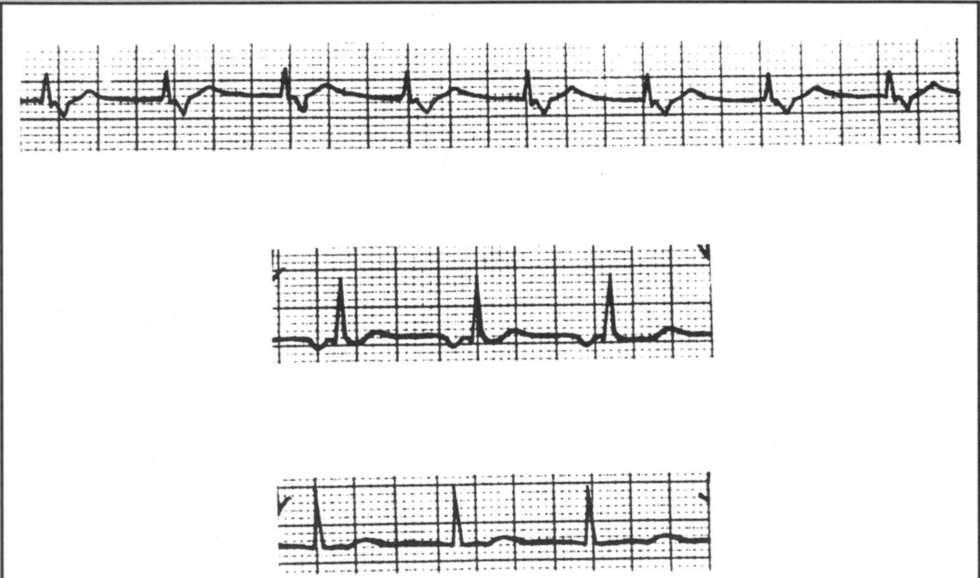

Eg. 40

6. Ventricular tachycardia

Types:

1. Paroxysmal - a) Non-sustained VT. Minimum of four consecutive VEBs with a maximum duration of 30 sec
   - b) Sustained VT

2. Non-paroxysmal VT (AIVR)

3. Fascicular tachycardia

4. Torsade de pointes

Criteria:

Type 1

1. Wide QRS complex (0.12 sec or more)

2. Regular QRS rate of 150 - 250/min

(Eg. 41a & b)

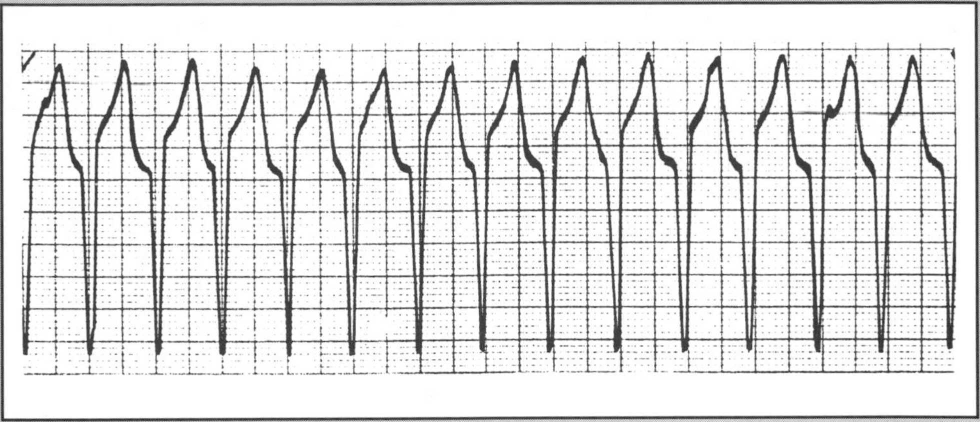

Eg. 41a

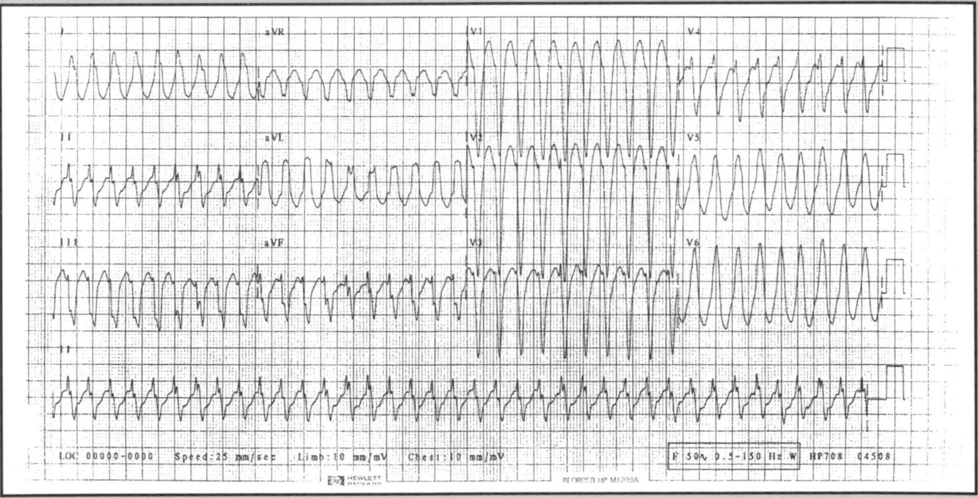
I
aVR
V1
V4
II
aVL
V2
V5
III
aVF
V3
V6
II
LOC 00000-0000 Speed:25 mm/sec Limb:10 mm/mV Chest:10 mm/mV
F 50~ 0.5-150 Hz W HP708 04508

Eg. 41b

Type 2

As for paroxysmal VT except that the QRS rate is between 60 - 130/min

(Eg. 42)

Type 3

1. Arises in left posterior fascicle.

2. QRS rate is dependent on whether it is paroxysmal (150-250/min) or non-paroxysmal (60-130/min).

3. QRS morphology can be near normal, but often becomes abnormally wide due to the development of RBBB and LAH.

4. Ventricular origin can be diagnosed if there is presence of - fusion beats: capture beats: AV dissociation and ventricular rate > atrial rate.

Type 4

1. QRS rate is between 200 - 250/min.

2. QRS axis keeps on changing.

3. Usually associated with a previously prolonged QTc interval.

(Eg. 43)

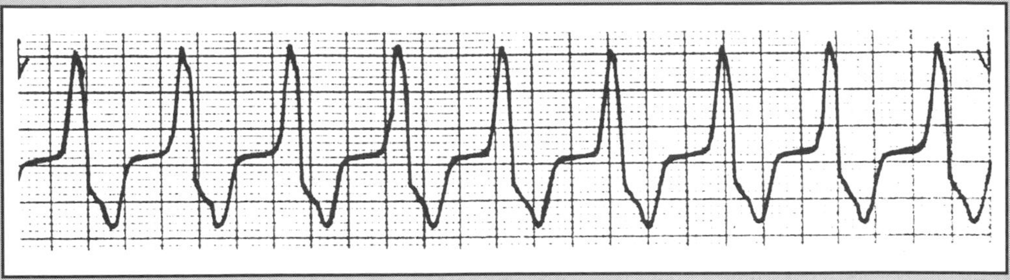

Eg. 42

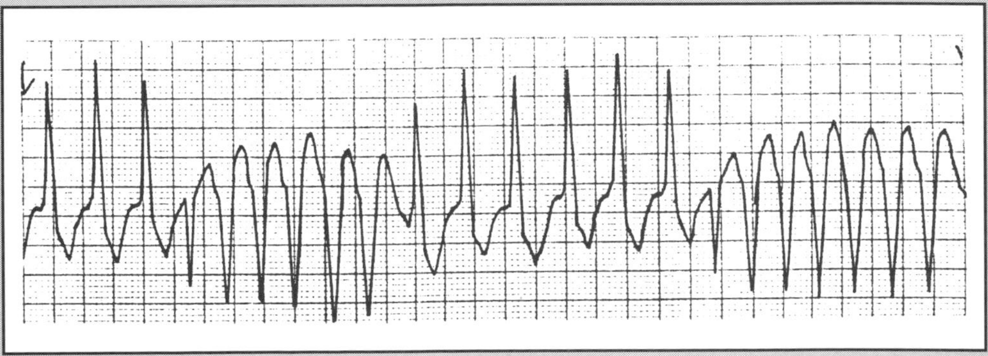

Eg. 43

6. Axis within -30 to -120 degrees.

7. QRS configuration in V1:

   a) R wave
   b) Rr wave
   c) RS wave
   d) Qs wave
   e) QR wave

(Eg. 54)

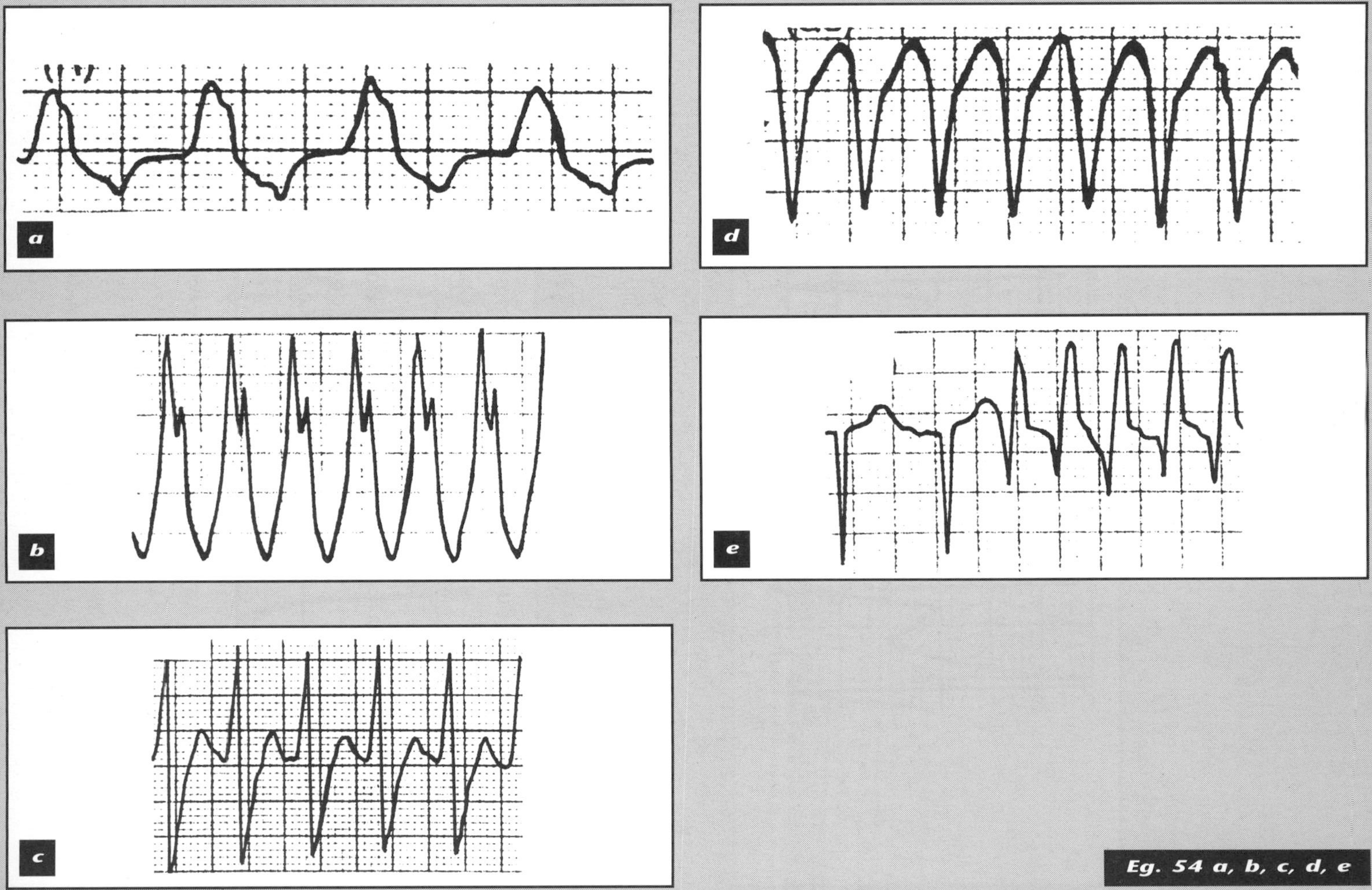

Eg. 54 a, b, c, d, e

Analysis of narrow complex tachycardia

1. Position of P wave in relation to QRS.
2. P wave axis.
3. Atrial rate.
4. Alternating changes of QRS complex.
5. Relationship between atrial and ventricular activity.

a) - (i) P following QRS: reciprocating tachycardia.
(ii) P in QRS: AV nodal tachycardia.

b) - (i) P wave axis (inferior-superior), i.e. negative P in II and III: AV nodal tachycardia and incessant atrial tachycardia using retrograde accessory pathway.
(ii) P is +ve or biphasic in II and -ve or biphasic in III: circus movement tachycardia.
(iii) Superior - inferior axis (+ve P in II and III): atrial tachycardia.

c) - Atrial rate: 170/min - reciprocating tachycardia or AVNT or atrial tachycardia.

300/min - atrial tachycardia
150/min - incessant tachycardia

d) - Alternation of QRS: reciprocating tachycardia.

e) - Majority of atrial flutter and 30% of atrial tachycardia have second-degree AV block. Occasional 1:1 atrial flutter can also occur. P:QRS ratio is 1:1 in the rest.

f) - If rate > 100/min and < 160/min with P waves before each QRS then it indicates sinus tachycardia.

g) - If flutter waves present then atrial flutter.

h) - If P waves regular and at 180 - 240/min and twice as much as QRS then it is atrial tachycardia with 2:1 AV block.

i) - Regular ventricular rate with no P waves at 180 - 240/min indicates AV nodal re-entrant tachycardia (common 'slow-fast' type).

j) - Regular ventricular rate at 180-240/min with one P wave to each QRS.

(i) R P' = P' R: atrial tachycardia with 2:1 AV block. **(Eg. 56)**

(ii) R P' < P' R: AVRT (involving bypass tract) or AVNRT. **(Eg. 57)**

(iii) R P' > P' R: AVNRT of the uncommon 'fast-slow' type. **(Eg. 58)**

k) - Irregular ventricular rate with no P waves - AF.

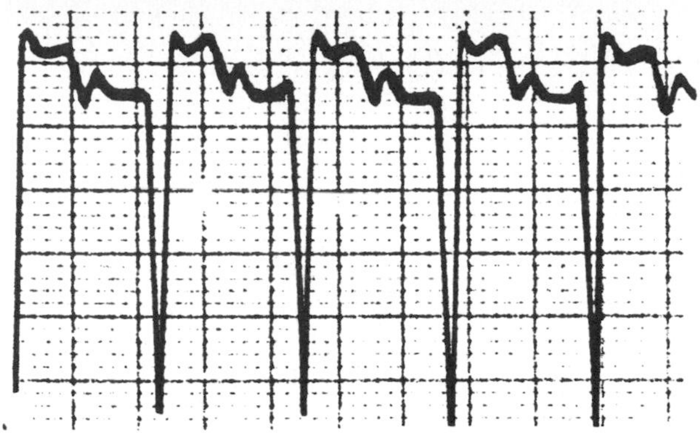

Eg. 56

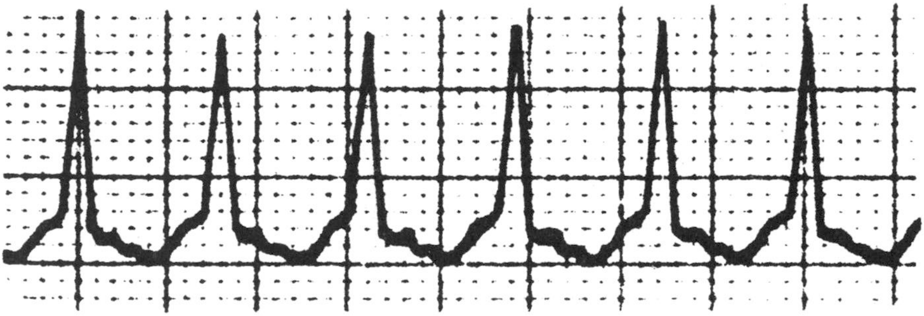

Eg. 57

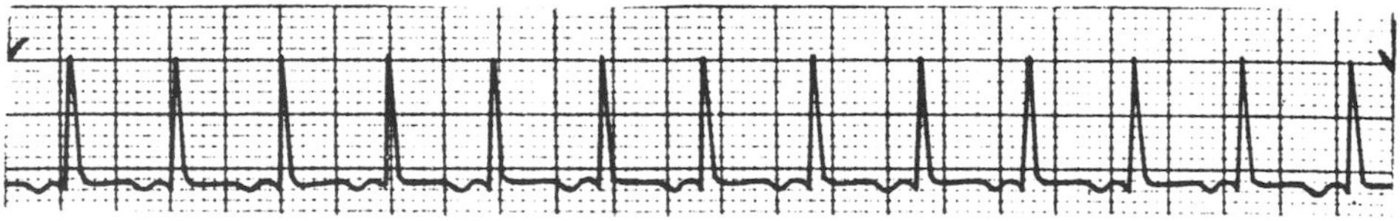

Eg. 58

IRREGULAR TACHYCARDIAS

1. **AF alone or with:** a) established BBB
   b) rate-dependent aberration
   c) accessory pathway conduction

Criteria for AF:

1. No P waves or flutter waves seen.

2. Atrial activity is either absent or irregular in amplitude and rate.

3. QRS complexes are irregular in amplitude and rate. **(Eg. 59a)**

A) Established BBB - if a previous trace is present showing BBB. **(Eg. 59b)**

B) Rate-dependent aberration - morphology of QRS is different if the preceding RR interval is long or short. **(Eg. 60)**

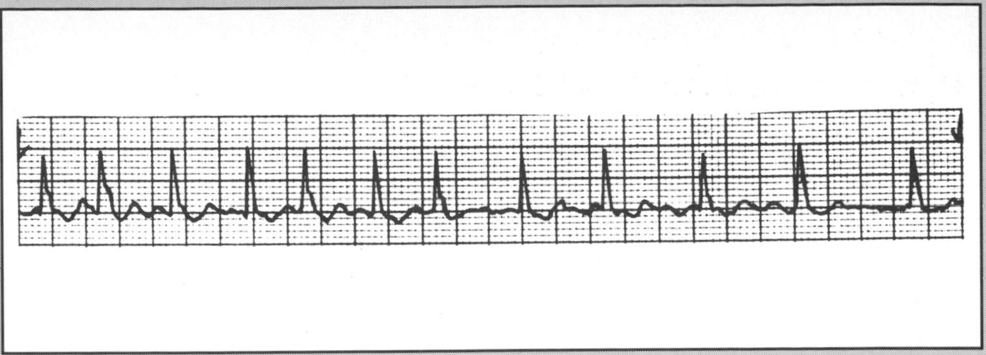

Eg. 59a

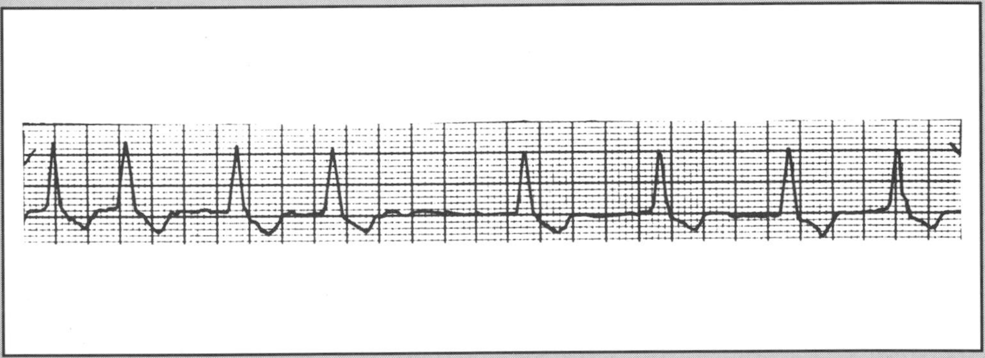

Eg. 59b

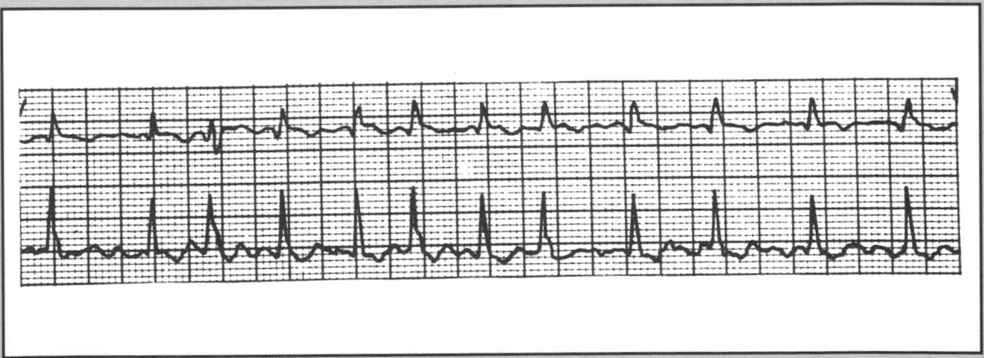

Eg. 60

C) ***Accessory pathway conduction*** - if RR interval is 260 msec or less than 6.5 small squares it indicates a ventricular rate of 230/min. If impulses are passing through the AV node then the ventricular rate will not rise above 200/min. So if the ventricular rate is above this then it means that the impulses probably are passing via an accessory conducting pathway. **(Eg. 61)**

NOTE: *when RR interval = or < 200 msec (five small squares), i.e. rate if 300/min: then there is a definite possibility that VF might develop.*

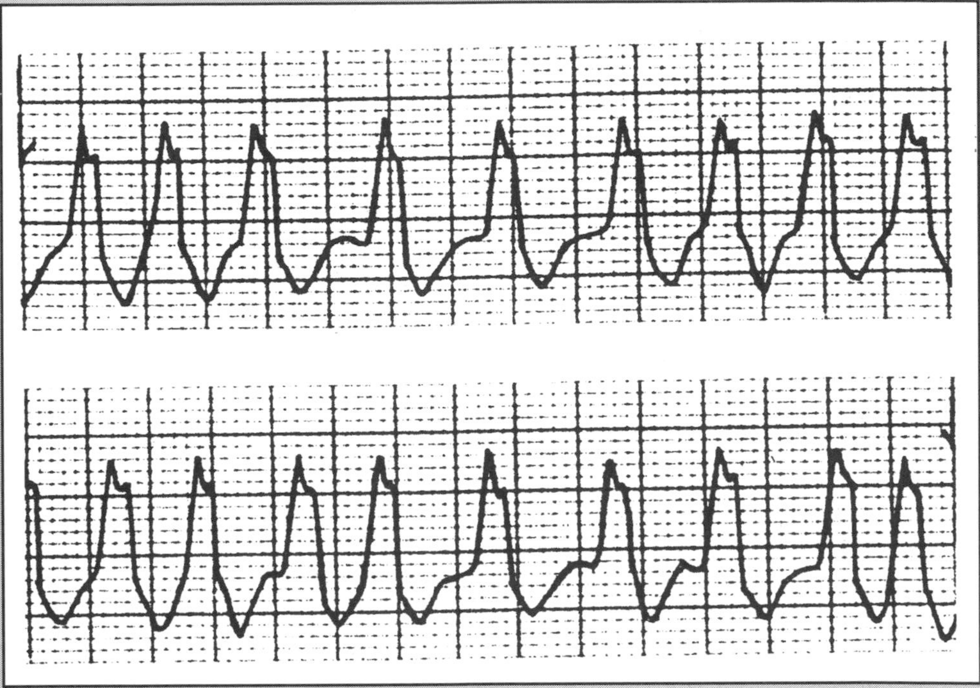

Eg. 61

2. **Atrial flutter with varying block**

Two categories according to Waldo and Maclean. **(Eg. 62)**

Types	*Atrial rate*	*Response to rapid atrial pacing*
I	230-350/min	Interrupted with restoration of sinus rhythm
II	340-430/min	Unresponsive to pacing

***NOTE:** atrial flutter must be remembered when considering a regular tachycardia of 150/min even if no flutter waves are seen.*

3. **Multiple atrial ectopics (Eg. 63)**

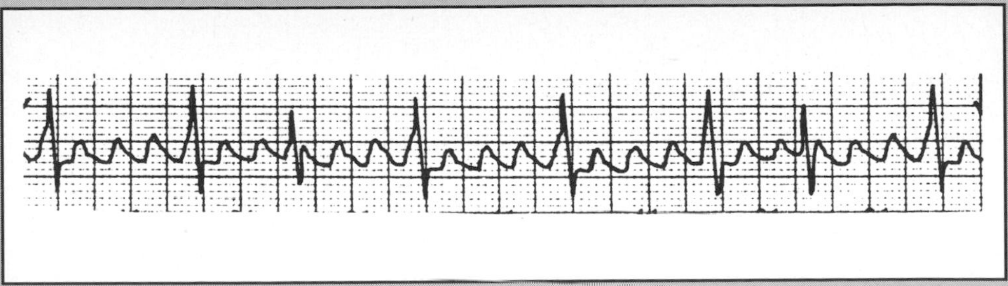

Eg. 62

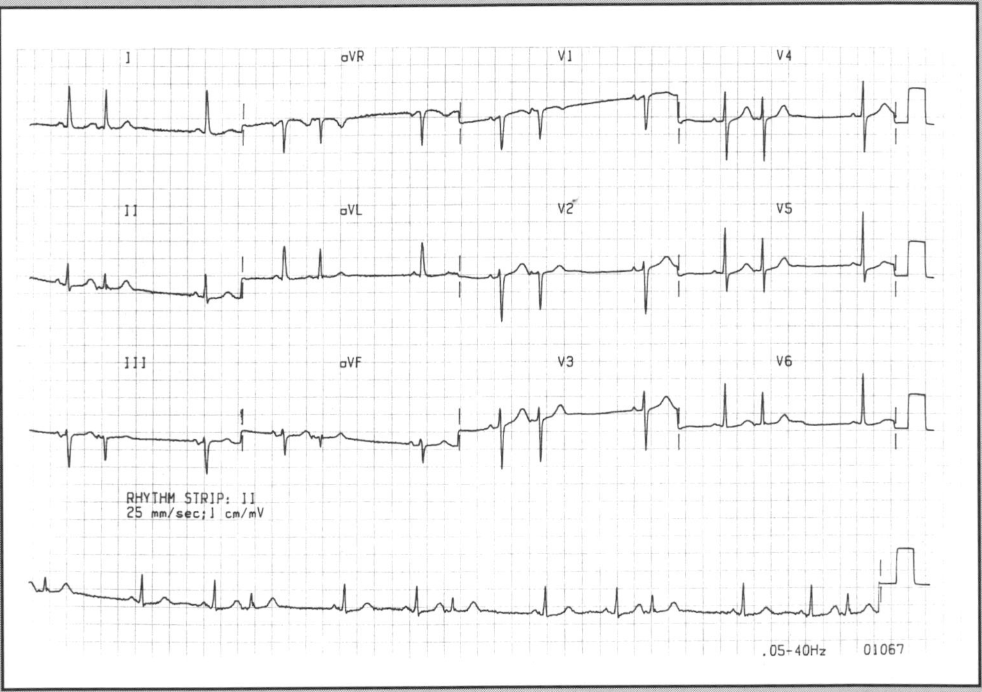

Eg. 63

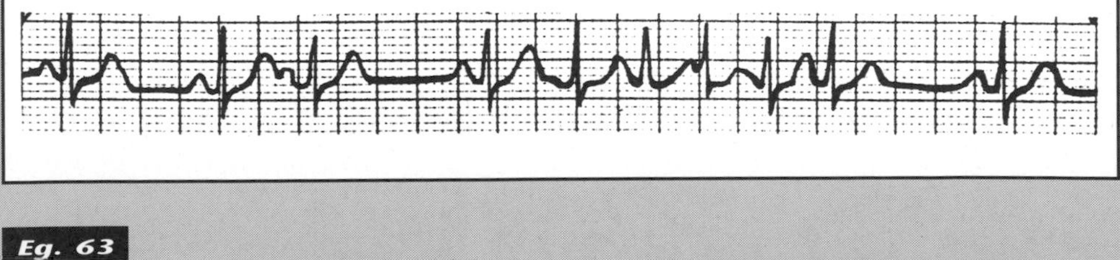

Eg. 63

4. **Multifocal atrial tachycardia (Eg. 64)**

Criteria:

a) At least three different P waves

b) Varying PR intervals

c) Rate is about 120/min

5. **Multiple ventricular ectopics (Eg. 65a)**

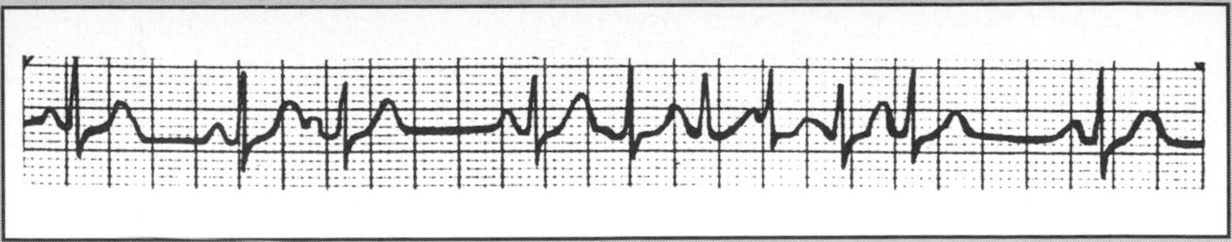

Eg. 64

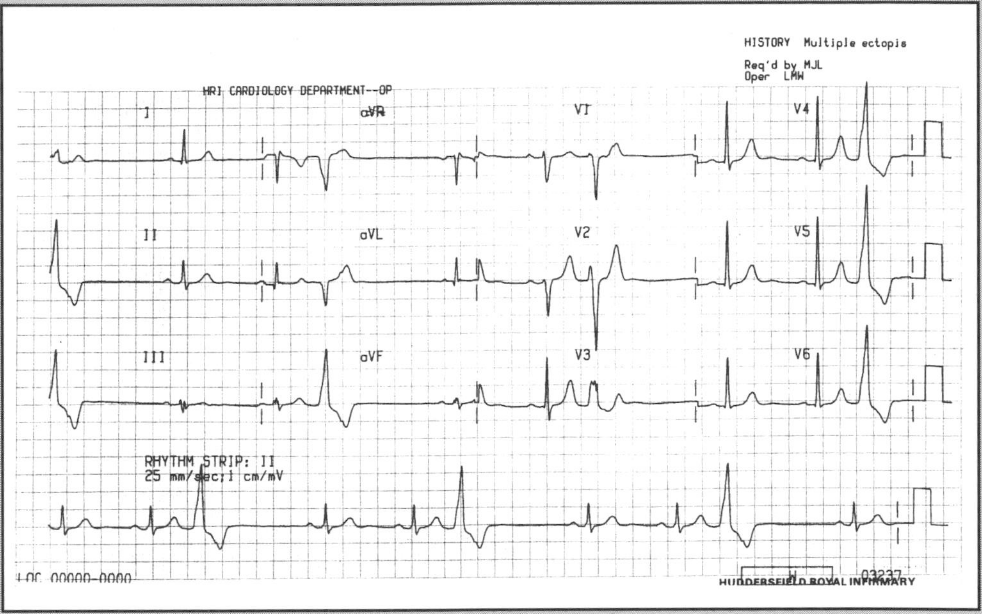

Eg. 65a

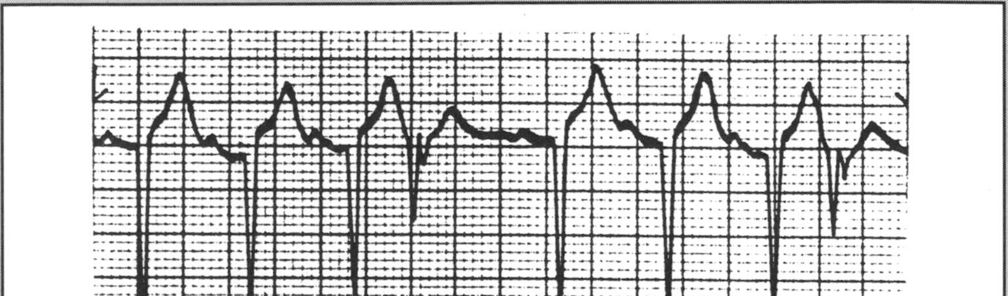

Eg. 65a

6. **Torsade de pointes (Eg. 65b)**

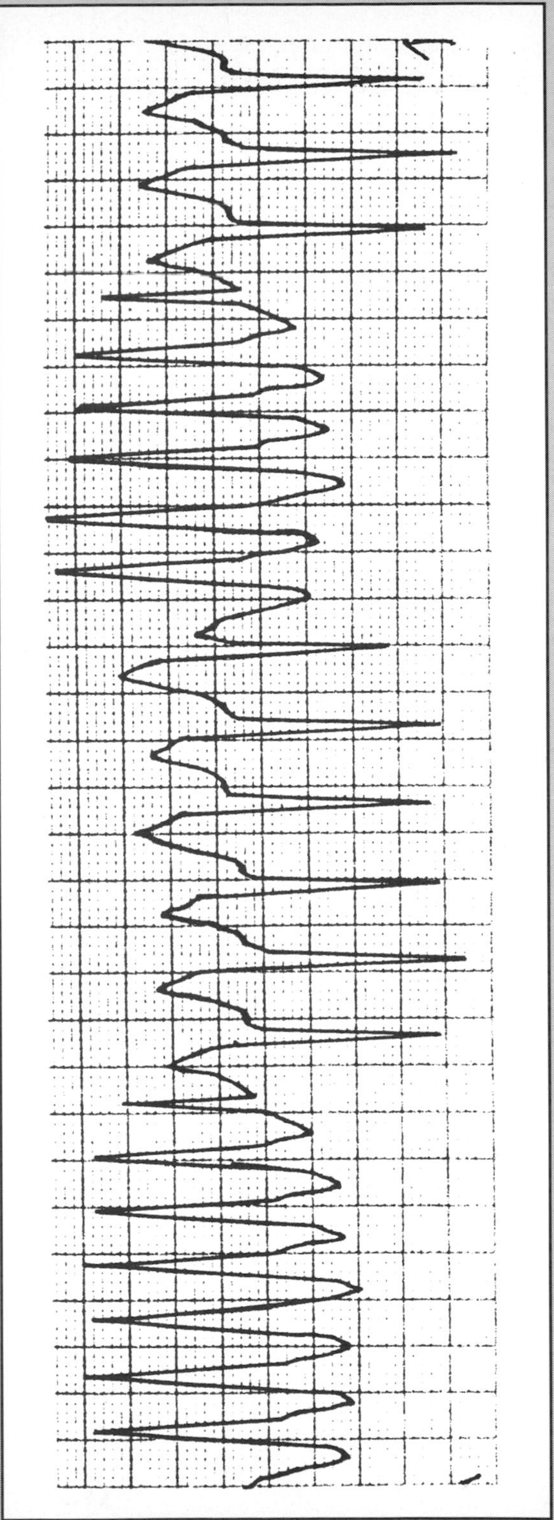

Eg. 65b

REGULAR BRADYCARDIAS

1. **Sinus bradycardia** - sinus rhythm with a rate below 60/min. (Eg. 66)

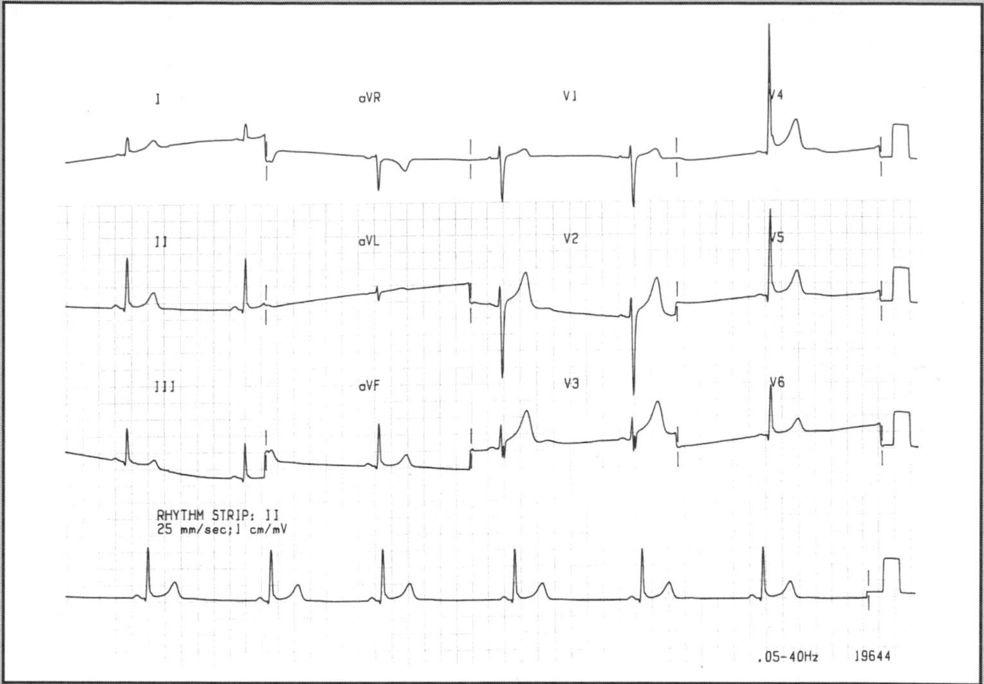
I
aVR
V1
V4
II
aVL
V2
V5
III
aVF
V3
V6
RHYTHM STRIP: II
25 mm/sec;1 cm/mV
.05-40Hz
19644

Eg. 66

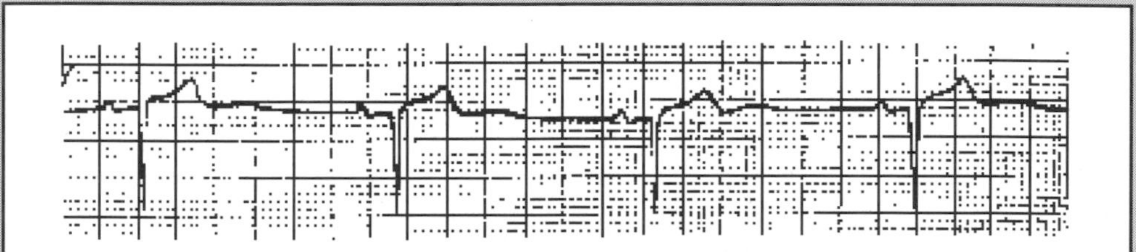

Eg. 66

2. **Second-degree heart block** - mobitz type II. **(Eg. 67)**

Criteria:

a) PR interval is constant.

b) Conduction to the ventricle is in a ratio of 2:1; 3:1 or 4:1 or higher.

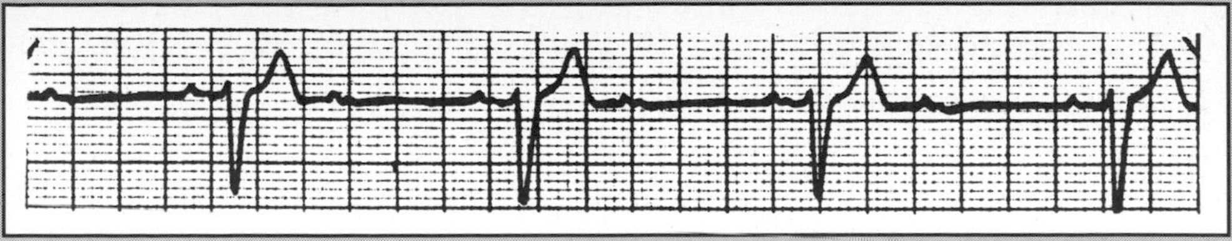

Eg. 67

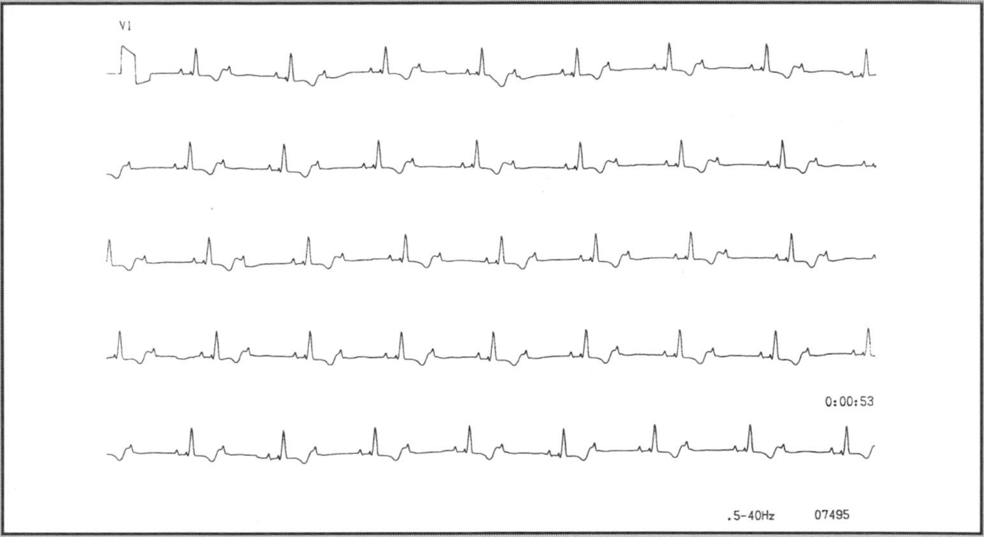

Eg. 67

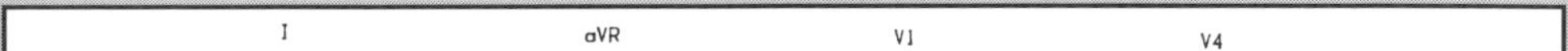

Eg. 67

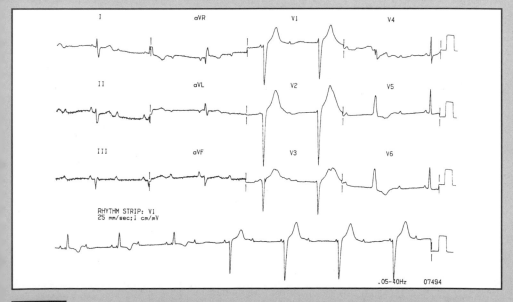

3. **Complete heart block**

With normal sinus discharges (Eg. 68)

Criteria:

a) P wave appear at a constant and faster rate than the ventricular rate.

b) QRS at a constant rate:

40-60/min if escape focus is higher;

30-40/min if escape focus is lower.

c) No relationship of the P waves to the QRS complex with the P waves moving in and out of the QRS complex.

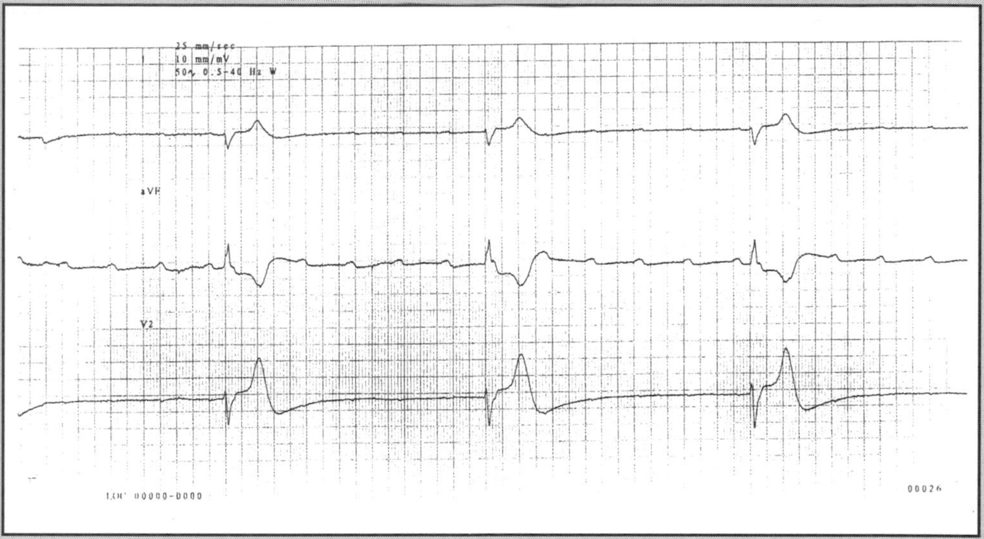

Eg. 68

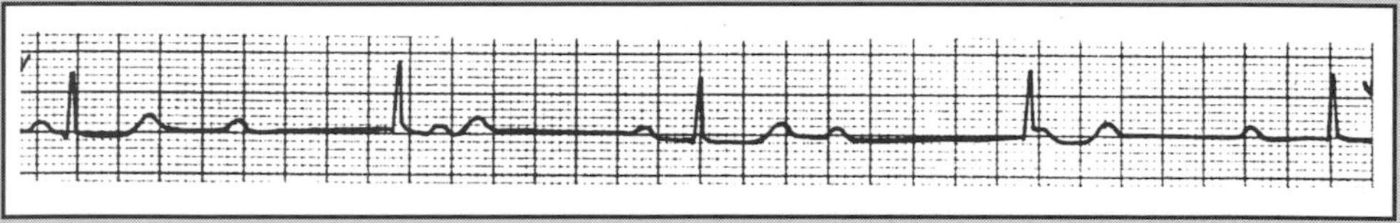

Eg. 68

With atrial fibrillation (Eg. 69)

Criteria:

a) No P waves seen - only fibrillary waves or undulating baseline.

b) Slow constant QRS complexes.

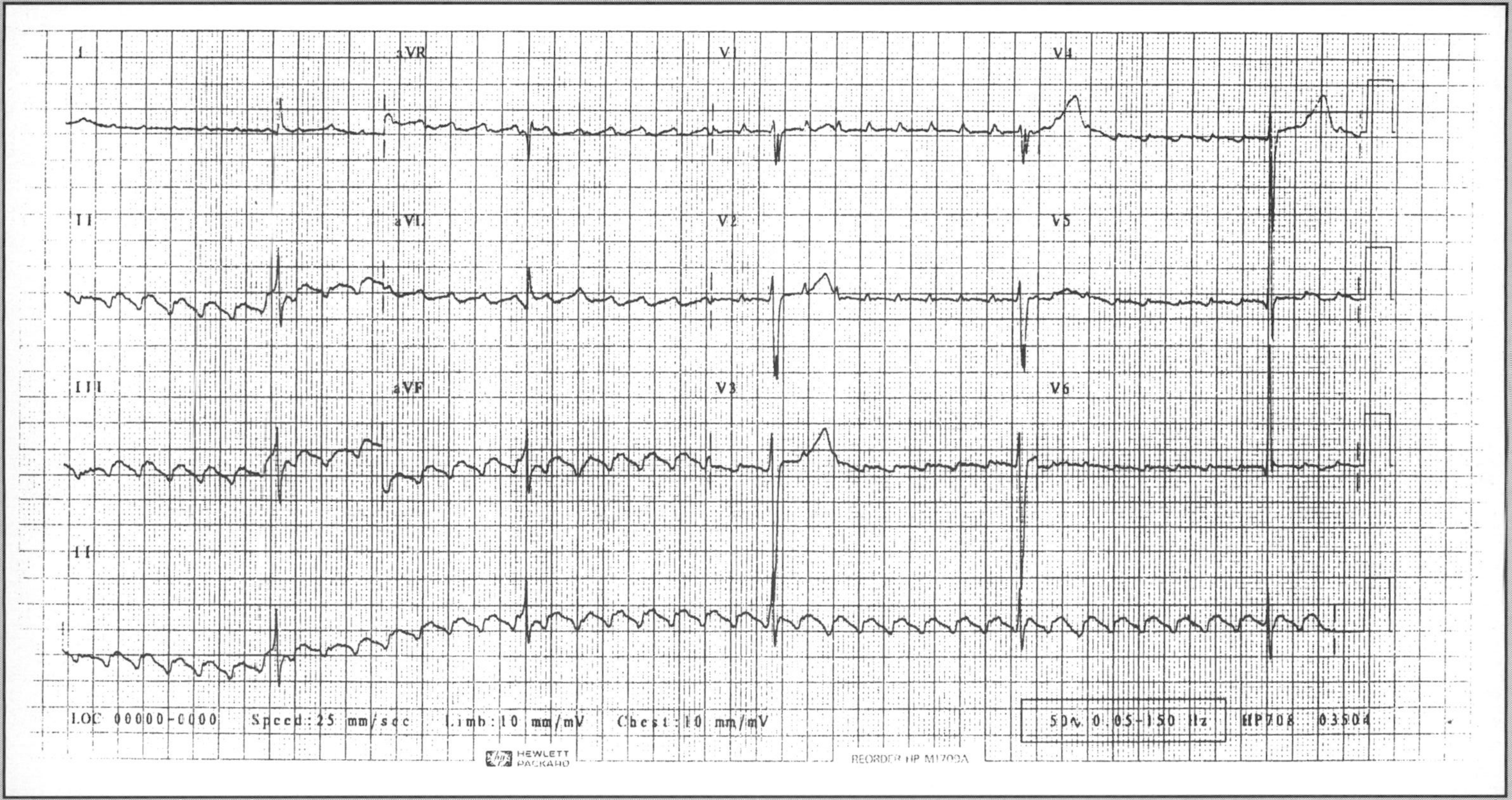
I
aVR
V1
V4
II
aVL
V2
V5
III
aVF
V3
V6
II
LOC 00000-0000
Speed: 25 mm/sec
Limb: 10 mm/mV
Chest: 10 mm/mV
50~ 0.05-150 Hz
HP708 03504
HEWLETT PACKARD
REORDER HP M1700A

Eg. 69

4. **Idioventricular rhythm: (Eg. 70)**

Criteria:

a) Regular QRS complex.

b) No P wave preceding the QRS complex.

c) P wave is absent or inverted or follows the QRS depending on the site of the junctional escape focus.

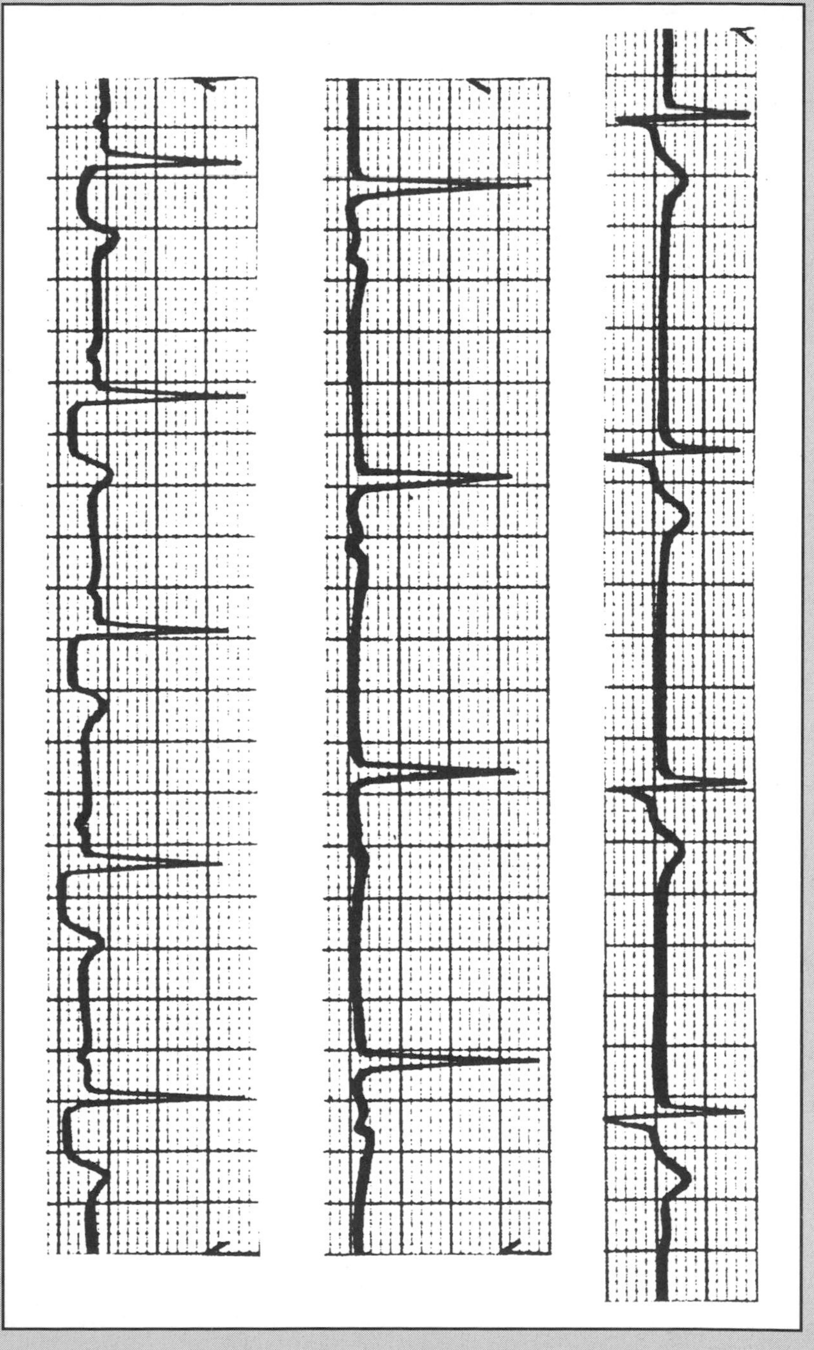

Eg. 70

IRREGULAR BRADYCARDIAS

1. **Wandering pacemaker (Eg. 71)**

Criteria:

a) Different P waves morphologies (at least three).

b) Different PR intervals.

c) Different P waves may have different rhythmicity.

2. **Atrial premature beats (APB)**

Types:

a) Blocked APB - early P wave not followed by a QRS complex. **(Eg. 72)**

b) Aberration - premature P wave comes sufficiently late for AV node to propagate the impulse but the distal conducting tissue has not recovered fully. Impulse therefore takes a different route to the ventricle usually having a BBB pattern. **(Eg. 73)**

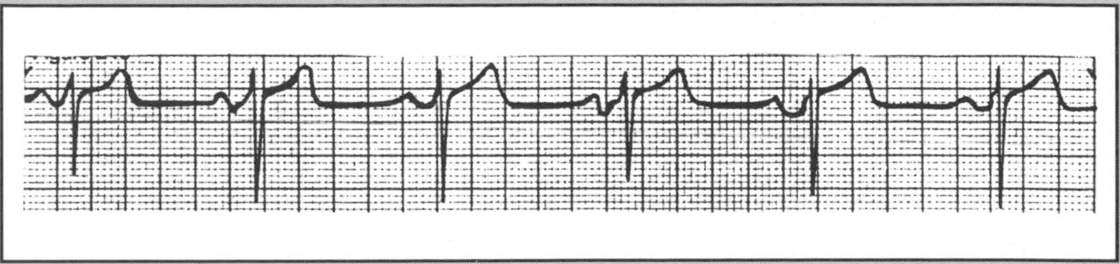

Eg. 71

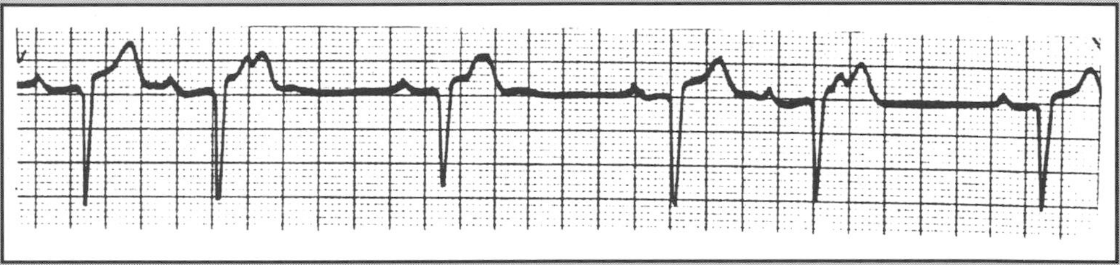

Eg. 72

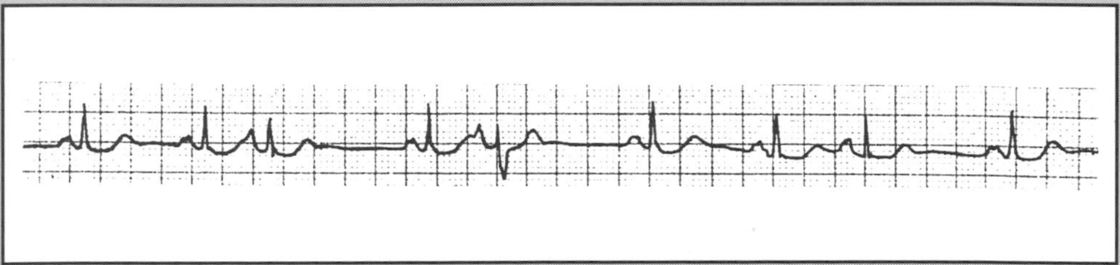

Eg. 73

c) Atrial bigeminy - APB if occurring every other beat is bigeminy. **(Eg. 74)** It is trigeminy if it occurs every third beat.

3. **Atrial parasystole (Eg. 75)**

Sinus beat or an ectopic beat cannot alter the rhythmicity of the parasystolic focus as a result of entrance block.

Criteria:

a) Variable coupling.

b) Fixed or multiples of interatrial ectopic interval.

c) Occasional fusion beats.

d) Capture of atria by ectopic focus.

NOTE: *exit block - parasystole is not always present and occasionally an ectopic discharge is absent when expected suggesting the possibility of an exit block.*

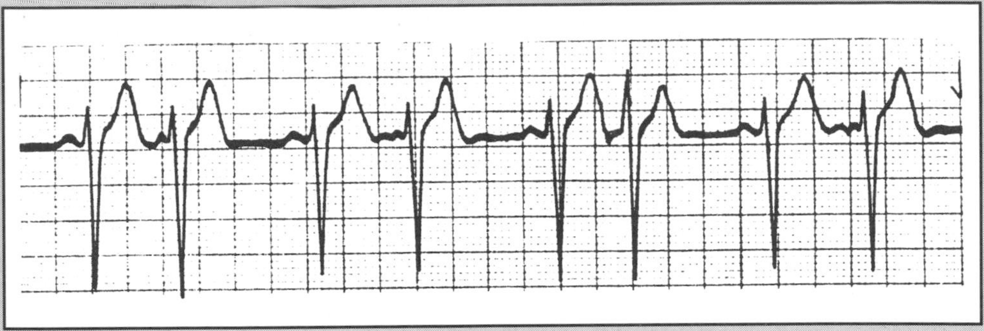

Eg. 74

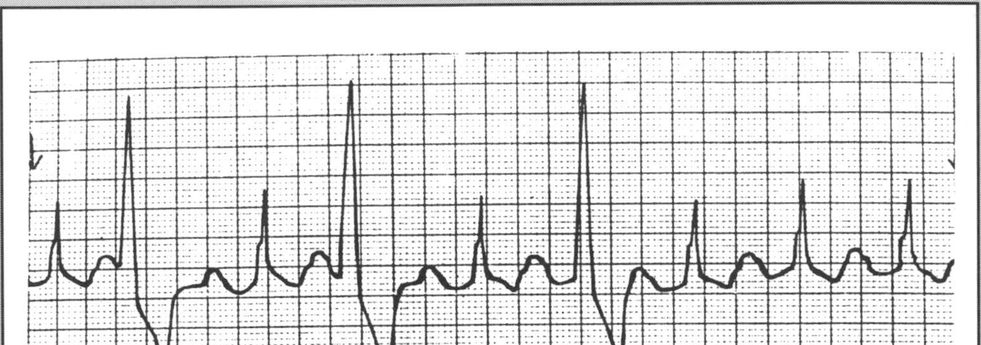

Eg. 75

4. **Sinoatrial block** (SA block: three degrees)

First degree: delay in impulse transmission from SA node to surrounding atrial tissue (cannot be diagnosed on surface ECG).

Second degree: delay in transmission with failure to conduct and loss of P waves.

Type I (Wenckebach block)

Criteria:
a) PP intervals gradually shorten.
b) PR interval remains constant.
c) Pause is present at the end of a cycle due to a blocked impulse leading to absent P wave.
d) Duration of pause is less than twice the shortest PP interval.
e) PP interval following the pause is longer than the PP interval before the pause.

Type II block

Criteria:
a) Fixed degree of block.
b) Sinus impulse fail to reach the atria in a fixed ratio i.e. 2:1/3:1.

Third degree: **(Eg. 76)**

Criteria:
a) Complete block of impulses from SA node and hence no P waves.
b) PP interval is usually twice the normal PP interval.

5. Sinus arrest (Eg. 77)

Criteria:
a) Failure of sinus node impulse formation.
b) The PP interval is not an integral multiple of the normal PP interval except by coincidence.

6. Sick sinus syndrome

Conglomeration of features that include problems of sinus node dysfunction and AV nodal conduction.

Criteria: Combination of:
1. Sinus bradycardia
2. Sinus arrest
3. SA block and asystole
4. Atrial tachyarrhythmia
5. Ventricular tachyarrhythmia

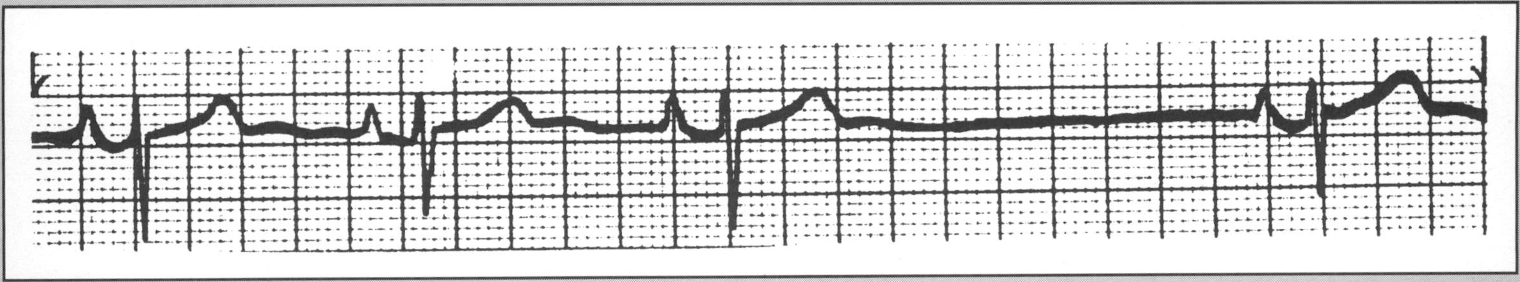

Eg. 76

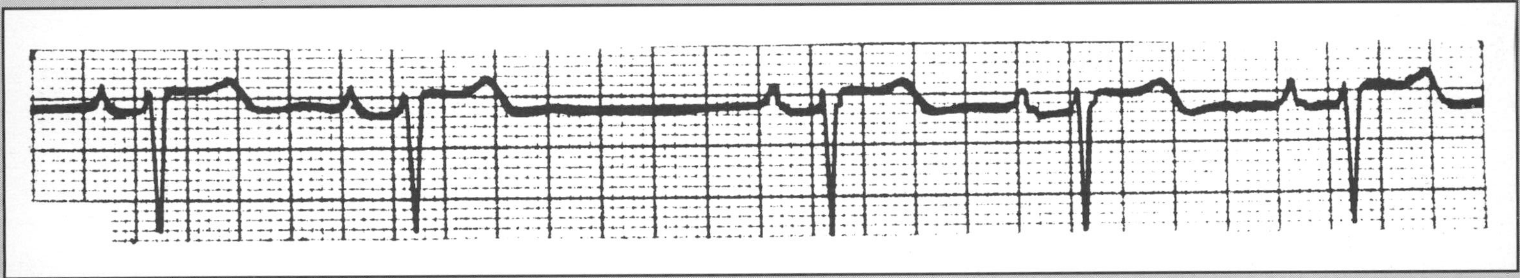

Eg. 77

7. Wenckebach phenomenon

Represents delay in AV node usually. Uncommonly in the distal conducting system.

Criteria:
a) PP interval is constant.
b) PR interval gradually increases.
c) RR interval gradually shortens and then a P wave fails to conduct to the ventricle.
d) Once QRS complex is dropped the duration of the PR interval and RR interval is again the same as the first beat in the series. **(Eg. 78)**

NOTE: *A 2:1 Wenckebach block cannot be differentiated from a Mobitz type-II block. A different grade of block is necessary to diagnose the Wenckebach phenomenon.*

Although the PR interval gradually increases the increment in the PR interval gradually falls and hence the RR interval progressively shortens until a QRS complex is dropped.

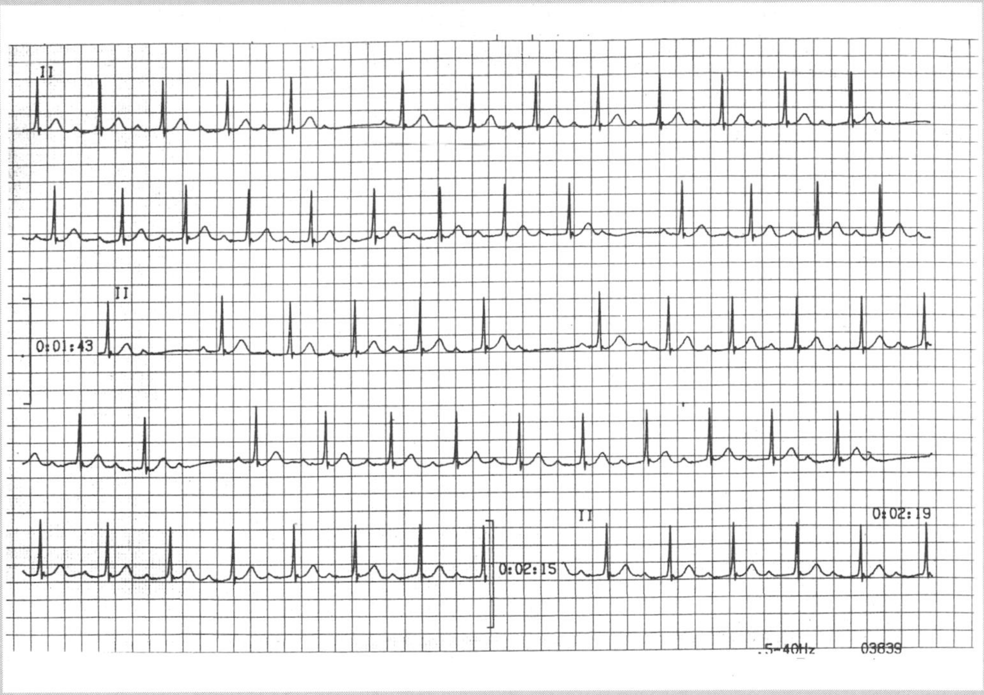

Eg. 78

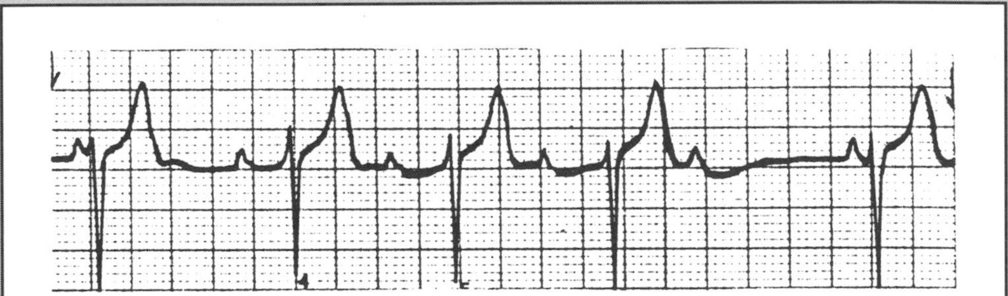

Eg. 78

8. Slow atrial fibrillation (Eg. 79)

9. Sinus arrhythmia

With inspiration there is increase in sinus rate. Expiration leads to slowing of the sinus rate. This is related to vagal tone which is inhibited by inspiration.

(Eg. 80)

10. Ventriculophasic sinus arrhythmia

In complete heart block the PP interval without QRS is longer than the one with the QRS. This is related to changes in autonomic tone affected by changes in stroke volume.

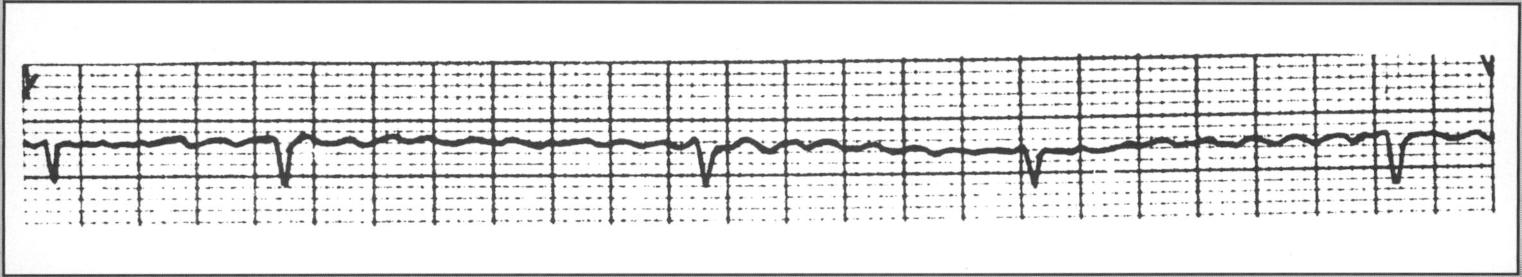

Eg. 79

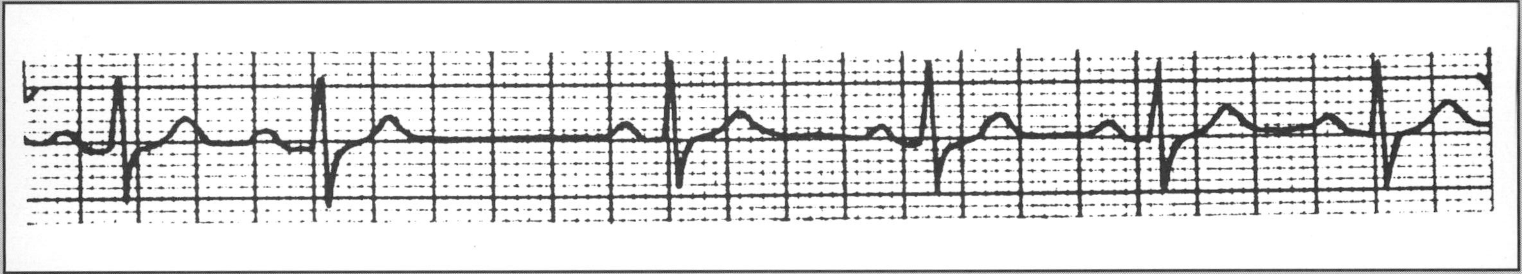

Eg. 80

Section IV

BASIC MANAGEMENT GUIDE FOR ARRHYTHMIAS

VENTRICULAR FIBRILLATION (Eg. 81, Algorithm I)

The most important problem of them all is ventricular fibrillation leading to cardiac arrest. Management protocol as recommended by the European Resuscitation Council 1992:

- If patient unconscious with no pulse in a large artery it is cardiac arrest.
- Give a precordial thump.
- Attach to a monitor and then shock successively with 200 joules for the first two shocks and then with 360 joules. Synchronise if VT and desynchronise if VF. Attempt to intubate and gain IV access if not achieved already. Institute cardiopulmonary resuscitation (CPR) with five chest compressions to one breath for 15 seconds.
- Give IV adrenaline 1 mg.
- Then three successive shocks at 360 joules each.
- Thereafter the cycle of adrenaline 1 mg, CPR and three DC shocks at 360 joules can be repeated.
- After every three cycles - other drugs may be used.
- To correct acidosis give sodium bicarbonate 50 mmol. Additional doses should only be given with the knowledge of the arterial or central venous pH.
- Anti-arrhythmic agents like lignocaine, amiodarone or bretylium tosylate may be given after every three cycles, but their use is not mandatory.
- Potassium, magnesium and calcium can be given in certain circumstances especially if there is a known deficiency.
- Resuscitation attempts may last between 10 minutes and 1 hour.

NOTE: *Method of CPR:- ball of palm over junction of lower 1/3 and upper 2/3 of sternum with elbows straight and locked. Depress 1.5" at 60/min. Oxygen via ambu bag at 12/min. Stop external cardiac massage (ECM) when inflating.*

Precautions and technique of delivering a shock:

- Paddle placed over apical area and upper right sternum.
- Electrode jelly under the paddle.
- No one should touch the patient or the metal cot or stand in a pool of liquid on the floor.
- All GTN patches should be removed.

NOTE: *failure to remove GTN patches might result in an explosion.*

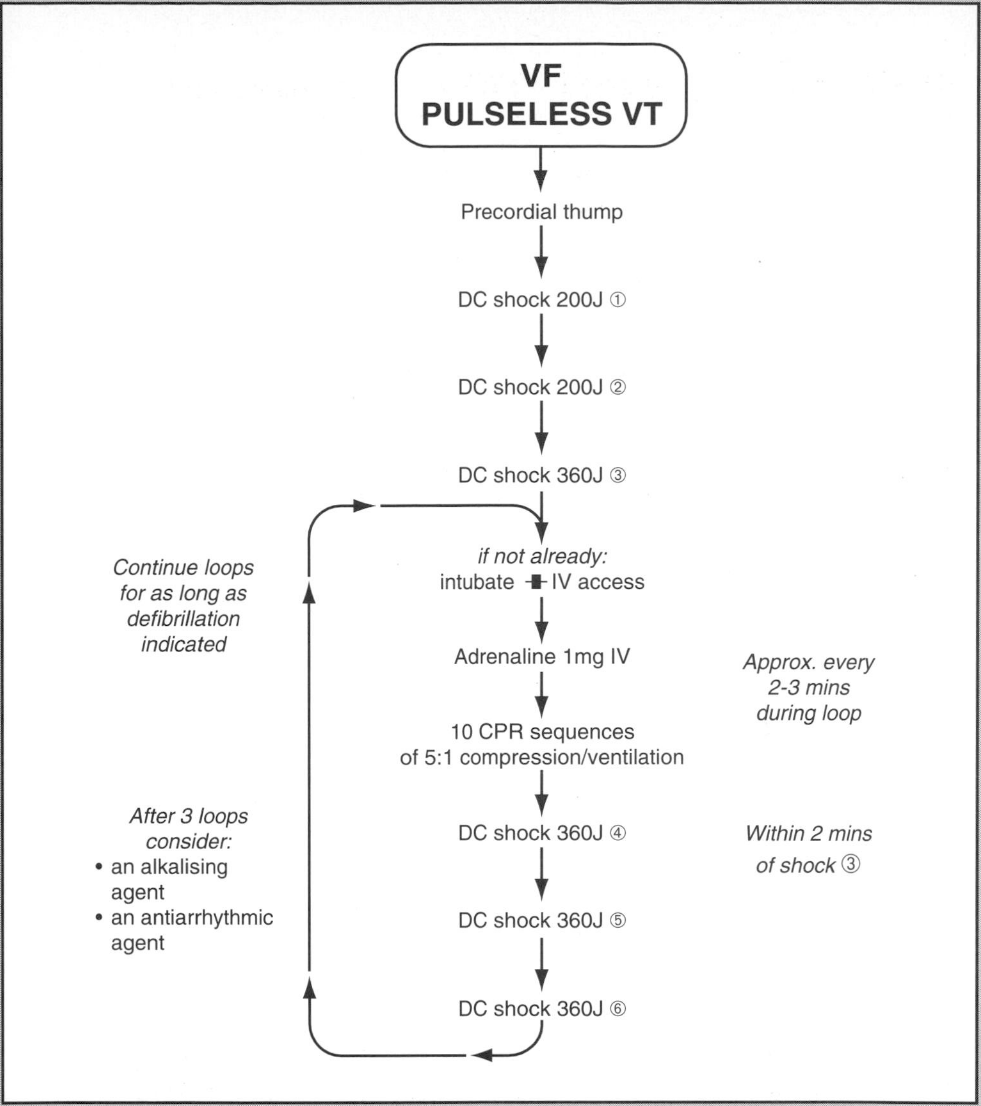
VF
PULSELESS VT
Precordial thump
DC shock 200J ①
DC shock 200J ②
DC shock 360J ③
if not already:
intubate + IV access
Adrenaline 1mg IV
10 CPR sequences
of 5:1 compression/ventilation
DC shock 360J ④
DC shock 360J ⑤
DC shock 360J ⑥
Continue loops for as long as defibrillation indicated
After 3 loops consider:
• an alkalising agent
• an antiarrhythmic agent
Approx. every 2-3 mins during loop
Within 2 mins of shock ③

Algorithm I

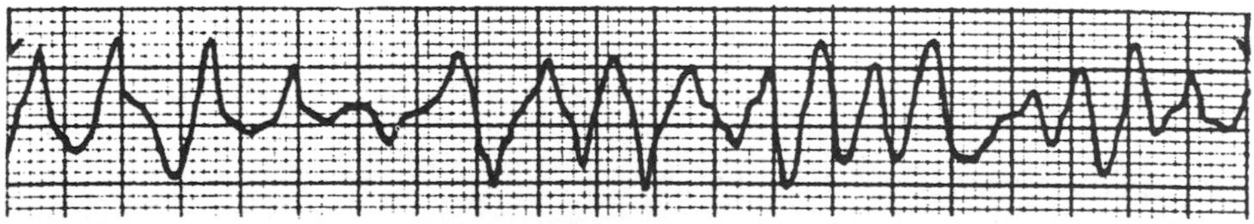

Eg. 81

Preferably all drugs should be given via a central line. Endotracheal instillation of drugs can be done after diluting with 10 ml of n/saline. Dose is two to three times higher than the conventional IV dose.

ASYSTOLE (Eg. 82, Algorithm II)

- Give precordial thump.
- Give two shocks at 200 joules and one at 360 joules just in case VF is present.
- Take care to desynchronise otherwise the machine will not deliver the shock.
- Intubate and gain IV access.
- Give adrenaline 1 mg IV.
- 10 CPR sequences with compression to ventilation ratio being 5:1.
- Atropine 3 mg IV once only to block the vagal tone.
- Pacing should be considered but only if electrical activity has recently been present.
- In the absence of electrical activity a further three cycles should be considered, following which adrenaline 5 mg IV should be tried.
- Recovery after 15 minutes of asystole is unlikely although hypothermia should be kept in mind.

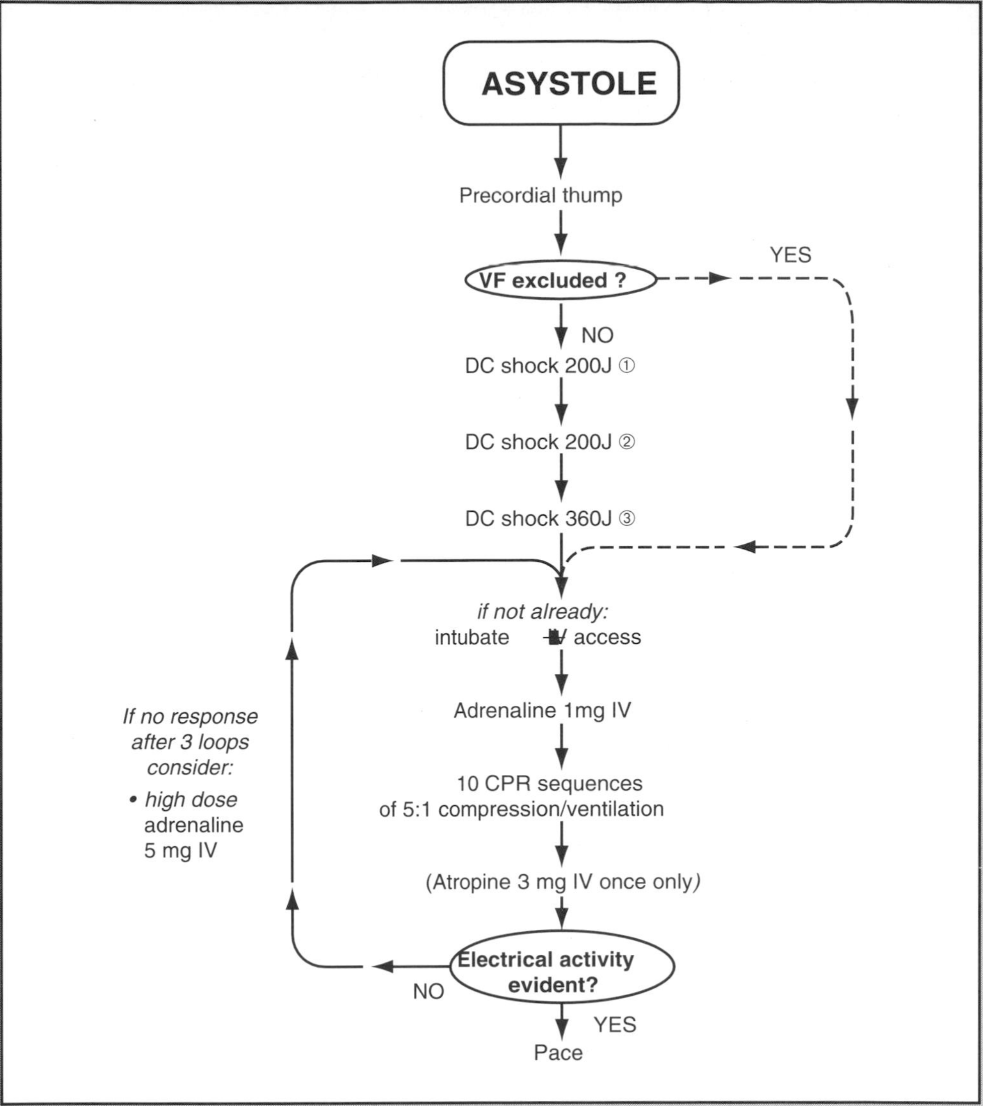
ASYSTOLE
Precordial thump
VF excluded ?
YES
NO
DC shock 200J ①
DC shock 200J ②
DC shock 360J ③
if not already:
intubate
IV access
Adrenaline 1mg IV
10 CPR sequences
of 5:1 compression/ventilation
(Atropine 3 mg IV once only)
Electrical activity evident?
NO
YES
Pace
If no response after 3 loops consider:
• high dose adrenaline 5 mg IV

Algorithm II

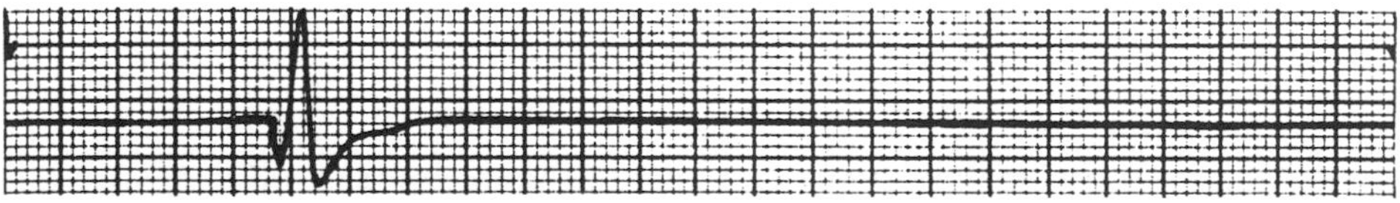

Eg. 82

REGULAR TACHYCARDIAS

1. Sinus tachycardia

Treat underlying disorder causing the tachycardia.

2. PSVT (Algorithm IV)

Brief attacks need no acute treatment.

Prolonged attacks should be treated and patient given long-term prophylaxis.

Vagal stimulation:

a) Carotid sinus massage - performed only when patient on monitor and sitting. One carotid artery massaged at a time for about 10-15 seconds. To stop immediately if there is sudden slowing.

b) Valsalva manoeuvre - expiration against a closed glottis (blowing into a balloon).

c) 'Diving reflex' - immersing face in ice cold water after patient has held his breath. Should be performed only under supervision as can lead to asystole.

d) Eyeball pressure - very painful and dangerous and hence not recommended.

Pharmacological agents:

a) IV adenosine - give 3 mg as a fast bolus. Then 6 mg and finally 12 mg at two-minute intervals. Adenosine triphosphate (ATP) can also be used.

   Half life of adenosine is extremely short at about 10 seconds and so any side-effects are short lived except in patients taking dipyridamole.

   Verapamil is preferable in asthmatics.

b) IV verapamil - 5-10 mg given in 0.5 to 1 min. Not to exceed 0.15 mg/kg

NOTE: *should not be used in patients on beta-blockers. Cause of failure is that verapamil has been given in too small a dose and too slowly. If patient already on beta-blockers then IV beta-blockers can be used instead (e.g. atenolol 5 mg). Digoxin may be tried if verapamil or beta-blockers fail.*

NARROW COMPLEX TACHYCARDIA
(Supraventricular tachycardia)

If not already done, give oxygen and establish IV access
Doses based on adult of average body weight

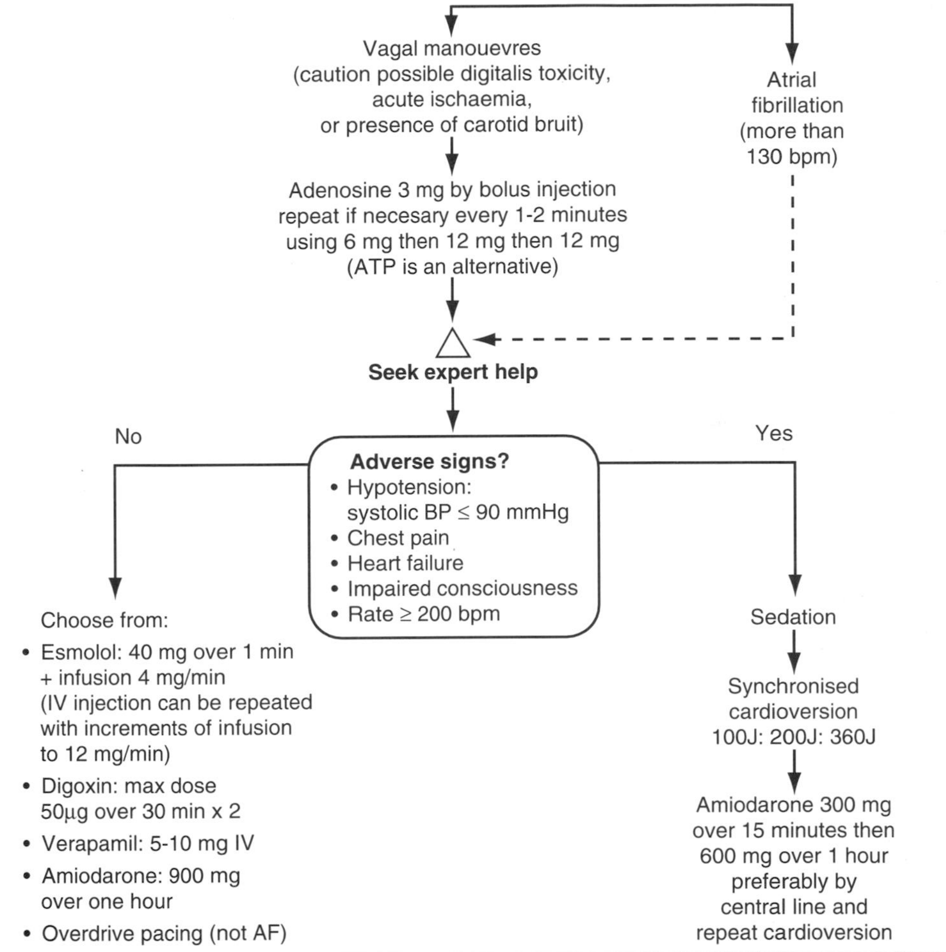

Vagal manouevres
(caution possible digitalis toxicity, acute ischaemia, or presence of carotid bruit)
Atrial fibrillation (more than 130 bpm)
Adenosine 3 mg by bolus injection repeat if necesary every 1-2 minutes using 6 mg then 12 mg then 12 mg (ATP is an alternative)
Seek expert help
No
Yes
Adverse signs?
• Hypotension: systolic BP ≤ 90 mmHg
• Chest pain
• Heart failure
• Impaired consciousness
• Rate ≥ 200 bpm
Choose from:
• Esmolol: 40 mg over 1 min + infusion 4 mg/min (IV injection can be repeated with increments of infusion to 12 mg/min)
• Digoxin: max dose 50µg over 30 min x 2
• Verapamil: 5-10 mg IV
• Amiodarone: 900 mg over one hour
• Overdrive pacing (not AF)
Sedation
Synchronised cardioversion 100J: 200J: 360J
Amiodarone 300 mg over 15 minutes then 600 mg over 1 hour preferably by central line and repeat cardioversion

Algorithm IV

4. Atrial flutter

a) Cardioversion is treatment of choice. Start with 25 joules and increase to 100 joules.

b) IV verapamil reduces the rapid ventricular rate and can occasionally convert to sinus rhythm.

c) Digoxin is the other drug which is useful. Other drugs which have a modest effect are class la, 1c and III anti-arrhythmic agents.

d) Right atrial overdrive pacing.

NOTE: *when atrial flutter is a component of sick sinus syndrome (SSS) then cardioversion should only be attempted after a temporary pacing wire has been inserted.*

5. Junctional tachycardia

a) If digoxin toxicity is suspected then stop the drug.

b) Drugs which block the AV node (i.e. adenosine, beta-blockers or verapamil) can be given.

c) Drugs which decrease automaticity are also useful, e.g. lignocaine and disopyramide.

6. Ventricular tachycardia

Sustained (Algorithm V)

Management depends on the circulatory state of the patient.

a) DC shock should be given in the following circumstances:

- Cardiac arrest
- Haemodynamic deterioration
- Failure of anti-arrhythmic drugs to control VT

b) IV anti-arrhythmic useful drugs are:

(i) Class I drugs e.g.:

a) disopyramide

b) mexiletine

c) flecainide acetate

(ii) Amiodarone

(iii) Beta-blockers

Following the publication of the CAST Trial, flecainide acetate is now indicated in life-threatening ventricular arrhythmias only.

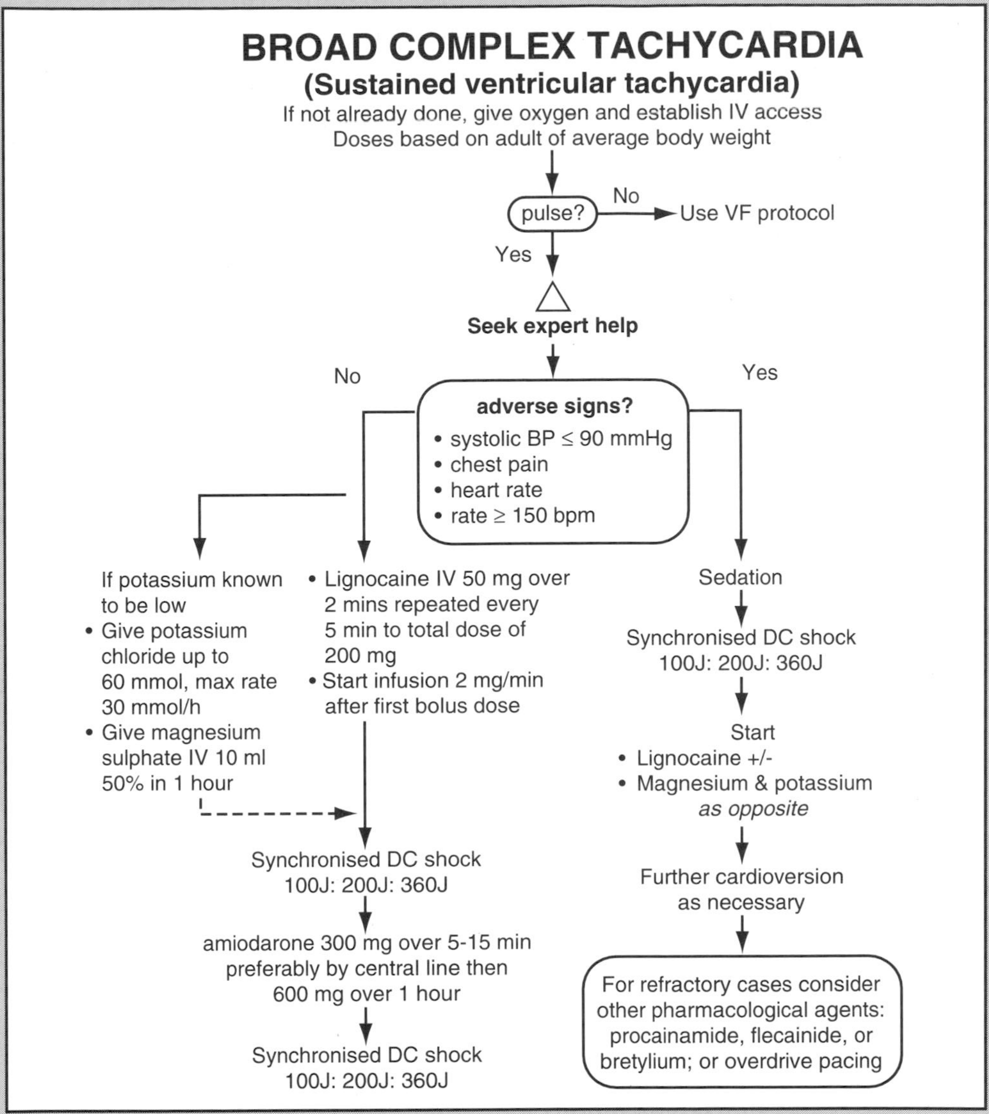
BROAD COMPLEX TACHYCARDIA
(Sustained ventricular tachycardia)
If not already done, give oxygen and establish IV access
Doses based on adult of average body weight
pulse?
No
Use VF protocol
Yes
Seek expert help
No
Yes
adverse signs?
• systolic BP ≤ 90 mmHg
• chest pain
• heart rate
• rate ≥ 150 bpm
If potassium known to be low
• Give potassium chloride up to 60 mmol, max rate 30 mmol/h
• Give magnesium sulphate IV 10 ml 50% in 1 hour
• Lignocaine IV 50 mg over 2 mins repeated every 5 min to total dose of 200 mg
• Start infusion 2 mg/min after first bolus dose
Synchronised DC shock 100J: 200J: 360J
amiodarone 300 mg over 5-15 min preferably by central line then 600 mg over 1 hour
Synchronised DC shock 100J: 200J: 360J
Sedation
Synchronised DC shock 100J: 200J: 360J
Start
• Lignocaine +/-
• Magnesium & potassium
as opposite
Further cardioversion as necessary
For refractory cases consider other pharmacological agents: procainamide, flecainide, or bretylium; or overdrive pacing

Algorithm V

NOTE: *digoxin is contraindicated if there is AF in presence of accessory conduction. This is because digoxin will increase the AV block and enhance the transmission of stimuli via the accessory path which can lead to VF. To prevent systemic embolism anticoagulation is mandatory.*

In: **a) rheumatic heart disease**
risk of stroke 17 times greater compared to a patient in sinus rhythm

b) non-rheumatic causes
risk of stroke five times greater

The AFASAK, BAATAF, SPAF and CAFA studies have all shown that patients with non-rheumatic AF also benefit from anticoagulation.

Suggested policy is:

1) Full dose anticoagulation to patients with structural heart disease.
2) Low dose anticoagulation (INR between 1.5 and 2.5) for patients over 65 years.
3) Low dose anticoagulation for younger patients with chronic lone AF.
4) Aspirin 325 mg/day to patients with episodes of paroxysmal AF only.

Paroxysmal AF

a) Flecainide and propafenone are effective but should be avoided in patients with ischaemic heart disease, heart failure and structural heart disease.

b) Sotalol hydrochloride is especially effective in older patients and those with organic heart disease.

c) Amiodarone effective in refractory paroxysmal AF especially in the elderly.

2. Torsade de pointes

a) Discontinuation of offending drugs such as:- quinidine; procainamide; disopyramide; phenothiazines, tricyclic antidepressants and H1 blockers.

b) Temporary ventricular pacing.

c) Correct hypocalcaemia and hypomagnesaemia.

d) Vasodilators, such as pinacidil and cromakalim, can be useful by decreasing the action potential duration.

3. Multiple atrial ectopics

a) If frequent then may herald the onset of AF.

b) They should be treated, especially in patients with:

  1. valvular heart disease
  2. post MI
  3. post cardiac surgery

c) Treated with beta-blocker as it will control ventricular rate if AF occurs.

d) If APB associated with alcohol or caffeine then these should be avoided.

e) Digoxin avoided as is likely to aggravate it.

4. Multiple ventricular ectopics

a) Unifocal and even frequent ventricular ectopics do not need treatment.

b) Multifocal salvoes of ventricular ectopics and R on T phenomenon occur in the setting of heart disease. These ectopics are independent risk factors and lead to increased cardiovascular mortality. However, suppression of these ectopics does not lead to improvement in prognosis. Anti-arrhythmic therapy is therefore only indicated for symptomatic reasons.

REGULAR BRADYCARDIAS (Algorithm VI)

1. Sinus bradycardia

In the symptomatic patient:

a) Give atropine 0.6 mg IV every five mins to a maximum of 1.8 mg.
b) Isoprenaline can also be given as an infusion at 1-2 μg/min to a maximum of 20 μg/min.
c) Atrial or ventricular pacing.

2. Second-degree heart block (Mobitz type II)

Initially insert a temporary pacing wire and then a permanent one. **(Eg. 84 shows a right ventricular paced rhythm)**

Criteria

1. No P waves.

2. Pacing spike before each bizarre, broad QRS complex.

3. QRS complex has LBBB pattern.

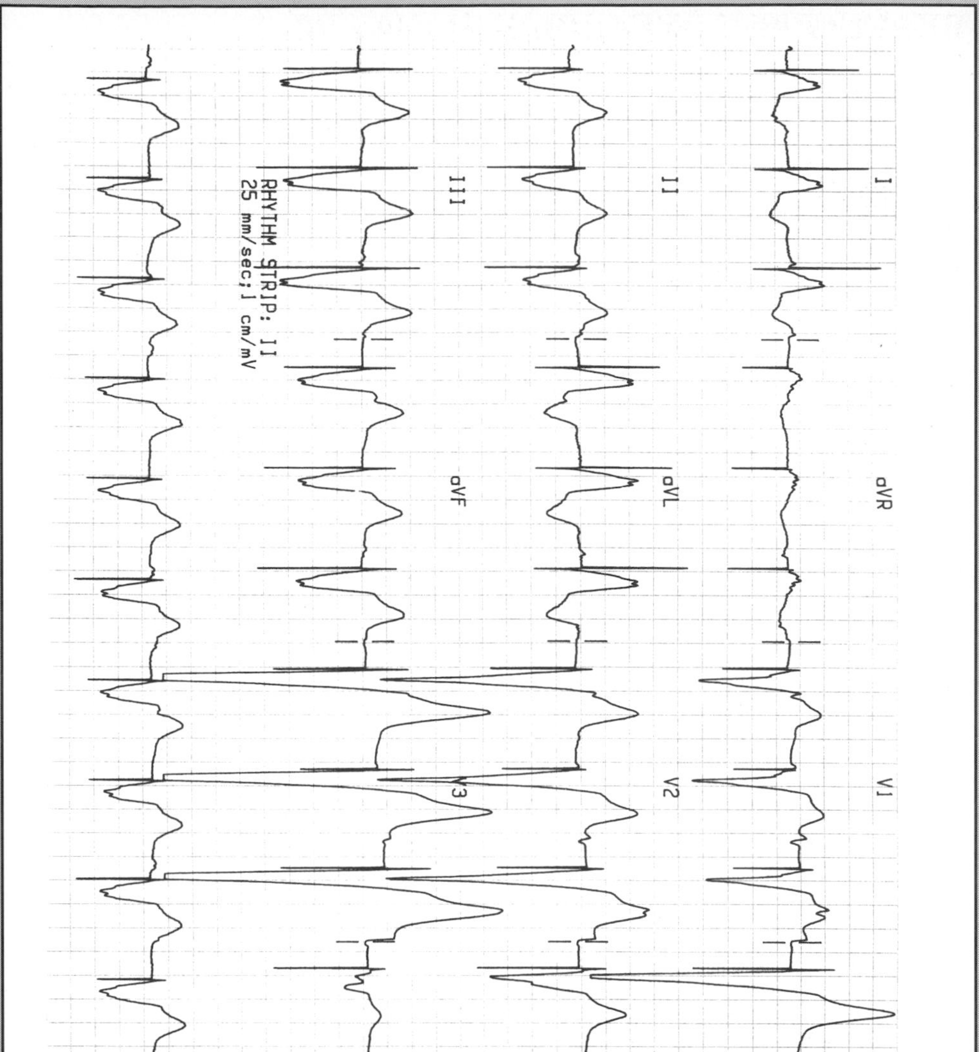
I
aVR
V1
V4
II
aVL
V2
V5
III
aVF
V3
V6
RHYTHM STRIP: II
25 mm/sec;1 cm/mV
.05-40Hz
19559

Eg. 84

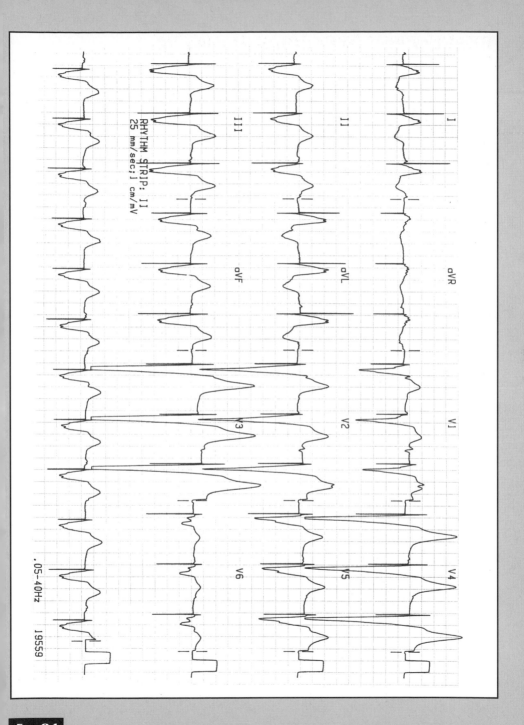

3. Complete heart block

Atropine 0.6 mg or isoprenaline infusion at 2μg/min given as a holding manoeuvre while preparations are being made to insert a pacing wire.

4. Idioventricular rhythm

Treatment is unnecessary.

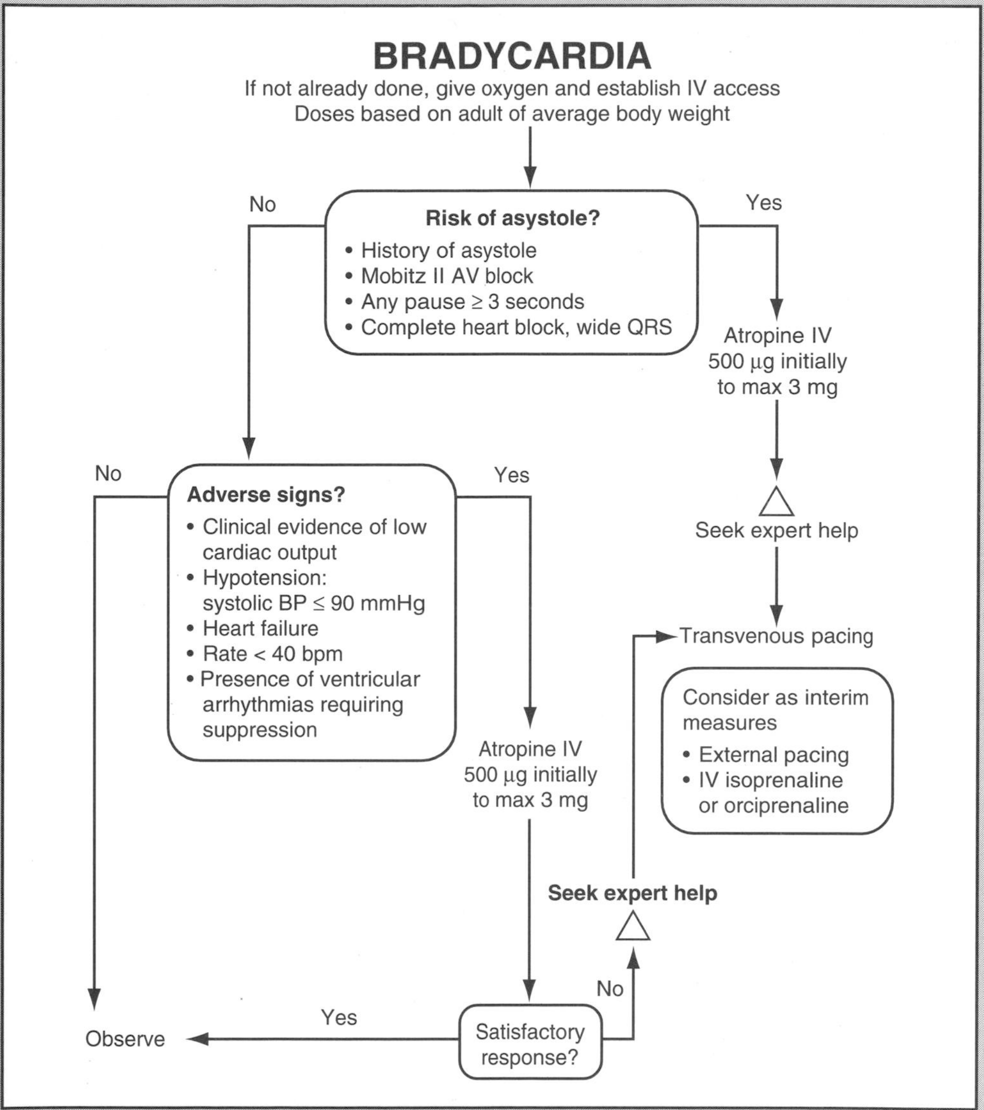

BRADYCARDIA
If not already done, give oxygen and establish IV access
Doses based on adult of average body weight
Risk of asystole?
• History of asystole
• Mobitz II AV block
• Any pause ≥ 3 seconds
• Complete heart block, wide QRS
No
Yes
Atropine IV
500 μg initially
to max 3 mg
Seek expert help
Transvenous pacing
Consider as interim measures
• External pacing
• IV isoprenaline or orciprenaline
Adverse signs?
• Clinical evidence of low cardiac output
• Hypotension: systolic BP ≤ 90 mmHg
• Heart failure
• Rate < 40 bpm
• Presence of ventricular arrhythmias requiring suppression
No
Yes
Atropine IV
500 μg initially
to max 3 mg
Seek expert help
No
Satisfactory response?
Yes
Observe

Algorithm VI

IRREGULAR BRADYCARDIAS

1. **SA block**

a) If transient no treatment is needed.

b) If patient is symptomatic then atropine or isoprenaline can be given as short-term measures.

c) Chronic problems need a permanent pacemaker.

2. **Sinus arrest**

Symptomatic patients may need a permanent pacemaker especially a dual chamber one.

(Eg. 85) shows a dual chamber paced rhythm

Criteria:

1. Small pacing spike before the P wave.

2. Large pacing spike before the QRS complex.

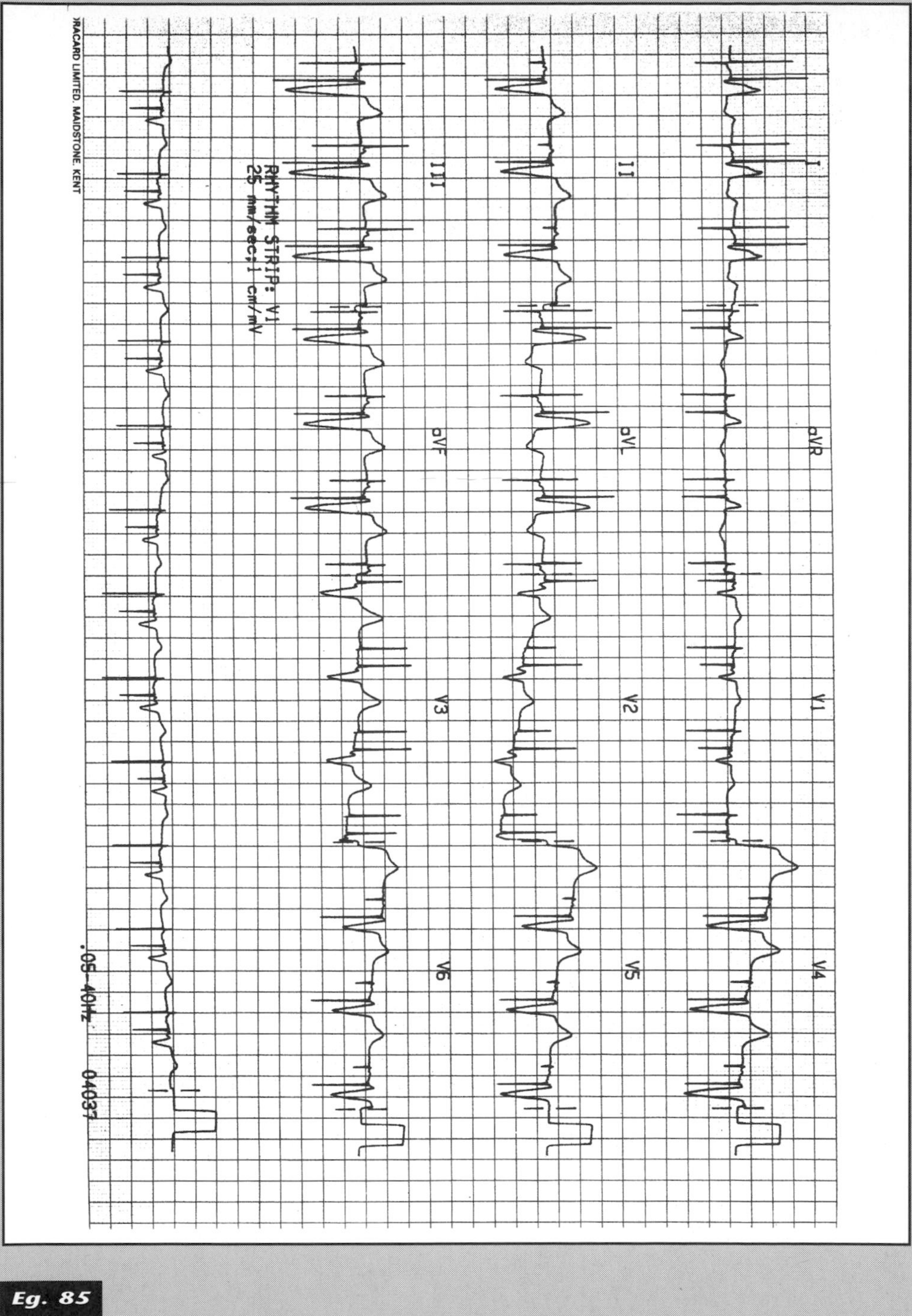
I
II
III
aVR
aVL
aVF
V1
V2
V3
V4
V5
V6
RHYTHM STRIP: V1
25 mm/sec;1 cm/mV
.05-40Hz
04037
RACARD LIMITED. MAIDSTONE. KENT

Eg. 85

3. Sick sinus syndrome (SSS)

a) Permanent pacemaker to control bradyarrhythmias and drugs such as digoxin to control tachyarrhythmias.

b) Dual chamber pacemaker.

4. Wandering atrial tachycardia

Treatment unnecessary.

5. Multifocal atrial tachycardia

a) Treat the underlying cause.

b) Verapamil may help.

c) Digoxin may worsen the arrhythmia.

6. Atrial parasystole

Treatment not needed as such; however, should be treated if leading to AF or atrial flutter.

Section V

INDEX

C Mathematics

1 Integers

Arithmetic check

Revised

- You need to know how to do basic arithmetic: addition, subtraction, multiplication and division of whole numbers.

Test Yourself 1

Work out these.

a $44 + 52$

b $67 - 48$

c 67×9

d $192 \div 12$

Solutions

Test Yourself 1

a $44 + 52 = 96$

b $67 - 48 = 19$

c $67 \times 9 = 603$

d $192 \div 12 = 16$

Multiples

Revised

- The multiples of a number are the numbers in its times table. For example, the multiples of 2, up to 10, are 2, 4, 6, 8 and 10.

2 4 6 8 10

Chief Examiner says

Remember to include 2 as a multiple of 2, 3 as a multiple of 3, and so on.

Test Yourself 2

List the multiples of 5, up to 30.

5 10 15 20 25 30

1 2 3 6 9 12 15 18 21 24 27 30

Solution

Test Yourself 2

5, 10, 15, 20, 25, 30

Factors

Revised

- The factors of a number are the numbers that divide exactly into it. For example, the factors of 6 are 1, 2, 3 and 6.

Chief Examiner says

Remember that 1 and 24 are factors of 24, 1 and 30 are factors of 30, and so on.

Test Yourself 3

a List the factors of 24.

b List the factors of 30.

Solutions

Test Yourself 3

a 24 can be written as 1×24, 2×12, 3×8 and 4×6.
So the factors of 24 are 1, 2, 3, 4, 6, 8, 12 and 24.

b The factors of 30 are 1, 2, 3, 5, 6, 10, 15 and 30.

Rounding numbers

Revised

- The most common rounding questions are:
  - round to the nearest 10
  - round to the nearest 100
  - round to the nearest 1000
- If the number is halfway you always round up. For example, 345 to the nearest 10 is 350.

Test Yourself 4

a Round 342 to the nearest 10.

b Round 7500 to the nearest 1000.

c Round 1847 to the nearest 10.

Solutions

Test Yourself 4

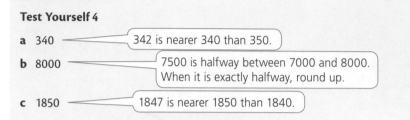

a 340 — 342 is nearer 340 than 350.

b 8000 — 7500 is halfway between 7000 and 8000. When it is exactly halfway, round up.

c 1850 — 1847 is nearer 1850 than 1840.

Multiplication and division

Revised

Multiplying and dividing by 10, 100, 1000, ...

- To multiply a whole number by 10, move the digits one place to the left and add a zero.
- To multiply a whole number by 100, move the digits two places to the left and add two zeros.
- To multiply a whole number by 1000, move the digits three places to the left and add three zeros.
- To divide a whole number by 10, move the digits one place to the right and take off a zero.
- To divide a whole number by 100, move the digits two places to the right and take off two zeros.
- To divide a whole number by 1000, move the digits three places to the right and take off three zeros.
- To multiply by a multiple of 10, 100 or 1000, use partitioning. For example, to multiply by 40, first multiply by 4 then multiply by 10.

Test Yourself 5

Work out these.

a 14×100

b 37×1000

c 26×10

d $65\,000 \div 1000$

e $290 \div 10$

f $8900 \div 100$

g 4×300

Solutions

Test Yourself 5

a $14 \times 100 = 1400$

b $37 \times 1000 = 37\,000$

c $26 \times 10 = 260$

d $65\,000 \div 1000 = 65$

e $290 \div 10 = 29$

f $8900 \div 100 = 89$

g $4 \times 300 = 4 \times 3 \times 100$

$= 12 \times 100$

$= 1200$

More difficult multiplications

Revised

- You need to know the basic multiplication tables.
- To multiply numbers, you may have learnt different methods, for example:
  - long multiplication
  - using a grid
  - using a lattice
- Make sure you know which method works for you.

Test Yourself 6

Work out these.

a 567×23

b 234×57

c 741×36

Solutions

Test Yourself 6

a Long multiplication

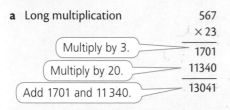

$$\begin{array}{r} 567 \\ \times\, 23 \\ \hline 1701 \\ 11340 \\ \hline 13041 \end{array}$$

Multiply by 3. (1701)

Multiply by 20. (11340)

Add 1701 and 11 340. (13041)

Using a grid

×	500	60	7
20	10 000	1200	140
3	1500	180	21

10 000 + 1200 + 140 + 1500 + 180 + 21 = 13 041

Using a lattice

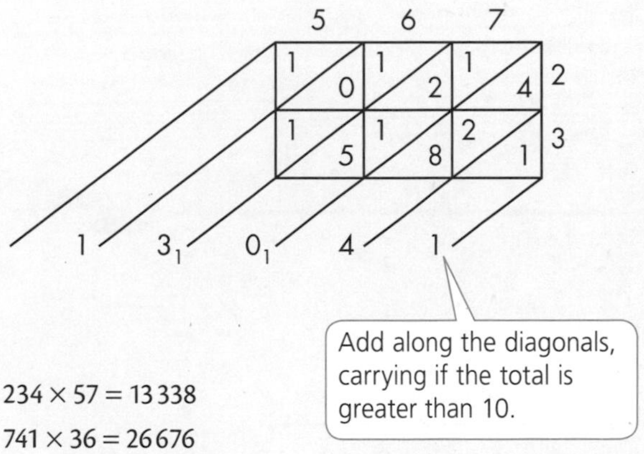

b $234 \times 57 = 13\,338$

c $741 \times 36 = 26\,676$

Squares, cubes, other powers and square roots

Revised

- You are expected to know the squares of counting numbers up to 15.

n	1	2	3	4	5	6	7	8	9	10	11	12	13	14	15
n^2	1	4	9	16	25	36	49	64	81	100	121	144	169	196	225

- You are also expected to know the corresponding square roots. For example, since $7^2 = 49$, then $\sqrt{49} = 7$.

$\sqrt{\ }$ means square root.

- You should know how to square numbers on your calculator. The key may look like [x^2] or [$\square^2$].
- You should know how to square root numbers on your calculator. The key may look like [$\sqrt{\ }$].
- You are expected to know the cubes of counting numbers up to 5 and of 10.

n	1	2	3	4	5	10
n^3	1	8	27	64	125	1000

- You should know how to cube numbers on your calculator. The key may look like [x^3] or you may need to use the [SHIFT] key or the [$\times$] key twice.
- Powers (or indices) are a short way of writing numbers multiplied by themselves. For example, $2^6 = 2 \times 2 \times 2 \times 2 \times 2 \times 2$.

Test Yourself 7

a Write down the value of each of these.

i $6^2 + 2^2$

ii $4^3 - 3^3$

iii $\sqrt{25}$

iv $\sqrt{64} - \sqrt{4}$

b Use your calculator to work out these.

i 19^2

ii $\sqrt{729}$

Solutions

Test Yourself 7

a i $36 + 4 = 40$

ii $64 - 27 = 37$

iii 5

iv $8 - 2 = 6$

b i [1] [9] [x^2] [=] 361

ii [$\sqrt{\ }$] [7] [2] [9] [=] 27

Negative numbers

Revised

- Numbers below zero are called negative numbers.
- To order negative and positive numbers, put them in the same order as they appear on the number line.

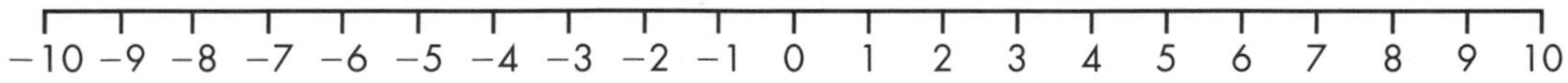

- To add and subtract with negative numbers, it is useful to draw a number line.
- You can also use these facts:
  - adding a negative number is the same as subtracting a positive number
  - subtracting a negative number is the same as adding a positive number.

Chief Examiner says

Notice that −4 is less than −1

Test Yourself 8

a Put these numbers in order, smallest first.

7, −3, 4, −1, −8, 2, −4

b The temperature at midnight is −6 °C.

At dawn the temperature has gone up by 7 degrees.

What is the temperature at dawn?

c Find the value of

i 4 − −2

ii 1 + −4

iii −1 − 5

Solutions

Test Yourself 8

a −8, −4, −3, −1, 2, 4, 7

b 1 °C — Start at −6 on the number line and count up 7.

c i 4 − −2 = 6

ii 1 + −4 = −3

iii −1 − 5 = −6

Use a number line. Start at the first number and move to the right to add or to the left to subtract. Alternatively, use the rules.

Unit A

2 Algebra 1

Using letters to represent numbers

Revised

- The line below consists of two parts, one red and one blue. An expression for its total length is 3 + 7.

3 7

- The line below consists of two parts, one red and one blue. An expression for its total length is $a + 7$.

a 7

- The line below consists of two parts, one red and one blue. An expression for its total length is $a + b$.

a b

Test Yourself 1

Write expressions for the total length of these lines.

a x 5

b 7 y

c x y

Solutions

Test Yourself 1

a $x+5$

b $7+y$

c $x+y$

Writing simple expressions

Revised

- You need to be able to write expressions to represent different situations.

Test Yourself 2

Write expressions for each of these situations.

a Gwen is 13 years old and Adam is x years old. What is their total age?

b Mariah is x years old and Carmine is y years old. What is their total age?

c Mika and Jenny have 13 pens in total. Jenny has x pens. How many pens does Mika have?

d In a nursery there are c children. There are g girls. How many boys are there?

Solutions

Test Yourself 2

a $13 + x$ years

b $x + y$ years

c $13 - x$

d $c - g$

Collecting like terms

Revised

- You need to be able to use algebraic notation. Here are some examples.
  - $a + a = 2a$, $a + a + a + a = 4a$
  - $4a + 3a = 7a$, $5a - 2a = 3a$
  - $2 \times a = 2a$, $5 \times a = 5a$
  - $a \times b = ab$, $3 \times a \times b = 3ab$
  - $a \times a = a^2$

Chief Examiner says

1a is the same as a.

Test Yourself 3

Simplify these.

a $p + p + p + p + p$

b $3p + 2p$

c $7 \times a$

d $3 \times p \times q$

e $x \times x$

Solutions

Test Yourself 3

a $5p$

b $5p$

c $7a$

d $3pq$

e x^2

Like and unlike terms

Revised

- Only like terms can be collected.
- $2a$ and $3a$ are like terms; $3a$ and $4c$ are unlike..

Test Yourself 4

Simplify where possible

a $2a + 3a$

b $3a - 4c$

c $4a + b - 3a$

Solutions

Test Yourself 4

a $5a$

b not possible

c $a + b$

3 Data collection

Collecting data

Revised

- Most things can be counted or measured.
- Data that are counted are called discrete data.
- Data that are measured are called continuous data.
- When collecting data it is often useful to use a tally chart to help make a frequency table.

Test Yourself 1

Here are the numbers of brothers that 25 children in one class have.

2	4	0	2	1
0	0	1	0	0
1	2	3	1	1
1	0	1	2	0
0	0	2	0	1

Show these data in a frequency table.

Chief Examiner says

It is easier to count the frequency if the tally is in 5s.

Solution

Test Yourself 1

Number of brothers	Tally	Frequency
0	卌 卌	10
1	卌 III	8
2	卌	5
Other	II	2

Data display

Revised

- Two ways of displaying discrete data are:
  - vertical line graphs
  - bar charts.

Test Yourself 2

Using the data in Test Yourself 1, draw

a a vertical line graph

b a bar chart.

Solutions

Test Yourself 2

a

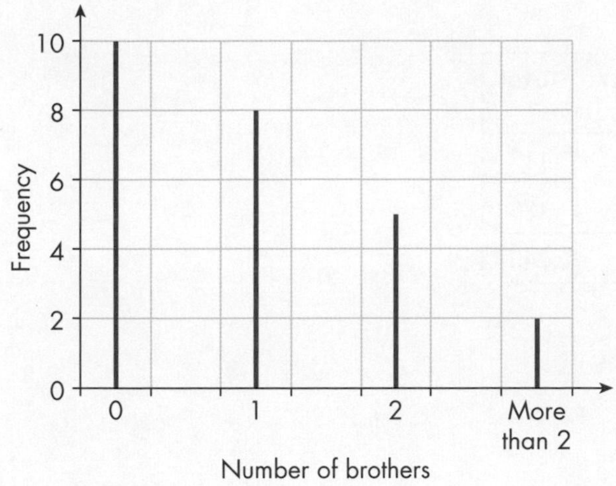

b

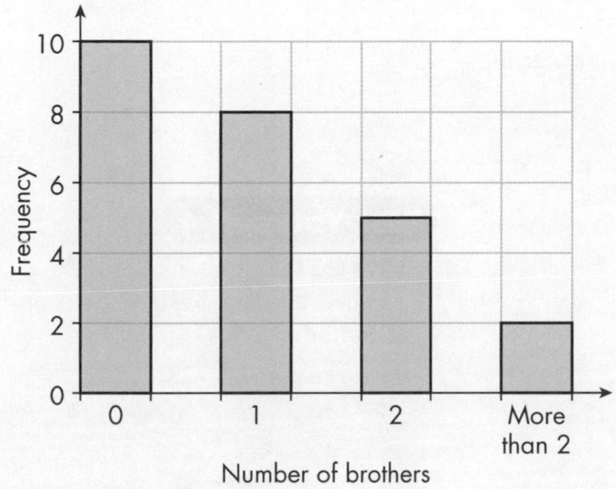

Two-way tables

Revised

- Two-way tables are useful ways of displaying different aspects of data.
- You need to be able to complete two-way tables and answer questions using the data in them.

Test Yourself 3

This two-way table gives some information on the country of manufacture and the material used for a sample of 240 food processors.

	Made in Europe	**Made in China**	**Made in other countries**	**Total**
Stainless steel		38	53	
Other material				123
Total	47		98	240

a Complete the table.

b How many food processors were made

i from stainless steel

ii in China?

Solutions

Test Yourself 3

a

	Made in Europe	Made in China	Made in other countries	Total
Stainless steel	26	38	53	117
Other material	21	57	45	123
Total	47	95	98	240

b **i** 117

ii 95

Grouping data

Revised

- When handling a lot of data it is useful to collect the data into groups.
- Grouped data is usually put into groups of equal width.

Solutions

Test Yourself 4

a

Time (min)	Tally	Frequency
21–30	~~IIII~~ IIII	9
31–40	~~IIII~~ ~~IIII~~	10
41–50	IIII	4
51–60	~~IIII~~ II	7

b

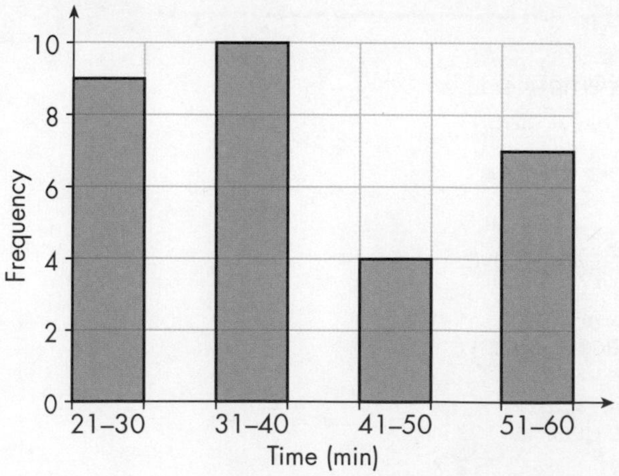

Test Yourself 4

Here are the times in minutes that 30 children claim to have spent on their homework.

26	48	52	23	21
59	29	31	26	33
23	33	37	44	29
26	21	45	31	60
52	51	39	54	37
39	40	52	39	48

a Show these data in a grouped frequency table.

b Draw a bar chart to show the data.

4 Decimals

Changing fractions to decimals

Revised

- In a decimal number, the places after the decimal point are $\frac{1}{10}$, $\frac{1}{100}$, $\frac{1}{1000}$, and so on.
- To change a fraction to a decimal, divide the numerator by the denominator. For example, $\frac{4}{5} = 4 \div 5 = 0.8$.

Test Yourself 1

a Write in words the place value of the digit 8 in each of these numbers.

i 280

ii 0.821

iii 0.408

b Write these fractions as decimals.

i $\frac{3}{10}$

ii $\frac{37}{100}$

iii $\frac{7}{28}$

Solutions

Test Yourself 1

a **i** eight tens

ii eight tenths

iii eight thousandths

b **i** 0.3

ii 0.37

iii $7 \div 28 = 0.25$

Multiplying and dividing decimals by 10, 100, 1000, ...

Revised

- See Unit A Chapter 1 for multiplying and dividing whole numbers by 10, 100, 1000, … .
- To multiply a decimal by 10, keep the decimal point in place and move the digits one place to the left.
- To multiply a decimal by 100, keep the decimal point in place and move the digits two places to the left.
- To multiply a decimal by 1000, keep the decimal point in place and move the digits three places to the left.
- If any of the places to the left of the decimal point are left empty, put zeros in them.
- To divide a decimal by 10, keep the decimal point in place and move the digits one place to the right.
- To divide a decimal by 100, keep the decimal point in place and move the digits two places to the right.
- To divide a decimal by 1000, keep the decimal point in place and move the digits three places to the right.
- If the units column or any of the places to the right of the decimal point are left empty, put zeros in them.

Solutions

Test Yourself 2

a $1.4 \times 100 = 140$
b $3.7 \times 1000 = 3700$
c $2.6 \times 10 = 26$
d $264.3 \div 100 = 2.643$
e $53.2 \div 10 = 5.32$
f $42.7 \div 1000 = 0.0427$

Test Yourself 2

Work out these.

a 1.4×100
b 3.7×1000
c 2.6×10
d $264.3 \div 100$
e $53.2 \div 10$
f $42.7 \div 1000$

Adding and subtracting decimals

Revised

- When adding or subtracting decimals,
  - make sure the decimal points are underneath each other
  - keep tenths under tenths, units under units, tens under tens, and so on
  - start from the column on the right.

Test Yourself 3

Work out these.

a $537.5 + 27.68$
b $53.78 - 24.9$

Solutions

Test Yourself 3

a

$$\begin{array}{r} 537.50 \\ +27.68 \\ \hline 565.18 \end{array}$$

b

$$\begin{array}{r} 53.78 \\ -24.90 \\ \hline 28.88 \end{array}$$

Add a zero so that there is the same number of decimal figures on each line.

Multiplying a decimal by an integer or another decimal

Revised

- To multiply a decimal by an integer or another decimal,
  - first multiply the numbers ignoring the decimal point
  - then count the total number of decimal places in the question
  - put a decimal point in the answer so that it has the same number of decimal places as in the question.

Test Yourself 4

Work out these.

a 26.4×7
b 1.53×4
c 0.42×8
d 47.3×1.5
e 4.68×0.6

Solutions

Test Yourself 4

a

$$\begin{array}{rrrrr} & & 2 & 6 & 4 \\ \times & & & & 7 \\ \hline & 1 & 8 & 4 & 8 \end{array}$$

So $26.4 \times 7 = 184.8$

There is one decimal place in the question, so there is one in the answer.

b

	1	5	3
×			4
	6	1	2

So $1.53 \times 4 = 6.12$

There are two decimal places in the question, so there are two in the answer.

c

	4	2
×		8
3	3	6

So $0.42 \times 8 = 3.36$

There are two decimal places in the question, so there are two in the answer.

d

$$\begin{array}{r} 473 \\ \times\ 15 \\ \hline 2365 \\ 4730 \\ \hline 7095 \end{array}$$

So $47.3 \times 1.5 = 70.95$

There are two decimal places in the question, so there are two in the answer.

e

	4	6	8
×			6
2	8	0	8

So $4.68 \times 0.6 = 2.808$

There are three decimal places in the question, so there are three in the answer.

Unit A

5 Formulae

Formulae written in words

Revised

- When using a formula that is written in words, remember to carry out the instructions in the order they are written.

Test Yourself 1

a To work out the cost, in pounds, of hiring a coach, Mrs Brown multiplies the number of miles by 2 and adds 40.

Find the cost for

i) 50 miles

ii) 140 miles.

b To work out the perimeter of a rectangle, add the length and the width and multiply the total by 2.

Find the perimeter of a rectangle with

i) length 6 cm, width 4 cm

ii) length 5.2 m, width 2.7 m.

Solutions

Test Yourself 1

a i $50 \times 2 + 40 = 100 + 40$

$= £140$

ii $140 \times 2 + 40 = 280 + 40$

$= £320$

b i $6 + 4 = 10$

Perimeter $= 2 \times 10 = 20$ cm

ii $5.2 + 2.7 = 7.9$

Perimeter $= 2 \times 7.9 = 15.8$ m

Formulae written using letters

Revised

- You do not need to write the × sign: $4 \times t$ is written $4t$.
- When being multiplied, the number is always written in front of the letter: $p \times 6 - 30$ is written $6p - 30$.
- You always start a formula with the single letter that you are finding: $2 \times l + 2 \times w = P$ is written $P = 2l + 2w$.
- When there is a division in a formula it is always written as a fraction: $y = k \div 6$ is written $y = \frac{k}{6}$.
- When writing your own formulae,
  - define your letters carefully, including any units
  - use brackets if you want addition and subtraction done before multiplication and division
  - use a fraction line not a ÷ sign for divide.

Chief Examiner says

Always use the shorthand form of an expression such as $2l + 2w$, not $2 \times l + 2 \times w$.

Remember that a formula needs an equals sign, for example: $P = 2l + 2w$.

Test Yourself 2

a Write a formula that could be used to find the cost (C pence) of x newspapers at 70p each.

b Write a formula that could be used to find the perimeter (P) of a square with length (l).

Solutions

Test Yourself 2

a $C = 70x$

b $P = 4l$

Chief Examiner says

Remember to define your letters.

Substituting numbers into a formula

Revised

- Substitution means replacing a letter with a number. For example, when $a = 5$, $4a = 4 \times 5 = 20$.
- When substituting in formulae, remember
  - expressions such as ab mean $a \times b$
  - multiplication and division are done before addition and subtraction unless there are brackets
  - expressions such as $3r^2$ mean $3 \times r^2$ so you square r and then multiply by 3.

Chief Examiner says

A common error is to work out $3r^2$ as $3r \times 3r$. That would be written $(3r)^2$.

Test Yourself 3

a If $P = 6n$, find P when $n = 5$.

b If $S = 4a + 10$, find S when $a = 2$.

c If $A = 2x + 5y$, find A when $x = 4$ and $y = 3$.

d If $C = 6b + 3a^2$, find C when $b = -3$ and $a = 5$.

e If $y = \frac{3a - 2b}{c}$, find y when

i $a = 2$, $b = -5$ and $c = 3$.

ii $a = \frac{1}{4}$, $b = \frac{3}{4}$ and $c = 2$.

Solutions

Test Yourself 3

a $P = 6 \times 5$

$= 30$

b $S = 4 \times 2 + 10$

$= 8 + 10$

$= 18$

c $A = 2 \times 4 + 5 \times 3$

$= 8 + 15$

$= 23$

d $C = 6 \times -3 + 3 \times 5^2$

$= -18 + 75$

$= 57$

e i $y = \frac{3 \times 2 - 2 \times -5}{3}$

$= \frac{6 + 10}{3}$

$= 5\frac{1}{3}$

ii $y = \frac{3 \times \frac{1}{4} - 2 \times \frac{3}{4}}{2}$

$= \frac{\frac{3}{4} - 1\frac{1}{2}}{2}$

$= \frac{-\frac{3}{4}}{2}$

$= -\frac{3}{8}$

6 Equations 1

Solving equations

Revised

- To solve an equation, you must always do the same to both sides of the equation.

Test Yourself 1

Solve these equations.

a $4g = 6$

b $s - 7 = 5$

c $2x = -8$

d $4 + 3g = 10$

e $3s - 2 = 7$

f $2x + 3 = 8$

Solutions

Test Yourself 1

a $4g = 6$

$g = 6 \div 4$ — Divide both sides by 4.

$g = 1.5$

b $s - 7 = 5$

$s = 5 + 7$ — Add 7 to both sides.

$s = 12$

c $2x = -8$

$x = -8 \div 2$ — Divide both sides by 2.

$x = -4$

d $4 + 3g = 10$

$3g = 10 - 4$ — Subtract 4 from both sides.

$3g = 6$

$g = 6 \div 3$ — Divide both sides by 3.

$g = 2$

e $3s - 2 = 7$

$3s = 9$ — Add 2 to both sides.

$s = 3$ — Divide both sides by 3.

f $2x + 3 = 8$

$2x = 5$ — Subtract 3 from both sides.

$x = 2.5$ — Divide both sides by 2.

Equations involving division

Revised

- To solve an equation with a fraction, multiply both sides of the equation by the denominator of the fraction.

Test Yourself 2

Solve these equations.

a $\frac{k}{3} = 16$

b $\frac{m}{2} = 9$

c $\frac{p}{4} = 4$

Solutions

Test Yourself 2

a $\frac{k}{3} = 16$

$k = 16 \times 3$ — Multiply both sides by 3.

$k = 48$

b $\frac{m}{2} = 9$

$m = 9 \times 2$ — Multiply both sides by 2.

$m = 18$

c $\frac{p}{4} = 4$

$p = 4 \times 4$ — Multiply both sides by 4.

$p = 16$

Word problems

Revised

- Writing your own equations is similar to writing your own formulae.

Test Yourself 3

Henri thinks of a number. He multiplies it by 4 and subtracts 7. His answer is 31.

Write an equation to represent this problem and solve it to find Henri's number.

Solution

Test Yourself 3

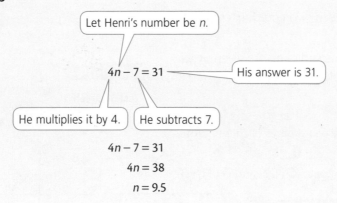

Let Henri's number be n.

$4n - 7 = 31$

His answer is 31.

He multiplies it by 4.

He subtracts 7.

$$4n - 7 = 31$$
$$4n = 38$$
$$n = 9.5$$

7 Coordinates

Points in all four quadrants

Revised

- On a flat surface (two dimensions) you need two coordinates to describe the position of a point.
- You may be asked to plot a point whose coordinates are given or to give the coordinates of a point which is plotted already.

Test Yourself 1

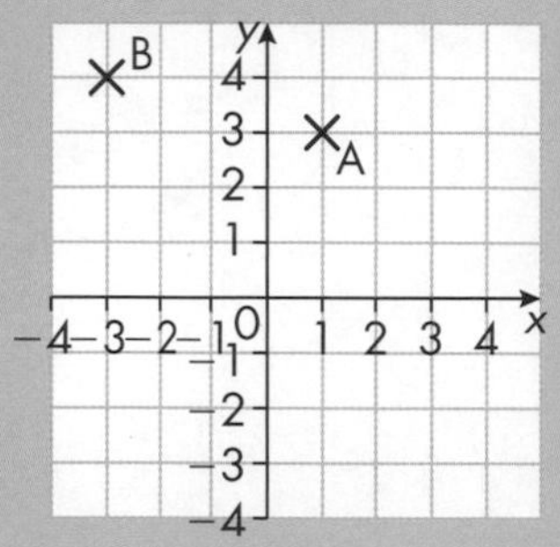

a State the coordinates of these points.

i A **ii** B

b Plot the points C (4, 2) and D (−2, −3)

Chief Examiner says

A common error is to write the coordinates the wrong way round. They are in alphabetical order.

Solutions

Test Yourself 1

a i (1, 3) **ii** (−3, 4)

b

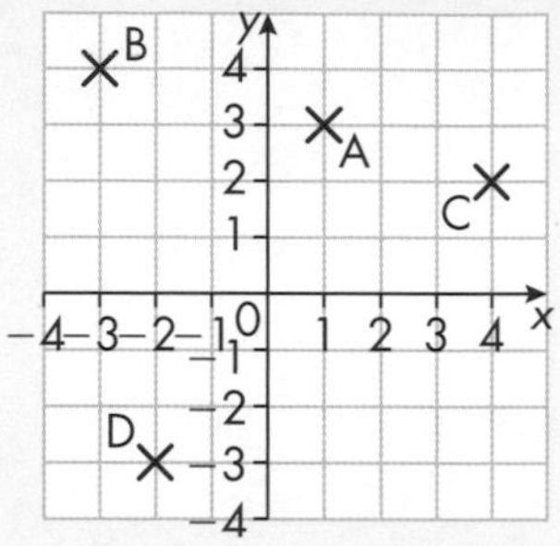

Lines parallel to the axes

Revised

- All horizontal lines have the equation $y =$ a number.

Chief Examiner says

Notice that the number in the equation is where the line crosses the *y*-axis.

- All vertical lines have equation $x =$ a number.

Test Yourself 2

Draw and label the following straight lines.

$x = 3$, $y = -2$, $y = 5$, $x = -4$

Chief Examiner says

Notice that the number in the equation is where the line crosses the *x*-axis.

Solution

Test Yourself 2

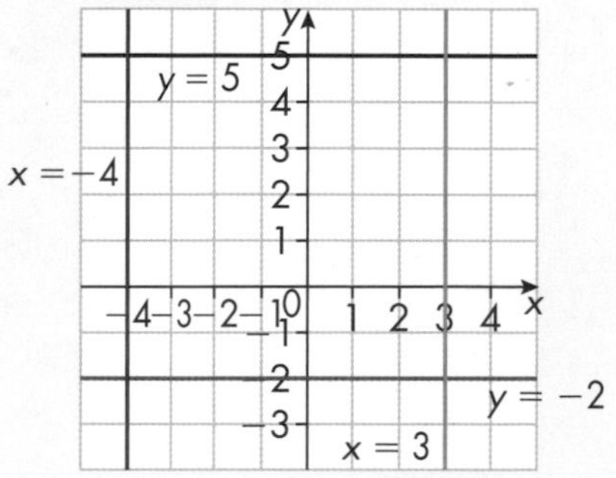

8 Statistical calculations 1

Median, mode and mean

Revised

- The median, mode and mean are all measures of 'average'.
- The median of a set of numbers is the middle value after they have been put in order, smallest to biggest. If there is an even number of values, there will be two middle values: the median is halfway between them.
- The mode of a set of data is the number, or value, that occurs most often.
- The mean is found by adding up all the values and dividing by the number of values.

Chief Examiner says

When there is a small number of values, the mode is a very poor measure of average.

Test Yourself 1

For this set of figures, find

a the mode

b the median

c the mean.

5 7 8 6 7 10 15 9 11 7

Solutions

Test Yourself 1

First put the numbers in order.

5 6 7 7 7 8 9 10 11 15

a The mode is 7. — 7 occurs more frequently than any of the other numbers.

b The median is 7.5. — There are two middle values, 7 and 8. The median is halfway between them.

c The mean $= \dfrac{5 + 6 + 7 + 7 + 7 + 8 + 9 + 10 + 11 + 15}{10}$

$= 85 \div 10$

$= 8.5$

Chief Examiner says

Even if the values are all whole numbers, the mean and median could be a fraction or a decimal.

Range

Revised

- The range is a measure of how spread out the data are.
- The range of a set of numbers is the difference between the smallest and largest values: (Largest – Smallest)
- When comparing sets of data always compare
  - one measure of average to see whether one set is generally higher than the others
  - a measure such as the range to see whether one set is more spread out than the others.

Test Yourself 2

Find the range of this set of figures.

5 7 8 6 7 10 15 9 11 7

Solution

Test Yourself 2

Range = 15 – 5
= 10

Modal class

Revised

- For grouped data with equal intervals, the modal class is the class with the highest frequency.

Test Yourself 3

The table shows the amounts of pocket money received by the members of Class 10H.

What is the modal class?

Money (£)	Frequency
0–3.99	3
4–7.99	10
8–11.99	12
12–15.99	5

Solution

Test Yourself 3

£8–£11.99

9 Sequences 1

Term-to-term rules

Revised

- A sequence is a group of terms linked by a rule. For example, the number of lines needed to make each of these pictures is:

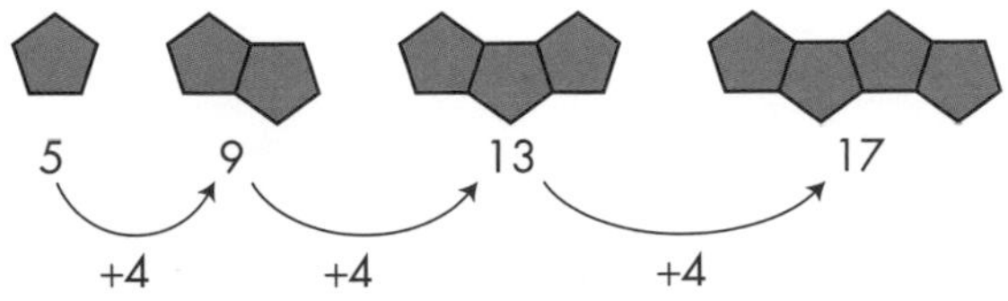

- The rule connecting the terms is +4.
- The next picture in the sequence would have $17 + 4 = 21$ lines.
- The rule that takes you from one term to the next is called the term-to-term rule.

Test Yourself 1

Find the term-to-term rule and the next number in each of these sequences.

a i

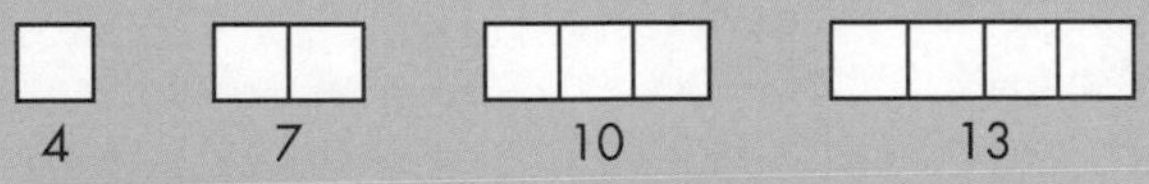

ii 15, 30, 45, 60 **iii** 100, 90, 80, 70 **iv** 2, 4, 8, 16

b i Draw the next diagram in this sequence.

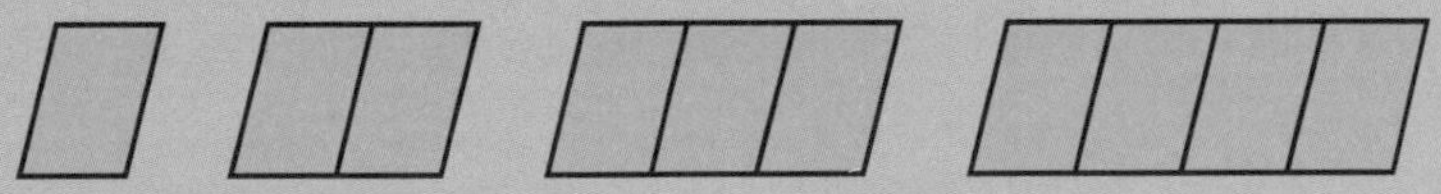

ii Count the number of lines in each diagram and find the term-to-term rule.

Solutions

Test Yourself 1

a i The term-to-term rule is +3. The next term is 16.
ii The term-to-term rule is +15. The next term is 75.
iii The term-to-term rule is −10. The next term is 60.
iv The term-to-term rule is ×2. The next term is 32.

b i

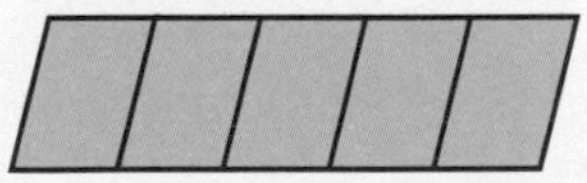

ii 4, 7, 10, 13, 16. The term-to-term rule is +3.

Position-to-term rules

Revised

- You can use a formula to give the terms in a sequence. For example, $n + 3$, $2n$, $3n + 1$.
- n stands for the number of a term (its position in a sequence), so for the first term $n = 1$, for the second term $n = 2$, and so on.

Test Yourself 2

a Write down the first four terms of each of these sequences.

i $n+3$ **ii** $2n$ **iii** $3n+1$

b Find the 20th term of the sequence with nth term $= 4n - 1$.

Solutions

Test Yourself 2

a i 4, 5, 6, 7 — $1 + 3, 2 + 3, 3 + 3, 4 + 3$

ii 2, 4, 6, 8 — $2 \times 1, 2 \times 2, 2 \times 3, 2 \times 4$

iii 4, 7, 10, 13 — $(3 \times 1) + 1, (3 \times 2) + 1, (3 \times 3) + 1, (3 \times 4) + 1$

b 79 — $(4 \times 20) - 1$

10 Measures

Using and reading scales

Revised

- To read a scale you need to decide what each division represents.

Test Yourself 1

a Write down the readings at A and B.

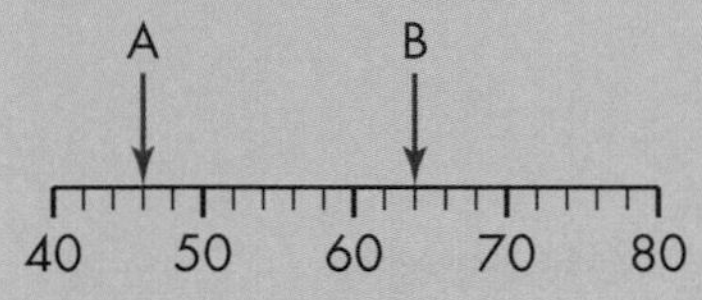

b On the scale, mark the point 76 and label it C.

Solutions

Test Yourself 1

a A is at 46. B is at 64.

b

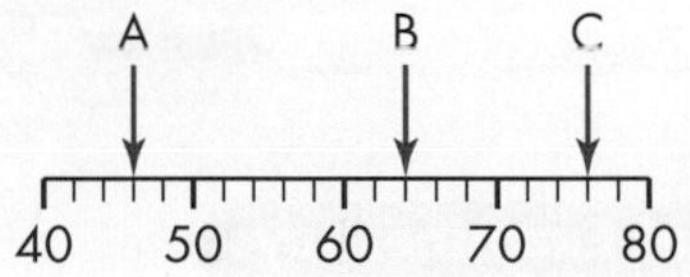

Changing from one unit to another

Revised

- You need to know how to change between the common metric units and how to work with a mixture of units.
  - Length
    1 cm = 10 mm
    1 m = 1000 mm
    1 m = 100 cm
    1 km = 1000 m
  - Mass
    1 tonne = 1000 kg
    1 kg = 1000 g
  - Capacity/Volume
    1 cl = 10 ml
    1 litre = 100 cl
    1 litre = 1000 ml
    1 litre = 1000 cm^3

Test Yourself 2

Change these units.

a 20 cm to mm

b 15 m to cm

c 2500 m to km

d 1.5 kg to g

e 4 litres to ml

Solutions

Test Yourself 2

a 20 cm = 20 × 10
= 200 mm (1 cm = 10 mm)

b 15 m = 15 × 100
= 1500 cm (1 m = 100 cm)

c 2500 mm = 2500 ÷ 1000
= 2.5 km (1 km = 1000 m)

d 1.5 kg = 1.5 × 1000
= 1500 g (1 kg = 1000 g)

e 4 litres = 4 × 1000
= 4000 ml (1 litre = 1000 ml)

Approximate equivalents

Revised

- Approximate equivalents between imperial and metric units are:
  - 1 km is about $\frac{5}{8}$ mile, 1 mile is about 1.6 km or 5 miles is about 8 km.
  - 1 m is about 40 inches, 1 inch is about $2\frac{1}{2}$ cm.
  - 1 foot is about 30 cm.
  - 1 kg is about 2 pounds.
  - 1 litre is about $1\frac{3}{4}$ pints or 4 litres is about 7 pints.
  - 1 gallon is about $4\frac{1}{2}$ litres.
- You will only need to find approximate equivalents.

Chief Examiner says

A more accurate approximation often used is, 1 kg is about 2.2 pounds.

Test Yourself 3

Change these imperial measures to rough equivalent metric measures.

a 30 miles

b 15 pounds

c 10 pints

Solutions

Test Yourself 3

a 30 miles = 30 × 1.6 = 48 km (1 mile = 1.6 km)

b 15 pounds = 15 ÷ 2 = 7.5 kg (2 pounds = 1 kg)

c 10 pints = 10 ÷ 1.75 = 6 litres (to the nearest litre) ($1\frac{3}{4}$ pints = 1 litre)

Estimating measures

Revised

- You need to use the appropriate units when measuring. For example, somebody's height is measured in metres or centimetres, rather than millimetres or kilometres.
- It is useful to know some common measures for comparison.
  - The mass of a bag of sugar is about 1 kg
  - Cans of drink hold about 300 ml
  - The height of an adult is about 1.5 m

Chief Examiner says

Do not try to be too accurate. For example, the length of a car is about 4 m, but 3 m or 5 m would also be accepted if you are not given more information.

Test Yourself 4

a Estimate the height of the giraffe. **b** Estimate the length of the whale.

Solutions

Test Yourself 4

a 5.5 m (Any answer from 5 m to 7 m is acceptable.)

b 7 m (Any answer from 6 m to 8 m is acceptable.)

11 Constructions 1

Measuring lengths

Revised

- You need to be able to measure lengths accurately.

Test Yourself 1

Measure the length of each of these lines.

a)
b)
c)
d)
e)
f)

Solutions

Test Yourself 1

a 4 cm **b** 9 cm **c** 7.5 cm

d 3.2 cm **e** 5.8 cm **f** 8.1 cm

Chief Examiner says

Answers 1 mm greater or 1 mm less will be acceptable.

Types of angle

Revised

- You need to be able to recognise and measure different types of angles.
  - Angles under 90° are called acute angles.

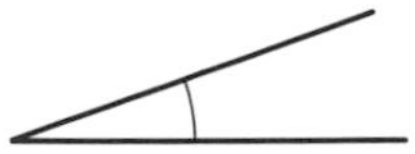

  - Angles between 90° and 180° are called obtuse angles.

  - Angles of 90° are called right angles.

  - Angles bigger than 180° are called reflex angles.

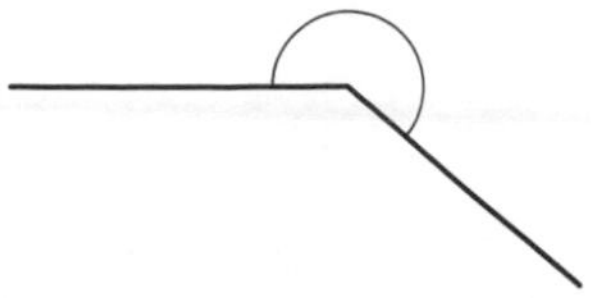

Test Yourself 2

State whether each of these angles is acute, obtuse or reflex.

a 32° **b** 185°
c 93° **d** 246°
e 141°

Solutions

Test Yourself 2

a Acute — Under 90°.
b Reflex — Over 180°.
c Obtuse — Between 90° and 180°.
d Reflex — Over 180°
e Obtuse — Between 90° and 180°.

Measuring angles

Revised

- To measure an angle, put your protractor or angle measurer with the 0° along one line and the centre at the point of the angle.
- Start at zero and go round the scale until you reach the other line making the angle. Read the scale to find the size of the angle.

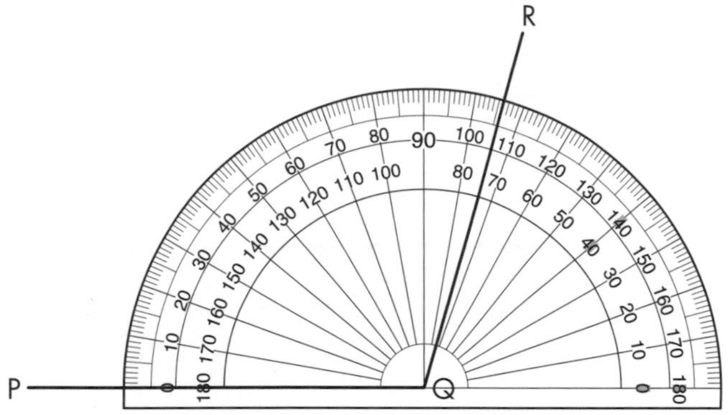

Chief Examiner says

To check that you have read off the correct scale, look at the angle and estimate its size. If it is acute, your answer should be less than 90°. If it obtuse, your answer should be between 90° and 180°.

Test Yourself 3

Measure these angles.

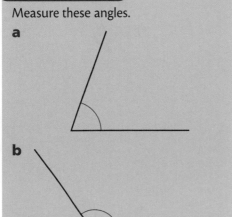

a

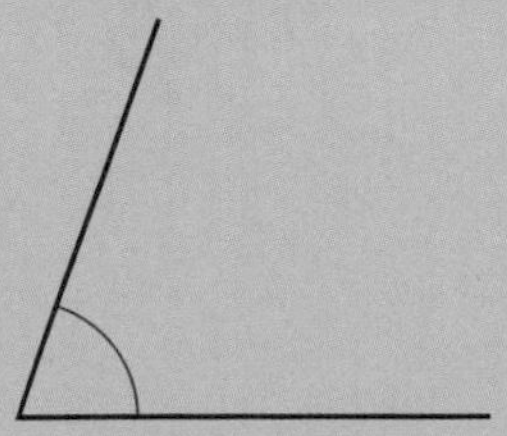

b

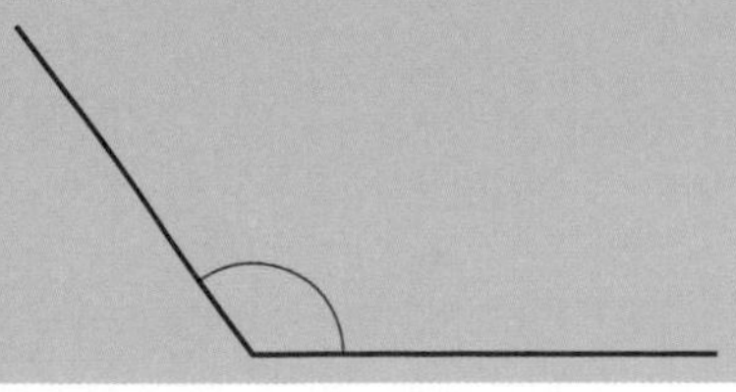

Solutions

Test Yourself 3

a 70°
b 125°

Drawing angles

Revised

- To draw an angle, first draw a line. Put your protractor or angle measurer with the 0° along the line and the centre at one end of the line.
- Start at zero and go round the scale until you reach the size of the angle you want to draw. Make a small mark on your paper at this point. Draw a line from the end of your line through the mark you have made.

Test Yourself 4

Draw these angles.

a 60°

b 135°

c 215

Solutions

Test Yourself 4

a

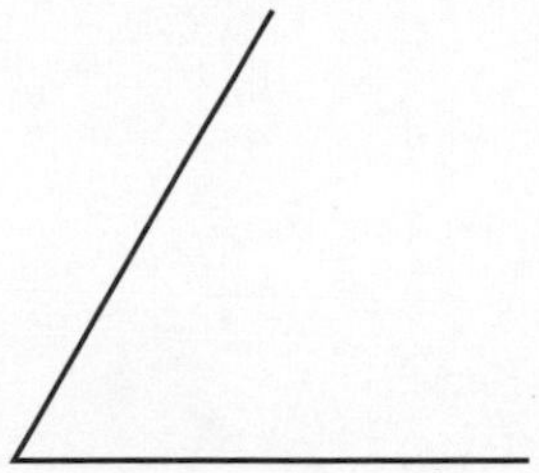

b

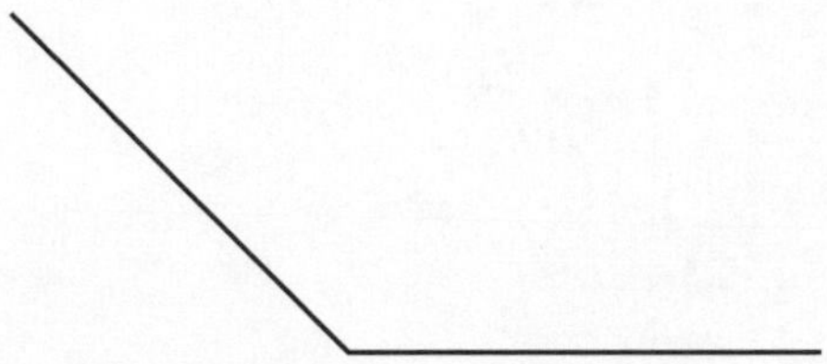

c

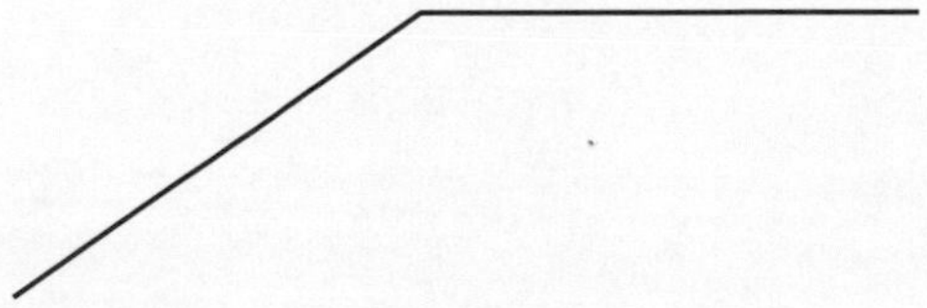

Drawing triangles

Revised

- You need to be able to construct a triangle given specific information.
  - Two sides and the angle between them

    Step 1: Draw line AB of given length.

    Step 2: Measure the angle at A.

    Step 3: Draw line AC of given length.

    Step 4: Join C to B.

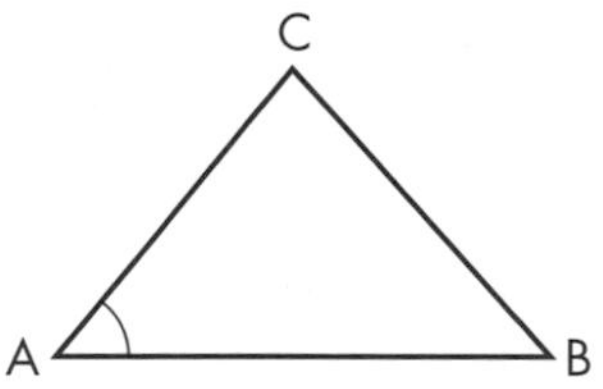

  - Two angles and one side

    Step 1: Draw line AB of given length.

    Step 2: Measure angles at A and B.

    Step 3: Draw lines AC and BC.

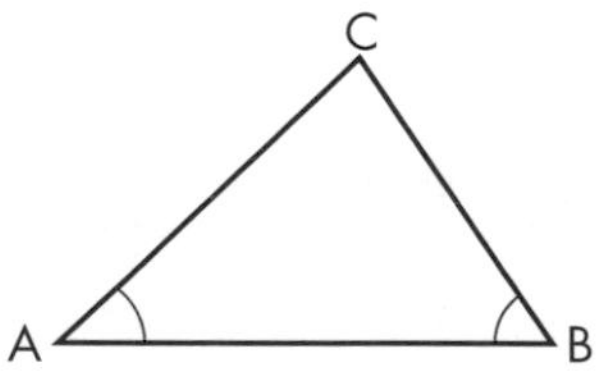

  - Three sides

    Step 1: Draw line AB of given length.

    Step 2: Use compasses to construct arcs AC and BC with the compasses set to the given lengths.

    Step 3: Draw AC and BC.

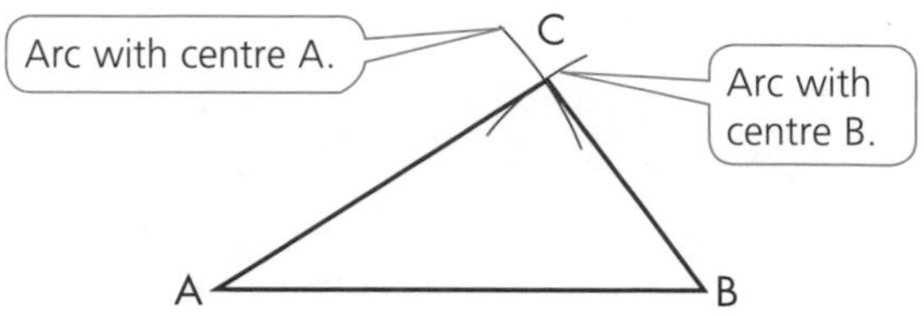

- Two sides and an angle

  Step 1: Draw line AB of given length.

  Step 2: Measure angle at A.

  Step 3: Draw a line from A towards C.

  Step 4: To fix C, draw an arc at B, the radius of the arc being the second given length. This construction may give two possible triangles, ABC or ABC′.

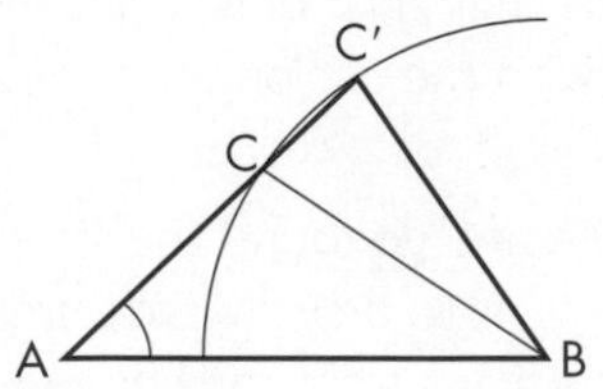

- You can use similar methods to construct quadrilaterals.

Chief Examiner says

When you do constructions, remember to leave in all your construction lines. Do not rub them out.

Test Yourself 5

a Construct an isosceles triangle ABC with sides AB = 4 cm, BC = 5 cm and AC = 5 cm.

b Measure angle ABC of the triangle.

Solutions

Test Yourself 5

a **Step 1:** Draw the 4 cm side of the triangle and label it AB.

Step 2: Set your compasses to 5 cm. With the compass point at A, make arcs above the centre of the line. Repeat with the point at B so that the arcs cross. This is point C.

Step 3: Draw AC and BC to complete the triangle.

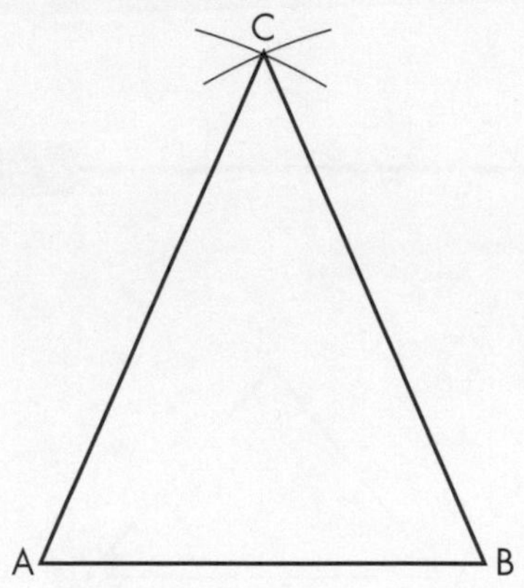

b Angle ABC = 66°

An angle of 65° to 68° is acceptable.

Scale drawings and maps

Revised

- If you give some directions using a street map, we say 'turn left' and so on.
- For more general directions, you can say 'Birmingham is south-west of Nottingham', for example.
- A scale is used to change the distance from a map or scale drawing to its real distance.

Solution

Test Yourself 6

On the map, AB = 3.2cm

So the distance from Ayton to Bowick = $3.2 \times 5 = 16$km

Test Yourself 6

Find the distance of Bowick (B) from Ayton (A).

Scale 1 cm to 5 km

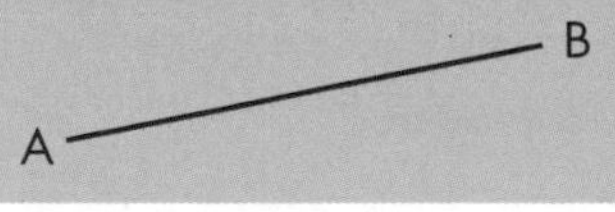

Scale drawings and bearings

Revised

- Bearings are measured clockwise from North and must have three figures. An angle of 27° would be written as a bearing of 027°.
- The bearing of B from A is the angle at A, measured clockwise from North to the line to B. It is marked x in the diagram. The bearing of A from B is the angle marked y in the diagram.

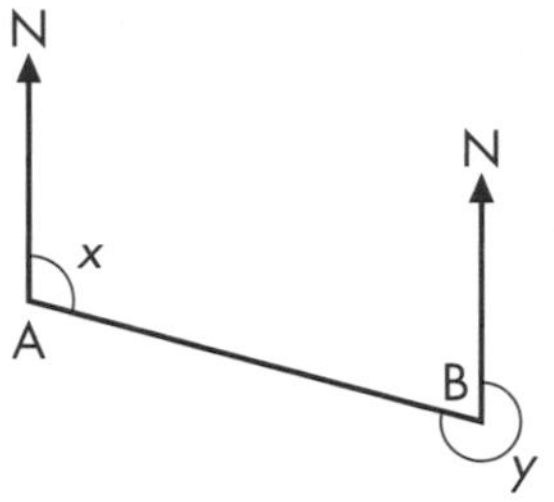

Chief Examiner says

A useful rule to remember is that the difference between the bearing of B from A and the bearing of A from B is 180°.

Chief Examiner says

Often, you will be asked to draw a diagram to find a place. It is important that you measure all distances and bearings accurately. It is also useful to do a sketch first.

- Scales are sometimes expressed as ratios. For example, a scale of 1:10000 on a map means that 1cm on the map represents 10000cm (which is 100m) on the ground.

Test Yourself 7

a Measure the bearings of A, B and C from O.

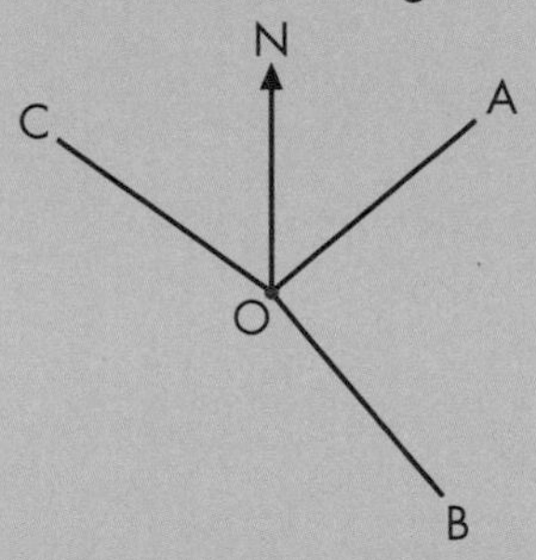

b Jim has drawn a scale plan of his house and garden. The scale is 1:200.

i On the plan, the length of the garden is 7cm. How long is the actual garden?

ii The house is 9m wide. How wide should it be on the plan?

Solutions

Test Yourself 7

a Bearing of A from O = 050°

Bearing of B from O = 140°

Bearing of C from O = 305°

b The scale is 1cm to 200cm. This is 1cm to 2m.

i The length of the garden is $7 \times 2 = 14$m.

ii The width of the house should be $9 \div 2 = 4.5$cm.

12 Using a calculator

Rounding numbers

Revised

- See Unit A Chapter 1 for rounding numbers to the nearest 10, 100, 1000.
- When you use a calculated number in further calculations, always use the more accurate version, rather than the rounded version. You can store the answer in your calculator.
- To round to the nearest whole number or a given number of decimal places,
  - look at the first digit not needed.
  - If the first digit not needed is 4 or less, then just ignore it. For example, 5.1246 correct to 2 decimal places is 5.12.

    The first digit not needed is 4, so write down the required digits.

  - If the first digit not needed is 5 or more, then add one to the last required digit. For example, 6.2873 correct to 2 decimal places is 6.29.

    The first digit not needed is 7, so add 1 to the last required digit, 8.

Rounding to a 1 significant figure

- In any number, the first digit from the left which is not 0 is the first significant figure.
- When rounding to 1 significant figure,
  - look at the first digit not needed, the second significant figure.
  - If the second significant figure is 4 or less, then just ignore it and, if necessary, include the correct number of zeros to show the size of the number. For example, 0.319 to 1 significant figure is 0.3 and 319 to 1 significant figure is 300.
  - If the second significant figure is 5 or more, add 1 to the first significant figure and, if necessary, include the correct number of zeros to show the size of the number. For example, 0.0685 to 1 significant figure is 0.07 and 685 to 1 significant figure is 700.

Chief Examiner says

The number 0.96 correct to 1 significant figure is 1, not 1.0, which has 2 significant figures. Extra zeros are used only to show the size of the number, as in 200 or 0.02, for example.

Test Yourself 1

a Write each of the following numbers correct to 1 decimal place.

i 0.234 **ii** 21.361

iii 14.19 **iv** 2.4075

v 243.95

b Write each of the following numbers correct to 1 significant figure.

i 3.658 **ii** 0.0543

ii 935.4 **iv** 47 510

Solutions

Test Yourself 1

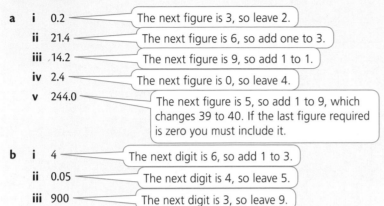

a **i** 0.2 — The next figure is 3, so leave 2.

ii 21.4 — The next figure is 6, so add one to 3.

iii 14.2 — The next figure is 9, so add 1 to 1.

iv 2.4 — The next figure is 0, so leave 4.

v 244.0 — The next figure is 5, so add 1 to 9, which changes 39 to 40. If the last figure required is zero you must include it.

b **i** 4 — The next digit is 6, so add 1 to 3.

ii 0.05 — The next digit is 4, so leave 5.

iii 900 — The next digit is 3, so leave 9.

iv 50 000 — The next digit is 7, so add 1 to 4.

Squares, square roots and other powers

Revised ☐

- Use the [x^2] key to find the square and the [$\sqrt{}$] key to find the square root.
  To find $\sqrt{3.2 + 4.6}$, you need to work out 3.2 + 4.6 first, so use brackets.
- Use the [∧] or [x^y] or [y^x] or [$x^?$] key to find powers.

Chief Examiner says

It is easy to press the wrong button when using a calculator. Do the calculation twice. Also, check if your answer seems sensible and find an estimate by approximating.

Test Yourself 2

Work out these.

Give your answers correct to 2 decimal places where appropriate.

a 1.5^2

b $\sqrt{21}$

c 6^7

d $4^5 - 3^4$

Solutions

Test Yourself 2

a [1] [.] [5] [x^2] [=] 2.25

b [$\sqrt{}$] [2] [1] [=] 4.582 …
= 4.58 (to 2 d.p.)

c [6] [∧] [7] [=] 279936

d [4] [∧] [5] [−] [3] [∧] [4] [=] 1105

Order of operations

Revised ☐

- When doing complex calculations with a calculator, you need to use brackets. For example, to work out $\frac{3.6 + 2.7}{1.4 + 5.2}$, you need to key in

[(] [3] [.] [6] [+] [2] [.] [7] [)] [÷]
[(] [1] [.] [4] [+] [5] [.] [2] [)] [=]

- Multiplication and division must be carried out before addition and subtraction. For example, to calculate, $3 + 4 \times 5$, you must work out 4×5 first. A calculator does this automatically, you can just key in [3] [+] [4] [×] [5] [=]
- Brackets must be worked out before multiplication and division. For example, to calculate $(3 + 4) \times 5$, you must work out $3 + 4$ first. If you key the calculation, including the brackets, into a calculator, it will do the whole calculation in one go.

Chief Examiner says

Remember that for every [(] there must be a [)].

Chief Examiner says

Calculators vary. The position of the keys and the symbols used on them are not always the same. The order in which the buttons have to be pressed may also vary. Make sure you know how your calculator works. Don't borrow a different calculator or change your calculator just before an exam. If you are unsure, ask your teacher.

Test Yourself 3

a Work out $\frac{4.2 + 3.6}{1.7}$ correct to 2 decimal places.

b Work out $4.7 \times 3.2 - 1.7 \times 6.1$

Solutions

Test Yourself 3

a [(] [4] [.] [2] [+] [3] [.] [6] [)] [÷] [1] [.] [7] [=] 4.588235 … = 4.59 (to 2 d.p.)

b [4] [.] [7] [×] [3] [.] [2] [−] [1] [.] [7] [×] [6] [.] [1] [=] 4.67

13 Statistical diagrams 1

Drawing pie charts

Revised

- To draw a pie chart,
  - first calculate the angle that represents one observation by dividing 360° by the total frequency
  - then multiply this amount by the frequency for each group.

Test Yourself 1

Class 10H had a choice of four events for their activity day.

The table shows the number who chose each activity.

Draw a pie chart to show this information.

Activity	Frequency
Ice skating	6
Paint balling	8
Horse riding	5
Theme park	11
Total	30

Solution

Test Yourself 1

360° ÷ 30 = 12°, so each member of the class is represented by 12°.

Calculate the angle of each sector.

Activity	Angle
Ice skating	$6 \times 12 = 72°$
Paint balling	$8 \times 12 = 96°$
Horse riding	$5 \times 12 = 60°$
Theme park	$11 \times 12 = 132°$
Total	360°

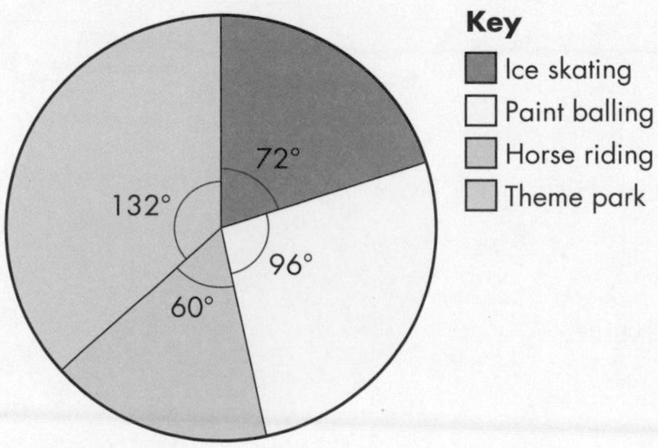

Chief Examiner says

Don't forget to label the sectors with the groups, not the size of the angles. The angles are labelled here as a check for you.

Interpreting pie charts

Revised

- To work out the number of items in each category,
  - measure the angle for each category
  - divide the total number of items by 360 to find the number of items represented by 1°
  - multiply each category angle by the number of items represented by 1°.

Test Yourself 2

The pie chart shows the type of fruit each of 1080 students in a school had one day.

Work out the number of students in each category.

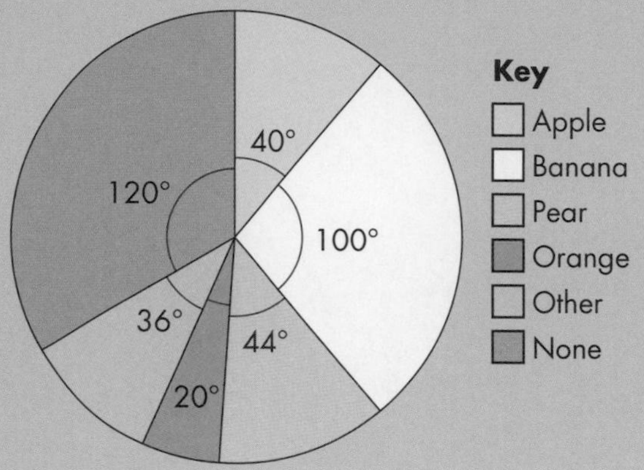

Solution

Test Yourself 2

1° represents 1080 ÷ 360 = 3 students.

Type of fruit	Number of students
Apple	40 × 3 = 120
Banana	100 × 3 = 300
Pear	44 × 3 = 132
Orange	20 × 3 = 60
Other	36 × 3 = 108
None	120 × 3 = 360

Drawing line graphs

Revised

- When drawing a vertical line graph, make sure each vertical line is the correct height.
- Joining the tops of the vertical lines creates the line graph.

Chief Examiner says

Always read scales carefully and make sure you know what each unit represents.

Test Yourself 3

The table shows monthly rainfall figures for Brisbane.

Month	Jan	Feb	Mar	Apr	May	Jun	Jul	Aug	Sep	Oct	Nov	Dec
Rainfall (mm)	160	158	141	93	74	68	57	46	46	75	97	133

a Draw a vertical line graph to show this data.

b Draw a line graph to show this data.

Solutions

Test Yourself 3

a

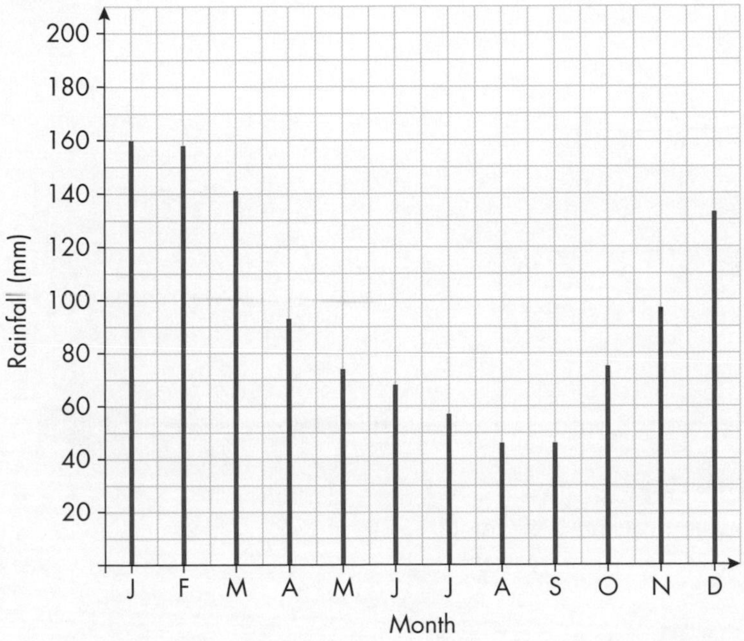

b

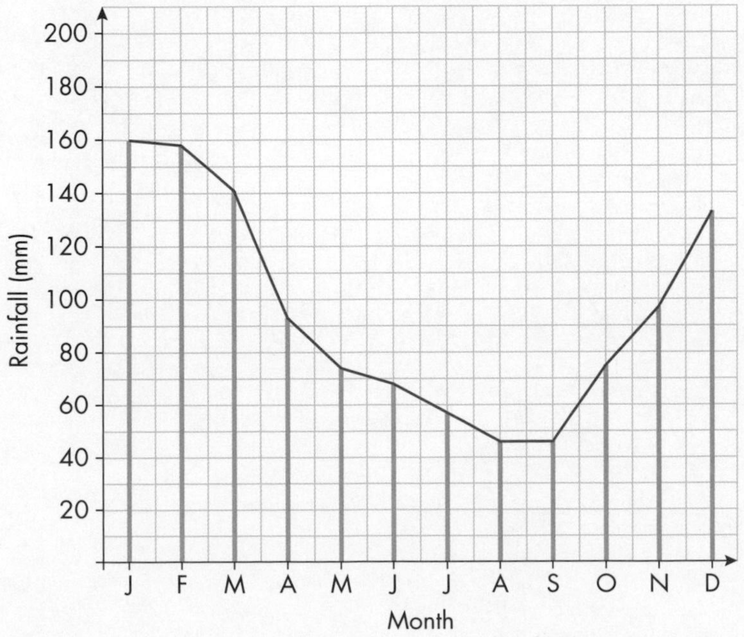

Chief Examiner says

If you are asked to draw a line graph without being asked to draw a vertical line graph as well, you don't draw the vertical lines.

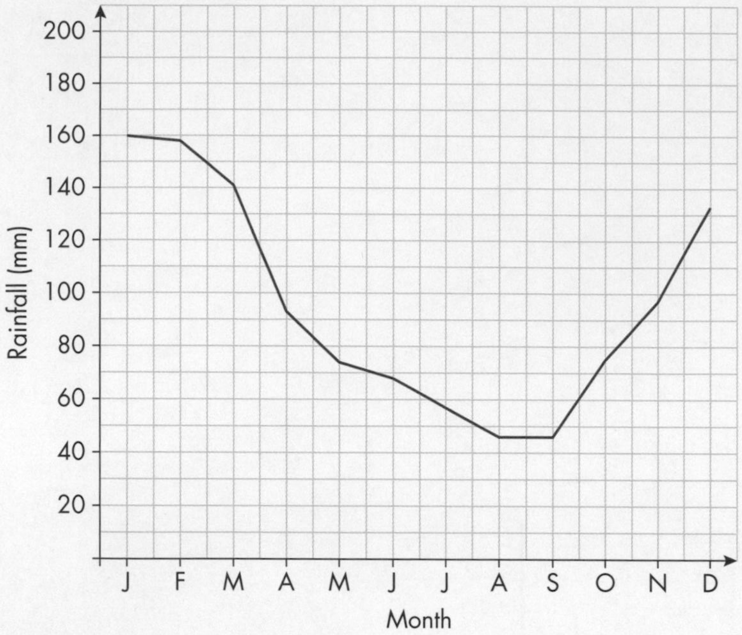

Interpreting line graphs

Revised

- The labels on the axes tell you what the graph is about.
- To read values from a line graph, you can draw vertical and horizontal lines from the axis to the line.

Test Yourself 4

This line graph shows the mean maximum monthly temperatures in Brisbane.

a In which month is the mean maximum temperature lowest?

b What is the mean maximum temperature in September?

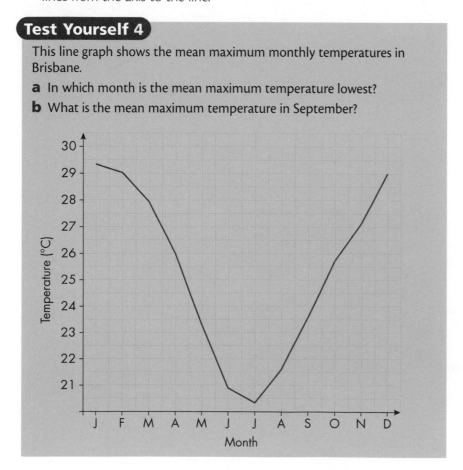

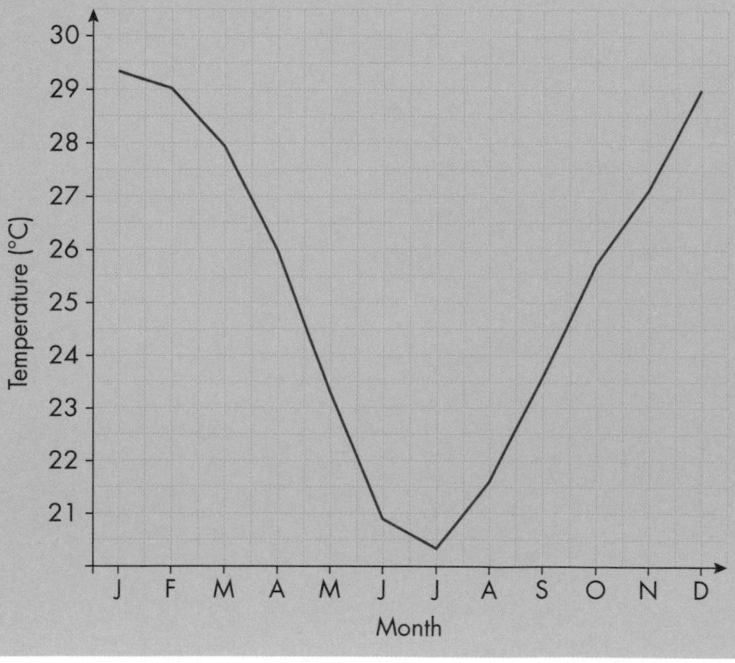

Solutions

Test Yourself 4

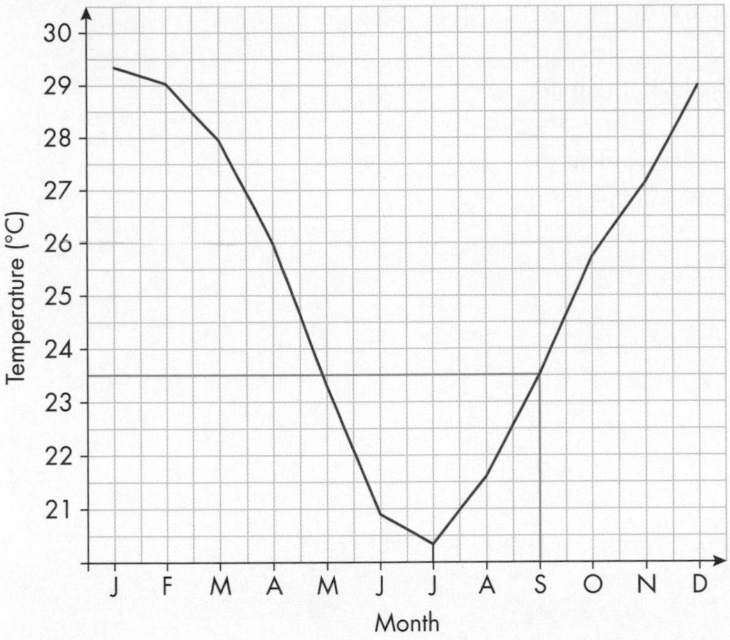

a July

b 23.5°C

Making comparisons

Revised

- When comparing two distributions make sure you use two statistics.
  - An average – either the mean, the median or the mode.
  - A measure of spread – usually the range.

Test Yourself 5

As part of annual medical checks, a company records the mass of each of its employees.

The results are shown in the table.

	Frequency	
Mass (*m* kg)	**Males**	**Females**
$45 < m \leqslant 50$	0	5
$50 < m \leqslant 55$	0	14
$55 < m \leqslant 60$	3	26
$60 < m \leqslant 65$	23	17
$65 < m \leqslant 70$	32	8
$70 < m \leqslant 75$	21	3
$75 < m \leqslant 80$	9	1
$80 < m \leqslant 85$	5	0
$85 < m \leqslant 90$	1	0

Compare the mass of the male and female employees.

Solution

Test Yourself 5

You should make at least one comparison concerning an average. Any of these three is acceptable.

- The group containing the median for the men is 10 kg higher than for the women.
- The modal group for the men is 10 kg higher than for the women.
- The mean mass for the men is 10 kg higher than the mean mass for the women.

You should also comment on the range.

- The range, 35 kg, is the same for men and women.

	Male	**Female**
Median	$65 < m \leqslant 70$	$55 < m \leqslant 60$
Mode	$65 < m \leqslant 70$	$55 < m \leqslant 60$
Mean	69	59
Range	35	35

14 Integers, powers and roots

Prime numbers and factors

Revised

- The factors of a number are the numbers that divide exactly into it. For example, the factors of 6 are 1, 2, 3 and 6.
- Prime numbers are numbers which have only two factors, 1 and the number itself.
- 1 is not a prime number.

Test Yourself 1

Write down the first five prime numbers.

Solution

Test Yourself 1

2, 3, 5, 7, 11

Writing a number as a product of its prime factors

Revised

- Prime factors are factors that are also prime numbers.
- You need to be able to write numbers as the product of their prime factors. For example, $12 = 2 \times 2 \times 3 = 2^2 \times 3$.
- There are different methods of finding a number as a product of its prime factors. Use the method you prefer.

Test Yourself 2

Write 48 as the product of its prime factors.

Solution

Test Yourself 2

Method 1

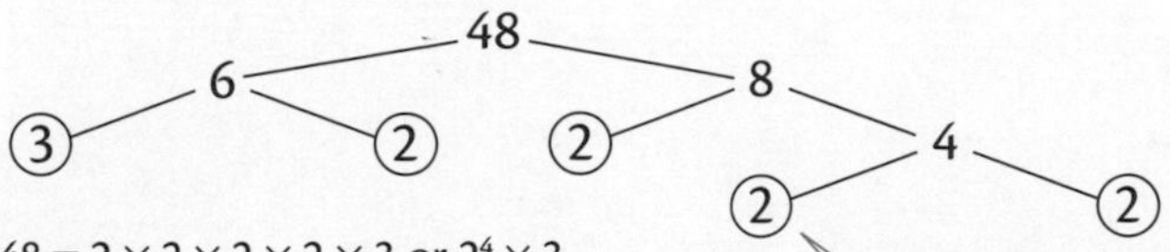

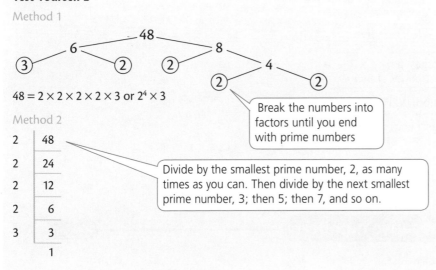

$48 = 2 \times 2 \times 2 \times 2 \times 3$ or $2^4 \times 3$

Break the numbers into factors until you end with prime numbers

Method 2

2	48
2	24
2	12
2	6
3	3
	1

Divide by the smallest prime number, 2, as many times as you can. Then divide by the next smallest prime number, 3; then 5; then 7, and so on.

Highest common factors and lowest common multiples

Revised

Highest common factor (HCF)

- The highest common factor of a set of numbers is the largest number that will divide into each of the numbers.
- To find the highest common factor,
  - write each number as the product of its prime factors
  - choose the factors that are common to all the given numbers
  - multiply them together.

Lowest common multiple (LCM)

- The lowest common multiple of a set of numbers is the smallest number that can be divided exactly by all the numbers.
- To find the lowest common multiple,
  - write each number as the product of its prime factors
  - choose the highest power of each of the factors that appear in the lists
  - multiply these numbers together.

Test Yourself 3

For the numbers 120, 36 and 84 find

a the highest common factor

b the lowest common multiple.

Solutions

Test Yourself 3

a $120 = (2) \times (2) \times 2 \times (3) \times 5$

$36 = (2) \times (2) \times (3) \times 3$

$84 = (2) \times (2) \times (3) \times 7$

2, 2 and 3 are common to all three numbers.

HCF is $2 \times 2 \times 3 = 12$.

Chief Examiner says

Check that 12 divides into 120, 36 and 84.

b $120 = 2^3 \times 3 \times 5$ — 120 has the largest power of 2 (2^3) and the largest power of 5 (5^1).

$36 = 2^2 \times 3^2$ — 36 has the largest power of 3 (3^2).

$84 = 2^2 \times 3 \times 7$ — 84 has the largest power of 7 (7^1).

LCM is $2^3 \times 3^2 \times 5 \times 7 = 2520$.

Multiplying and dividing by negative numbers

Revised

- When multiplying and dividing, use these rules.
  - $+ \times + = +$ • $+ \div + = +$
  - $- \times - = +$ • $- \div - = +$
  - $+ \times - = -$ • $+ \div - = -$
  - $- \times + = -$ • $- \div + = -$
- Combine the numbers and signs separately. A number with no sign is positive.

Solutions

Test Yourself 4

a $-4 \times 3 = -12$ — $- \times + = -$

b $24 \div -8 = -3$ — $+ \div - = -$

c $-12 \div -6 = 2$ — $- \div - = +$

Test Yourself 4

Work out these.

a -4×3

b $24 \div -8$

c $-12 \div -6$

Squares, square roots, cubes and cube roots

Revised

- See Unit A, Chapters 1 and 12 for more on squares, square roots, cubes and cube roots.
- There may be cube and cube root functions on your calculator. The keys may look like this: [x^3] and [$\sqrt[3]{\ }$]. You may need to use the [SHIFT] key.
- When you square root a number, there are two solutions. For example $\sqrt{4} = 2$ or -2.
- Your calculator will only give you the positive solution when you use the square root function.

Test Yourself 5

Work out these. Where necessary, give your answer to 2 decimal places.

a 3.7^3

b $\sqrt[3]{6.2}$

Solutions

Test Yourself 5

a [3] [.] [7] [x^3] [=] 187.4161

b [$\sqrt[3]{\ }$] [6] [.] [2] [=] 1.84 (2 d.p.)

Reciprocals

Revised

- The reciprocal of x is $\frac{1}{x}$.
- The reciprocal of $\frac{a}{b}$ is $\frac{b}{a}$.
- Use the [1/x] or the [x^{-1}] button.

Test Yourself 6

Work out the reciprocal of each of these.

a 4

b $\frac{2}{3}$

c 0.1

d 40

e $1\frac{2}{3}$

Solutions

Test Yourself 6

a $\frac{1}{4}$ or 0.25

b $\frac{3}{2}$ or $1\frac{1}{2}$

c [0] [.] [1] [1/x] [=] 10

d [4] [0] [1/x] [=] 0.025

e [1] [$a\frac{b}{c}$] [2] [$a\frac{b}{c}$] [3] [1/x] [=] $\frac{3}{5}$

15 Algebra 2

Expanding brackets

Revised

- When expanding brackets, multiply every term within the brackets by the term immediately in front of the bracket.
- Like terms can be added and subtracted.

Test Yourself 1

Expand and simplify these.

a $7(x - 4)$

b $4(x + 2y)$

c $a(x + y)$

d $3(2a + 3b) - 2(a - 2b)$

Chief Examiner says

'Multiply out', 'expand' and 'remove the brackets' all mean the same thing.

Solutions

Test Yourself 1

a $7x - 28$ — The x and 4 terms are each multiplied by 7.

b $4x + 8y$ — The x and $2y$ terms are each multiplied by 4.

c $ax + ay$ — The x and y terms are each multiplied by a.

d $6a + 9b - 2a + 4b = 4a + 13b$ — First multiply out the brackets, taking care over $-2 \times -2b = +4b$, then collect the terms.

Collecting like terms

Revised

- When simplifying, only the same type of terms can be collected.
- $2a$ and $3a$ are the same type; $3a$ and $4c$ are different types.

Test Yourself 2

Simplify these.

a $3a - 2b + 4b + a$

b $3ab - 2ac + 4ab + ac$

c $a^2 - 2a + 3a + b^2 - 2a^2 + 3b^2$

Solutions

Test Yourself 2

a $4a + 2b$ — The a and b terms are each collected.

b $7ab - ac$ — The ab and ac terms are each collected.

c $a - a^2 + 4b^2$ — The a, a^2 and b^2 terms are each collected.

Factorising

Revised

- To factorise an expression, look for every number and letter that is common to every term and write these outside a bracket. Inside the bracket, write the terms that will give the original terms when the bracket is expanded.

Test Yourself 3

Factorise these.

a $3a + 6$

b $2x^2 - 3xy$ **c** $4a - 8ac + 16a^2b$

Solutions

Test Yourself 3

a $3(a + 2)$ **b** $x(2x - 3y)$

c $4a(1 - 2c + 4ab)$ — Note that $4a = 4a \times 1$ so 1 must be in the bracket.

Index notation

Revised

- You can use index notation in algebra: $x \times x \times x \times x = x^4$.

Test Yourself 4

Write these using index notation.

a $b \times b \times b$

b $x \times x \times y \times y \times y$ **c** $2x \times 3x$

Solutions

Test Yourself 4

a b^3 **b** x^2y^3

c $6x^2$ — Multiply the numbers together, then multiply the letters together.

16 Statistical diagrams 2

- See Unit A, Chapter 3 for more on grouping data.
- See Unit A, Chapter 8 for more on statistical calculations.
- See Unit A, Chapter 13 for more on statistical diagrams.

Frequency diagrams

Revised

- For grouped data with equal intervals, a frequency diagram can be drawn.
- The height of each bar is equal to the frequency.

Test Yourself 1

The table shows the amounts of pocket money received by the members of Class 10H.

Draw a frequency diagram to show this information.

Money (£)	Frequency
0–3.99	3
4–7.99	10
8–11.99	12
12–15.99	5

Solution

Test Yourself 1

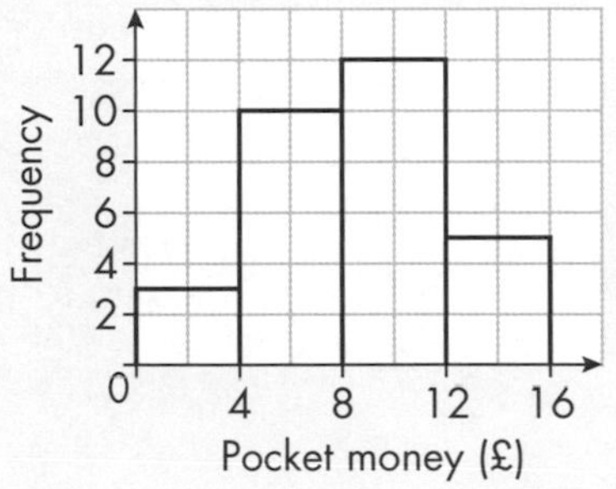

Frequency polygons

Revised

- To draw a frequency polygon,
  - plot the values of the frequency at the midpoints of the intervals
  - join with straight lines.

Test Yourself 2

The table shows the amount of pocket money received by members of Class 10H.

Draw a frequency polygon to show this information.

Amount (£)	0–3.99	4–7.99	8–11.99	12–15.99
Frequency	3	10	12	5

Solution

Test Yourself 2

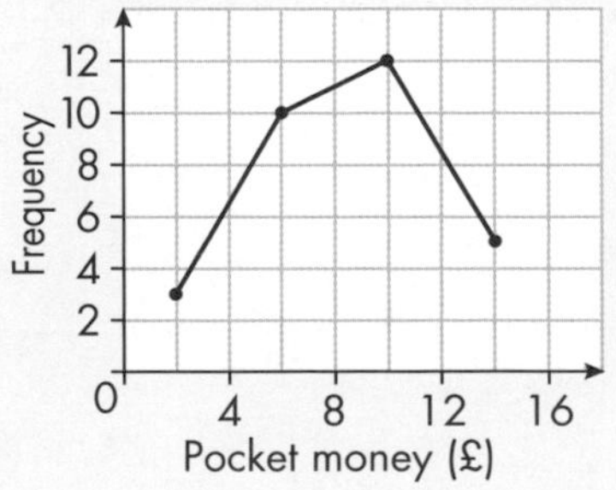

Stem-and-leaf diagrams

Revised

- You can display a large number of two-digit data items in a stem-and-leaf diagram.
- You write the tens digit (the stem) in the left-hand column.
- You write the units digits (the leaves) in the right-hand column.
- To draw a stem-and-leaf diagram,
  - first work through the data and write the 'leaf' for each value in turn
  - then redraw the diagram with the 'leaves' ordered.
- You can also use a stem-and-leaf diagram with, for example, units as the 'stem' and the first decimal place as the 'leaves'.
- Always give a key, for example 3 | 2 represents 32.
- You can find the median by counting up to the middle value.

Test Yourself 3

Here are the test marks of a group of students.

63	54	34	42	38	76	69
52	45	54	67	71	64	43
57	59	47	66	57	63	

a Draw a stem-and-leaf diagram to show this information.

b Find the median mark.

Solutions

Test Yourself 3

a Unordered

3	4	8				
4	2	5	3	7		
5	4	2	4	7	9	7
6	3	9	7	4	6	3
7	6	1				

Ordered

3	4	8				
4	2	3	5	7		
5	2	4	4	7	7	9
6	3	3	4	6	7	9
7	1	6				

Key 3 | 4 represents 34

b Since there are 20 values there are two middle values, the 10th and 11th.
They are both 57, so the median is 57.

17 Equations 2

- See Unit A, Chapter 6 for more on solving equations.

Solving equations

Revised

- When you solve an equation, you must always do each operation to the whole of both sides of the equation.
- An equation with an x^2 term usually has two solutions.

Chief Examiner says

Remember that $5x^2$ means $5 \times x^2$ not $(5x)^2$.

Test Yourself 1

Solve these equations.

a $3x - 4 = 20$

b $5x^2 = 80$

Solutions

Test Yourself 1

a $3x - 4 = 20$

$3x = 24$ — First add 4 to both sides.

$x = 8$ — Then divide both sides by 3.

b $5x^2 = 80$

$x^2 = 16$ — First divide both sides by 5.

$x = \pm 4$ — Then find the square root of each side.

Solving equations with a bracket

Revised

- If the equation has a bracket, multiply out the bracket first.

Test Yourself 2

Solve the equation $2(x + 4) = 13$.

Solution

Test Yourself 2

$2\,(x + 4) = 13$

$2x + 8 = 13$ — Multiply out the bracket.

$2x = 5$ — Subtract 8 from both sides of the equation.

$x = \frac{5}{2}$ — Divide both sides by 2.

Equations with *x* on both sides

Revised

- If the 'unknown' is on both sides of the equation, rearrange the equation so that the numbers are on one side and the 'unknown' is on the other side.

Test Yourself 3

Solve the equation $5x + 4 = 2x + 19$.

Solution

Test Yourself 3

$5x + 4 = 2x + 19$

$5x = 2x + 15$ — First subtract 4 from both sides.

$3x = 15$ — Then subtract $2x$ from both sides.

$x = \frac{15}{3}$ — Then divide both sides by 3.

$x = 5$

Fractions in equations

Revised

- If an equation involves a fraction, multiply both sides of the equation by the denominator.

Test Yourself 4

Solve these equations.

a $\frac{3x}{4} = 12$

b $\frac{x}{5} + 7 = 10$

Solutions

Test Yourself 4

a $\frac{3x}{4} = 12$

$3x = 48$ — Multiply both sides by 4.

$x = \frac{48}{3}$ — Divide both sides by 3.

$x = 16$

b $\frac{x}{5} + 7 = 10$

$\frac{x}{5} = 3$ — Subtract 7 from both sides.

$x = 15$ — Multiply both sides by 5.

18 Ratio and proportion

Ratios

Revised

- If two quantities are in proportion to one another so that for x parts of the first there are y parts of the second, then the ratio is x to y.
- The ratio x to y is written as $x : y$.
- To write a ratio in its lowest terms (or simplest form), both parts need to be in the same units. You then divide both sides of the ratio by the same number until they have no common factors.
- To write a ratio in the form $1 : n$, divide the second part by the first.

Test Yourself 1

Write each of these ratios

i in its lowest terms

ii in the form $1 : n$

a 6 : 9

b 50p : £4

c 5 m : 40 cm

Solutions

Test Yourself 1

a **i** 2 : 3 (Divide both sides by 3.) **ii** 1 : 1.5 (Divide both sides by 2.)

b **i** 50 : 400 = 1 : 8 (Change to pence and divide both sides by 50.) **ii** 1 : 8

c **ii** 500 : 40 = 25 : 2 (Change to cm and divide both sides by 20.) **ii** $1 : \frac{2}{25} = 1 : 0.08$ (Divide both sides by 25.)

Using ratios

Revised

- If two quantities are in the ratio $1 : n$
  - to find the second quantity, you multiply the first quantity by n.
  - to find the first quantity, you divide the second quantity by n.
- If two quantities are in the ratio $m : n$
  - to find the second quantity, you multiply the first quantity by $\frac{n}{m}$.
  - to find the first quantity, you multiply the second quantity by $\frac{m}{n}$.

Test Yourself 2

In a recipe, flour and fat are used in the ratio 5 : 2.

a How much fat is needed when 480 g of flour is used?

b How much flour is needed when 300 g of fat is used?

Solutions

Test Yourself 2

a Quantity of fat $= 480 \times \frac{2}{5}$
$= 192\text{g}$

b Quantity of flour $= 300 \times \frac{5}{2}$
$= 750\text{g}$

Dividing a quantity in a given ratio

Revised

- To share in a given ratio,
  - add the parts of the ratio together
  - divide the amount to be shared by this total to find the multiplier
  - multiply each part of the ratio by the multiplier.
- If you are given a ratio and one of the quantities,
  - divide the quantity given by its part of the ratio to find the multiplier
  - multiply the other parts of ratio by the multiplier to find the other quantities
  - or multiply the total number of parts by the multiplier to find the total quantity.

Chief Examiner says

If the multiplier is not an exact amount, leave it as a fraction and round the final answer if necessary.

Test Yourself 3

£150 is shared in the ratio 2 : 3 : 5. How much is each part.

Test Yourself 4

In a school students must study one foreign language but cannot study more than one.

Students from one year group chose French, Spanish, Latin or German in the ratio 6 : 5 : 2 : 3.

42 students study French.

How many students are there in the year group?

Solutions

Test Yourself 3

Total of parts is $2 + 3 + 5 = 10$

Multiplier is $150 \div 10 = 15$

Parts are $2 \times 15 = £30$,

$3 \times 15 = £45$, $5 \times 15 = £75$

Chief Examiner says

Check that $30 + 45 + 75 = 150$.

Test Yourself 4

Multiplier $= 42 \div 6 = 7$

Students studying French ÷ French ratio

Total ratio $= 6 + 5 + 2 + 3 = 16$

Total number of students $=$
$16 \times 7 = 112$

Best value

Revised

To compare value, you need to compare either

- how much you get for a certain amount of money; the better value item has a greater amount per penny (or pound).
- how much a certain quantity costs; the better value item has a lower unit cost.

Test Yourself 5

Which of these packets is the better value?

Chief Examiner says

In a question that asks for the best value, if you show no working, you will score no marks, even if you pick the correct item.

Solution

Test Yourself 5

Large pack: $750 \div 259 = 2.895\ 75...$

Small pack: $450 \div 169 = 2.662\ 72...$

The large pack is the better value because it gives more grams per penny.

19 Statistical calculations 2

- See Unit A, Chapter 8 for more on statistical calculations.

The mean from a frequency table

Revised

- To calculate the mean from a frequency table,
  - multiply each observation (x) by its frequency
  - then add up these results
  - finally, divide by the total frequency.
- You can add an extra row or column to the table to calculate $x \times f$.

Chief Examiner says

You are often told the total frequency in the question.

Test Yourself 1

The table shows the number of letters delivered one morning to a street of 100 houses. Find the mean number of letters.

Number of letters	0	1	2	3	4	5
Frequency	8	19	28	25	17	3

Solution

Test Yourself 1

No. of letters (x)	0	1	2	3	4	5	Total
Frequency (f)	8	19	28	25	17	3	100
$x \times f$	0	19	56	75	68	15	233

Mean = 233 ÷ 100 = 2.33

Chief Examiner says

Check that the total frequency matches that given in the question.

Grouped data and Continuous data

Revised

- For grouped discrete data, use the middle of the interval for the value of x to represent each group. For example, the middle value of the group 0–9 is 4.5.
- For continuous data, again, use the middle of the interval for the value of x to represent each class. For example, the middle value of the class $0 \leqslant x < 10$ is 5.
- The value of the mean in these cases will only be an estimate.

Test Yourself 2

The table shows the number of widgets produced per hour on one machine in a factory.

Calculate an estimate of the mean number of widgets produced per hour by the machine.

Number of widgets produced per hour	Frequency
120–139	1
140–159	10
160–179	17
180–199	9
200–219	3

Solution

Test Yourself 2

Number of widgets produced per hour	Frequency (f)	Middle value (x)	$f \times$ middle x
120–139	1	130	$1 \times 130 = 130$
140–159	10	150	$10 \times 150 = 1500$
160–179	17	170	$17 \times 170 = 2890$
180–199	9	190	$9 \times 190 = 1710$
200–219	3	210	$3 \times 210 = 630$
Total	40		6860

Estimate of the mean = $6860 \div 40 = 171.5$ widgets per hour

Test Yourself 3

The table shows the duration, in minutes, of 120 telephone calls.

Calculate an estimate of the mean duration of the telephone calls.

Duration (m minutes)	Frequency
$0 < m \leqslant 5$	26
$5 < m \leqslant 10$	38
$10 < m \leqslant 15$	20
$15 < m \leqslant 20$	20
$20 < m \leqslant 25$	12
$25 < m \leqslant 30$	4

Solution

Test Yourself 3

Duration (m minutes)	**Frequency (f)**	**Middle value (m)**	**$f \times$ middle m**
$0 < m \leqslant 5$	26	2.5	$26 \times 2.5 = 65$
$5 < m \leqslant 10$	38	7.5	$38 \times 7.5 = 285$
$10 < m \leqslant 15$	20	12.5	$20 \times 12.5 = 250$
$15 < m \leqslant 20$	20	17.5	$20 \times 17.5 = 350$
$20 < m \leqslant 25$	12	22.5	$12 \times 22.5 = 270$
$25 < m \leqslant 30$	4	27.5	$4 \times 27.5 = 110$
Total	120		1330

Estimate of the mean $= 1330 \div 120 = 11.08$ minutes (11 minutes and 5 seconds)

20 Pythagoras' theorem

Pythagoras' theorem and Using Pythagoras' theorem

Revised

- In a right-angled triangle, labelled like this, Pythagoras' theorem states that $a^2 = b^2 + c^2$.
- The longest side of a right-angled triangle is called the hypotenuse.

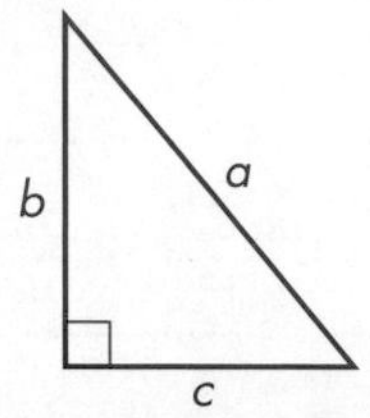

Chief Examiner says

As a check, remember that in a right-angled triangle the longest side, the hypotenuse, is always opposite the right angle.

Chief Examiner says

It is a good idea to label the triangles, using letters for the sides, and to write down the rule; then substitute the actual values for the sides before rearranging, if that is needed.

Test Yourself 1

Calculate the length of the unknown side in each of these triangles.

a

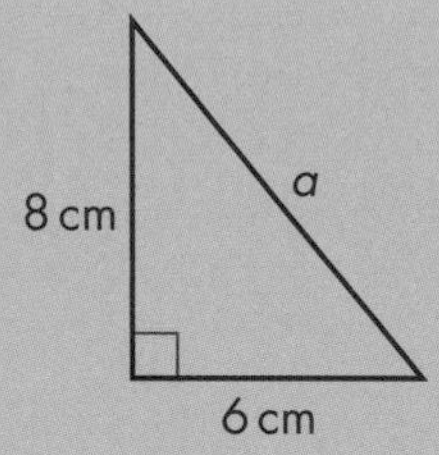

b

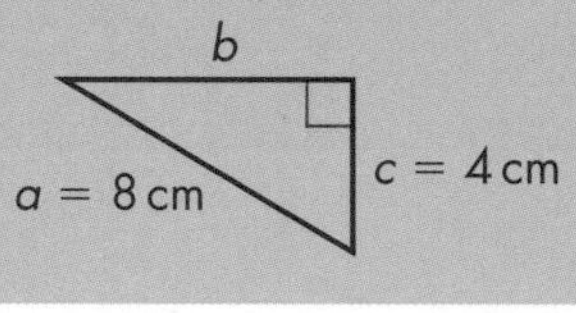

Solutions

Test Yourself 1

a $a^2 = b^2 + c^2$ (*a* is the hypotenuse.)

$= 8^2 + 6^2$

$= 64 + 36$

$= 100$

$a = \sqrt{100}$

$a = 10\,\text{cm}$

b $a^2 = b^2 + c^2$

$8^2 = b^2 + 4^2$

$64 = b^2 + 16$

$b^2 = 64 - 16$

$b^2 = 48$

$b = \sqrt{48}$

$b = 6.9\,\text{cm}$ (to 1 d.p.)

Pythagorean triples

Revised

- The numbers *a*, *b* and *c* form a Pythagorean triple if $a^2 + b^2 = c^2$.
- If the three sides of a triangle form a Pythagorean triple then the triangle is right-angled.

Test Yourself 2

Work out whether or not these triangles are right-angled.

a

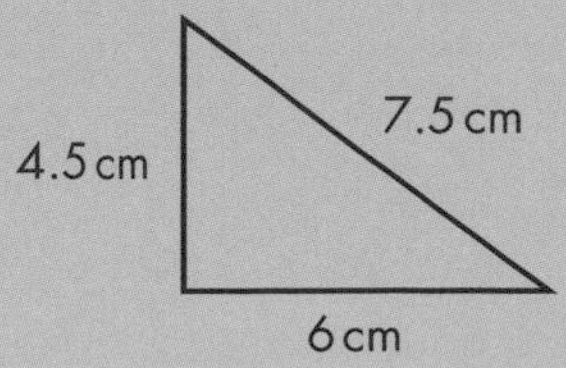

b

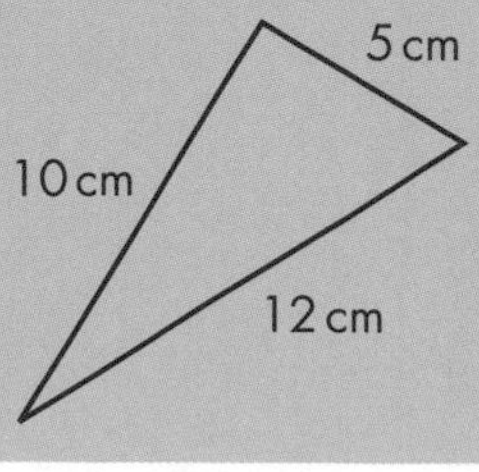

Solutions

Test Yourself 2

a $4.5^2 + 6^2 = 20.25 + 36 = 56.25$
$7.5^2 = 56.25$, so the triangle is right-angled.

b $5^2 + 10^2 = 25 + 100 = 125$
$12^2 = 144$, so the triangle is not right-angled.

Line segments

Revised

- A line segment is the part of a line between two points. It has a finite length.
- The midpoint of a line is the point halfway along the line.
- You can find the midpoint of a line segment using this formula:
  $\left(\frac{\text{add the } x \text{ coordinates}}{2}, \frac{\text{add the } y \text{ coordinates}}{2}\right)$
- To find the length of the line segment joining A and B, use Pythagoras' theorem. The difference in the *x* coordinates and the difference in the *y* coordinates give you the lengths of the two shorter sides.

Test Yourself 3

A is the point (1, 5) and B is the point (7, 2).

Calculate

a the midpoint of AB

b the length of AB.

Solutions

Test Yourself 3

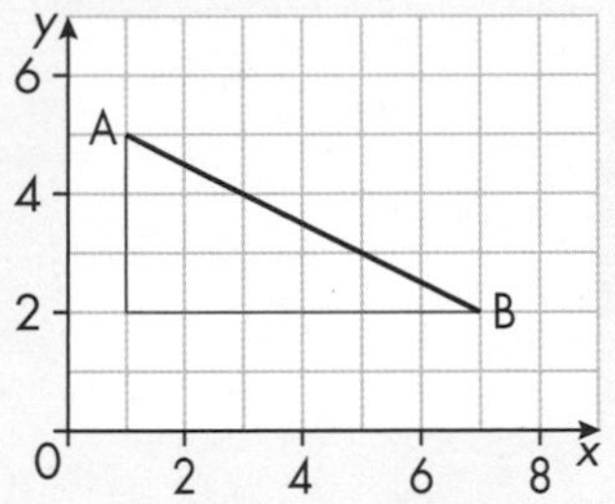

a The midpoint of AB is $\left(\frac{1+7}{2}, \frac{5+2}{2}\right) = \left(\frac{8}{2}, \frac{7}{2}\right) = (4, 3.5)$

b $AB^2 = (7 - 1)^2 + (5 - 2)^2$
$AB^2 = 6^2 + 3^2$
$AB^2 = 45$
$AB = \sqrt{45}$
$AB = 6.7$ units (correct to 1 d.p.)

Chief Examiner says

You don't have to draw a diagram.

21 Planning and collecting

Different types of data

Revised

- Primary data is data that you collect yourself, by counting, measuring and so on.
- Secondary data is data you get from elsewhere, such as newspapers, books or databases.

Test Yourself 1

Which of the following are examples of primary data and which are secondary data?

a Using newspapers to find the number of hours of sunshine in different places

b Using the internet to find out how long kings and queens reigned

c Measuring how good people are at estimating height

Solutions

Test Yourself 1

a Secondary data

b Secondary data

c Primary data

Designing a questionnaire

Revised

- Questions should be short, clear, easy to understand and relevant.
- Questions should give a choice of possible answers. This avoids a large number of vague answers that are difficult to analyse.
- Questions should not cause embarrassment.

Test Yourself 2

Why are these not good questions?

a What do you like about this shop?

b Do you come here often?

c Are you married?

Solutions

Test Yourself 2

a It is too vague. There is a wide range of possible answers.

b Is is not precise. What does 'often' mean?

c It is personal and probably not relevant.

22 Sequences 2

- See Unit A, Chapter 9 for more on sequences.

Using rules to find terms of a sequence

Revised

- If you know one term and the term-to-term rule, you can generate other terms of a sequence.
- If you know the position and the formula for the *n*th term of a sequence, you can generate other terms of the sequence.

Test Yourself 1

a For a sequence, $T_1 = 42$ and $T_{n+1} = T_n - 3$.
Find the first five terms of the sequence.

b The formula for the *n*th term of a sequence is $2n + 5$.
Find the 29th term of the sequence.

Solutions

Test Yourself 1

a $T_1 = 42$
$T_2 = 42 - 3 = 39$
$T_3 = 39 - 3 = 36$
$T_4 = 36 - 3 = 33$
$T_5 = 33 - 3 = 30$
The first five terms are 42, 39, 36, 33, 30.

b $T_{29} = 2 \times 29 + 5 = 63$

Finding the *n*th term of a linear sequence

Revised

- The terms of a linear sequence increase or decrease by the same number each time.
- This number is called the common difference.
- Linear sequences which go up for example by 3 each time have an *n*th term of the form $3n + b$
- Linear sequences which go down for example by 2 each time have an *n*th term of the form $-2n + b$
- You can find b by substituting 1 for n and comparing the result with the first term.
- You can also work more formally by saying: The *n*th term of a linear sequence = Common difference × n + (First term – Common difference)
- You can write this as *n*th term = $An + b$
  - where A is the common difference
  - and b is the first term – the common difference

Test Yourself 2

a Find the nth term of the sequence 7, 11, 15, 19, ...

b Find the 50th term of this sequence.

Solutions

Test Yourself 2

a The terms increase by 4 each time so the nth term $= 4n + b$.
Substituting $n = 1$ gives $4 + b$. The first term is 7 so $b = 3$.
So nth term $= 4n + 3$.

b 50th term $= 4 \times 50 + 3 = 203$

Some special sequences

- Linear sequences, that is those that increase or decrease by a constant amount, for example
  - 2, 5, 8, 11, 14, ... (nth term $3n - 1$)
  - 6, 4, 2, 0, −2 ... (nth term $8 - 2n$)
- Linear sequences include even numbers (nth term $2n$) and odd numbers (nth term $2n - 1$)
- Square numbers: 1, 4, 9, 16, ... (nth term n^2)
- Powers of 2: 2, 4, 8, 16, ... (nth term 2^n)
- Powers of 10: 10, 100, 1000, 10000, ... (nth term 10^n)
- Triangle numbers: 1, 3, 6, 10, 15, ... (nth term $\frac{n(n+1)}{2}$)

23 Constructions 2

- See Unit A, Chapter 11 for how to construct angles and triangles.

Constructions

Revised

- **The perpendicular bisector of a line segment**

  AB is the given line.

  Step 1: Draw two arcs of the same radius above and below the line, centred on A and B.

  Step 2: Join the intersections of the arcs. This line is the perpendicular bisector of the line AB.

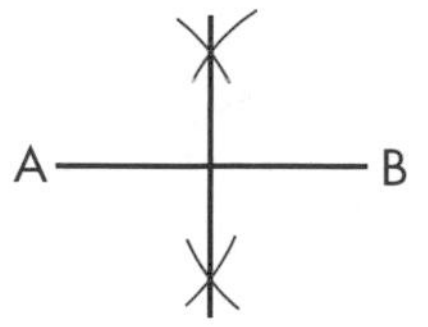

- **The perpendicular from a point on a line**

  AB is the given line. P is the given point.

  Step 1: Draw an arc, centred on P, to cut AB twice.

  Step 2: Open your compasses to a larger radius. Draw two arcs of the same radius, centred on the points of intersection of the first arc and AB, to cut each other above the line.

  Step 3: Join the point of intersection of the two arcs to P. This line is perpendicular to AB.

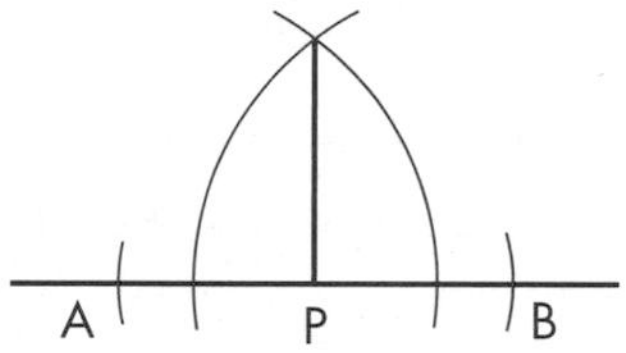

- **The perpendicular from a point to a line**

  AB is the given line. P is the given point.

  Step 1: Draw an arc, centred on P, to cut AB twice.

  Step 2: Draw two more arcs of the same radius, centred on the points of intersection of the first arc and AB, to cut each other below the line (on the opposite side from P).

  Step 3: Join the point of intersection of the two arcs to P. This line is perpendicular to AB.

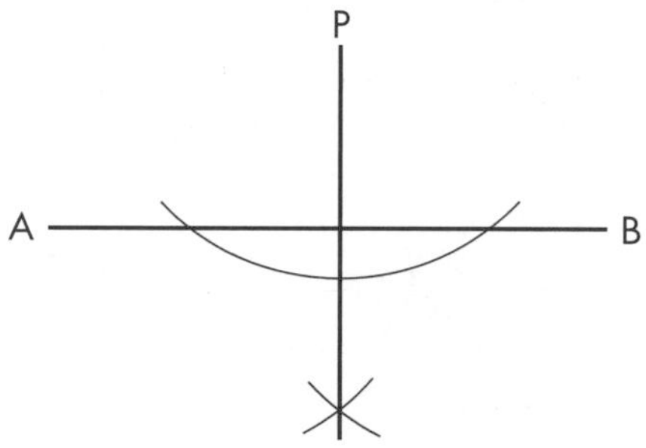

- **The bisector of an angle**

  AB and AC are the two lines making the given angle.

  Step 1: Draw two arcs of the same radius, centred on A, to cut AB and AC.

  Step 2: Draw two more arcs of the same radius, centred on B and C, to cut each other between AB and AC.

  Step 3: Join the point of intersection of the two arcs to A. This line is the bisector of angle A.

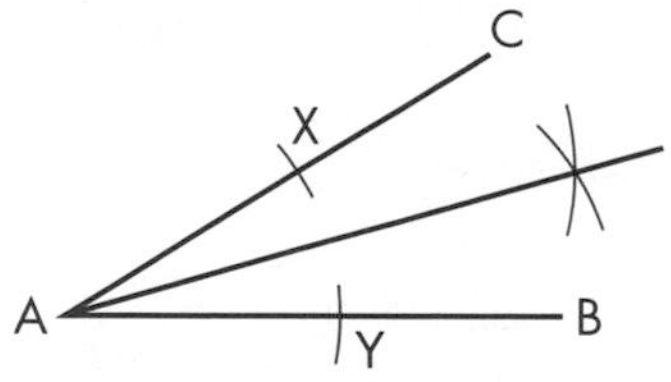

Test Yourself 1

Draw any triangle. Use ruler and compasses to bisect all its angles.

Solution

Test Yourself 1

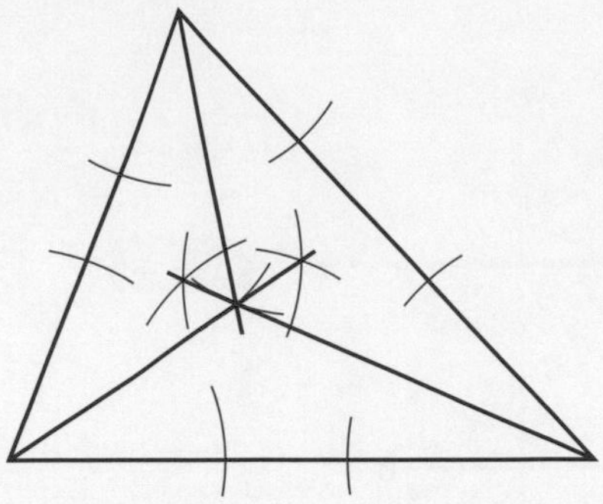

Chief Examiner says

If your construction is accurate, you should find that all the bisectors meet at one point. (This point is, in fact, the centre of a circle which has all the vertices of the triangle on it – you can check by drawing this circle, if you wish.)

Constructing a locus

Revised

- A locus is a path or region where a point can move according to a rule.
- The locus of a point which moves so that it is always 3 cm from a fixed point A is a circle, centre A, radius 3 cm.

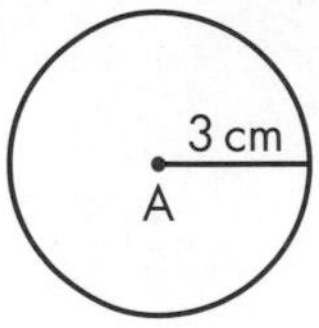

- The locus of a point which moves so that it is always less than 3 cm from a fixed point A is the region inside a circle, centre A, radius 3 cm.

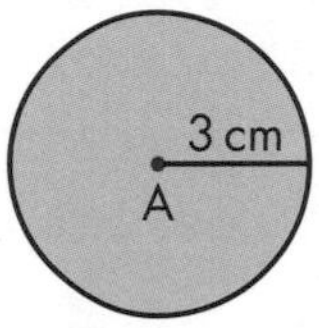

- The locus of a point which moves so that it is always more than 3 cm from a fixed point A is the region outside a circle, centre A, radius 3 cm.

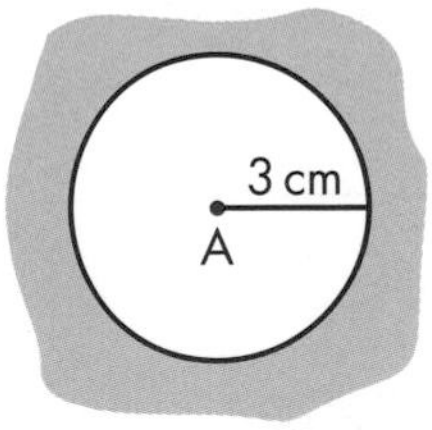

- The locus of a point which is an equal distance from two given points is the perpendicular bisector of the line joining the two points.

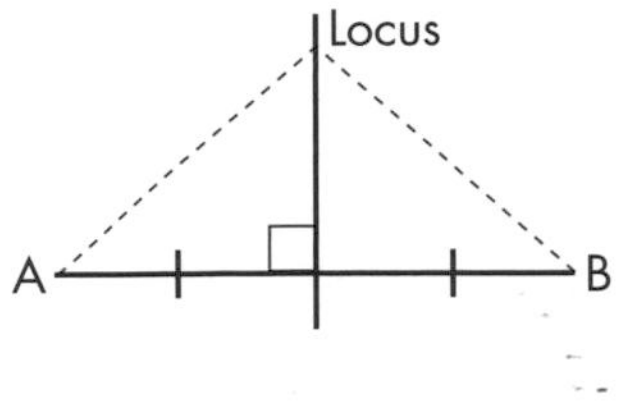

- The locus of a point which is an equal distance from two given intersecting lines is the angle bisectors of the angles between the lines.

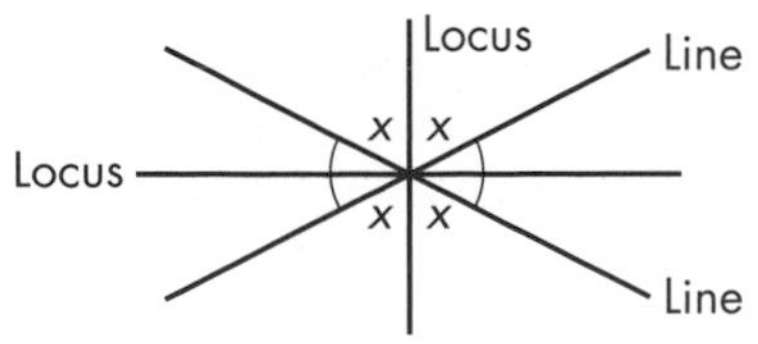

- The locus of a point which is 2 cm from a given straight line is the pair of lines parallel to that line.

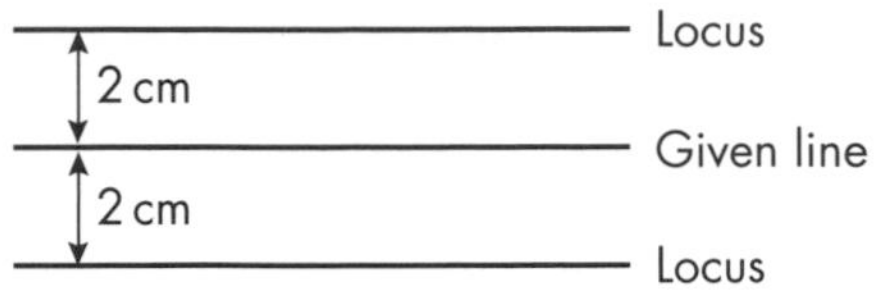

- The locus of a point which is 2 cm from a given line segment AB is the pair of parallel lines to that line segment joined by semicircles with centres at A and B and radius 2 cm.

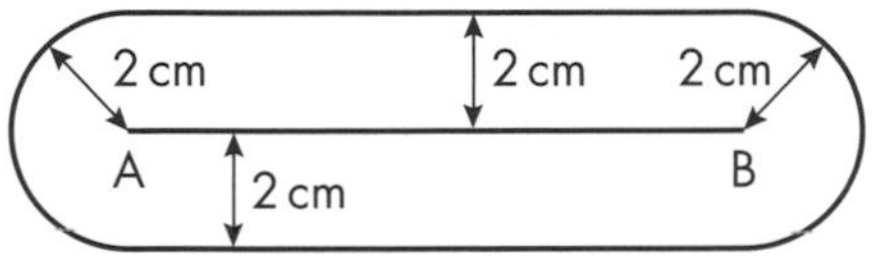

Test Yourself 2

A goat is tethered by a 2 m rope to a rail 3 m long, which is fixed in a field of grass. The rope can slide along the rail. Draw a scale diagram to show the region of grass which the goat can eat.

Solution

Test Yourself 2

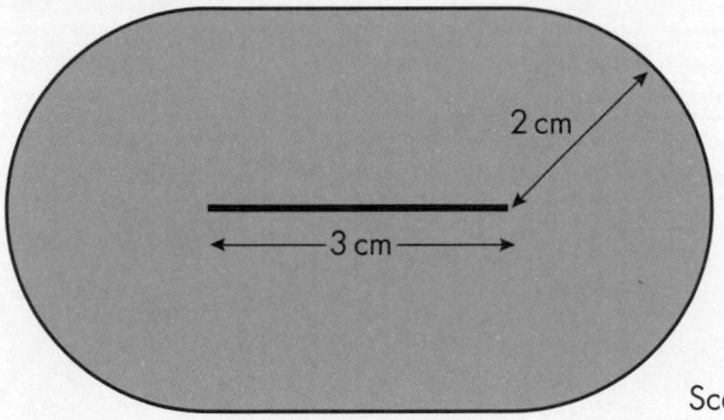

Scale: 1 cm to 1 m

Intersecting loci

Revised

- Exam questions often involve more than one locus.
- Draw one locus at a time.
- Show the final required region or points clearly by labelling, together with shading if necessary.

Test Yourself 3

Find the locus of points equidistant from A, B and C.

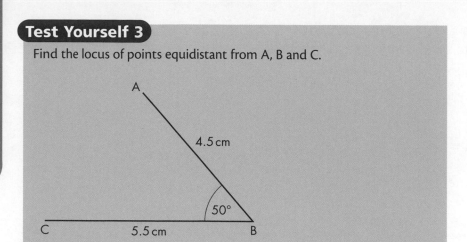

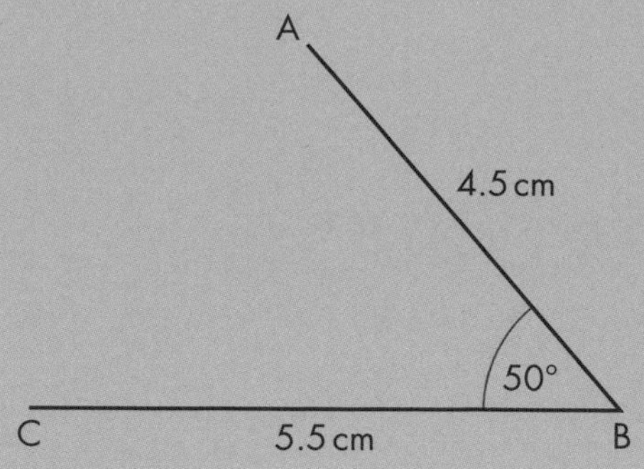

Solution

Test Yourself 3

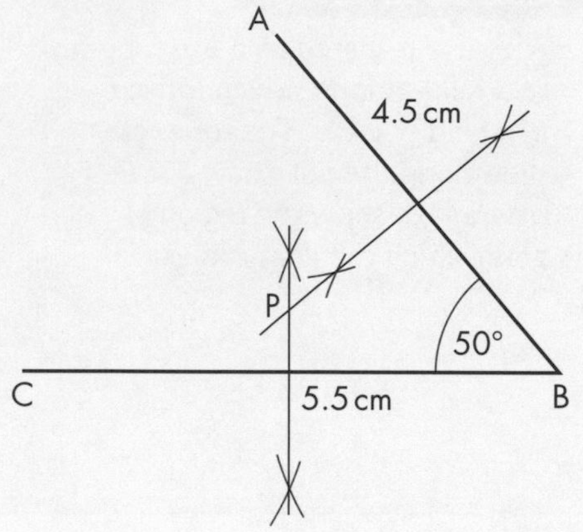

The locus of points equidistant from A and B is the perpendicular bisector of AB.
The locus of points equidistant from B and C is the perpendicular bisector of BC.
The required locus is where these two lines meet. It is marked P.

24 Rearranging formulae

Rearranging formulae

Revised

- To change the subject of a formula, use the equation rule of doing the same to both sides to get the new subject on one side of the formula.

Chief Examiner says

Remember: always do the same operation to both sides.

Test Yourself 1

a Make a the subject of $v = u + at$

b Make u the subject of the formula $s = \frac{t(u+v)}{2}$

Solutions

Test Yourself 1

a $v = u + at$

$v - u = at$ — Take u from both sides.

$\frac{v-u}{t} = a$ — Divide both sides by t. The fraction line acts as a bracket.

$a = \frac{v-u}{t}$ — Rewrite with a on the left.

b $s = \frac{t(u+v)}{2}$

$2s = t(u+v)$ — Multiply both sides by 2.

$2s = tu + tv$ — Multiply out the bracket.

$2s - tv = tu$ — Subtract tv from both sides.

$\frac{2s-tv}{t} = u$ — Divide both sides by t.

$u = \frac{2s-tv}{t}$ — Rewrite with u on the left.

1 Working with numbers

Chief Examiner says

In Unit B you are not allowed to use a calculator.

Ordering integers

Revised

Chief Examiner says

Be careful – some questions ask you to list numbers starting with the smallest, others ask you to start with the largest number.

- For whole numbers, the more digits a number has the larger it is.
- When two numbers have the same number of digits, the first digit tells you which number is bigger. If the first digits are the same, check the second digits. If the second digits are the same, check the third digits, and so on.

Test Yourself 1

Write these numbers in order, smallest first.

21 424, 2655, 2831, 2645, 2283

Solution

Test Yourself 1

2283, 2645, 2655, 2831, 21 424

Integer complements

Revised

- A complement is the number which you need to add to make the total a round number such as 100. For example, the complement of 58 is 42 because 58 + 42 = 100.

Test Yourself 2

Find the complement to 100 of these.

a 27
b 99
c 5

Solutions

Test Yourself 2

a 73 **b** 1 **c** 95

Multiplication and division facts

Revised

- You need to know the basic multiplication tables.

Adding and subtracting mentally

Revised

- There are various methods you can use to do addition and subtraction mentally. These include:
  - partitioning
  - using complements
  - counting on.
- When you are adding decimals it is usually easier to deal with the decimal parts first and then add the integer parts.

Solution

Test Yourself 3

Method 1

$16.3 - 10 = 6.3$ — But 10 is 0.3 too much so add this back.

$6.3 + 0.3 = 6.6$

Method 2

$9.7 + 0.3 = 10$

$10 + 6.3 = 16.3$

$0.3 + 6.3 = 6.6$ — Counting on in two steps, 0.3 and 6.3, giving 6.6.

Test Yourself 3

Find the difference between 16.3 and 9.7.

Written methods for adding and subtracting decimals

Revised ☐

- When adding or subtracting decimals,
  - make sure the decimal points are underneath each other
  - keep tenths under tenths, units under units, tens under tens and so on
  - start from the column on the right.

Test Yourself 4

Work out these.

a $537.5 + 27.68$

b $53.78 - 24.9$

Solutions

Test Yourself 4

a

537.50
+27.68
565.18

b

53.78
−24.90
28.88

Add a zero so that there is the same number of decimal places in each number.

Multiplying and dividing decimals

Revised ☐

- For a multiplication involving decimals,
  - first multiply the numbers ignoring the decimal point
  - then count the total number of decimal places in the question
  - put a decimal point in the answer so that it has the same number of decimal places as in the question.
- To divide a decimal by a whole number, line up the calculation so the decimal points are underneath each other.
- To divide by a decimal with one decimal place, multiply both numbers by 10 so that the number you are dividing by is a whole number.
- To divide by a decimal with two decimal places, multiply both numbers by 100 so that the number you are dividing by is a whole number.

Test Yourself 5

Work out these.

a 47.3×1.5

b 2.7×0.04

c $12.9 \div 3$

d $4.68 \div 0.6$

e $20.4 \div 0.12$

Solutions

Test Yourself 5

a

```
      4 7 3
  ×     1 5
  ---------
    2 3 6 5
    4 7 3 0
  ---------
    7 0 9 5
```

So 47.3 × 1.5 = 70.95

There are two decimal places in the question, so there are two in the answer.

b

```
      2 7
  ×     4
  -------
    1 0 8
```

So 2.7 × 0.04 = 0.108

There are three decimal places in the question, so there are three decimal places in the answer.

c

```
3 | 1 2 . 9
```

12.9 ÷ 3

```
      4 . 3
   ---------
3 | 1 2 . 9
```

Set out the division calculation with the decimal points lined up.

12.9 ÷ 3 = 4.3

d 4.68 ÷ 0.6 = 46.8 ÷ 6

Multiply both numbers by 10.

```
       7 . 8
   ----------
6 |  4 6 . 8
    -4 2 . 0
   ----------
       4 . 8
      -4 . 8
      -------
           0
```

4.68 ÷ 0.6 = 7.8

e 20.4 ÷ 0.12 = 2040 ÷ 12

Multiply both numbers by 100.

```
        1 7 0
    ---------
12 | 2 0 4 0
    -1 2
    -----
       8 4
       8 4
      -----
         0
```

20.4 ÷ 0.12 = 170

2 Angles, triangles and quadrilaterals

Angles

Revised

- See Unit A, Chapter 11 for types of angles and drawing and measuring angles.

Triangles

Revised

- A triangle has three sides.
- A triangle can have one angle equal to 90°.

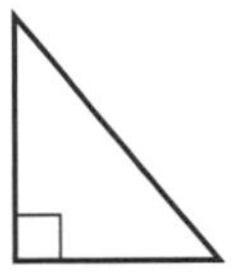

Right-angled

- A triangle with two sides equal is called isosceles and also has two angles equal. Little lines may be marked on the sides to show that they are equal.

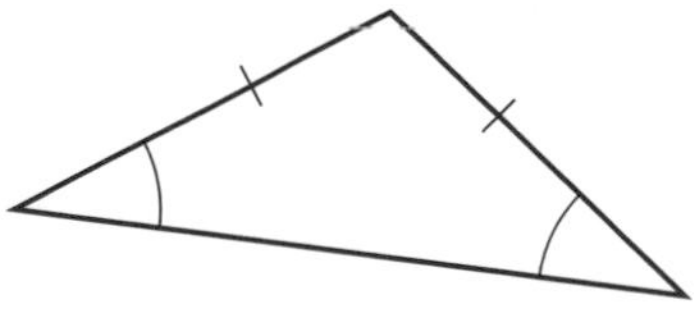

- A triangle with all three sides equal is called equilateral and also has three angles equal to 60°.

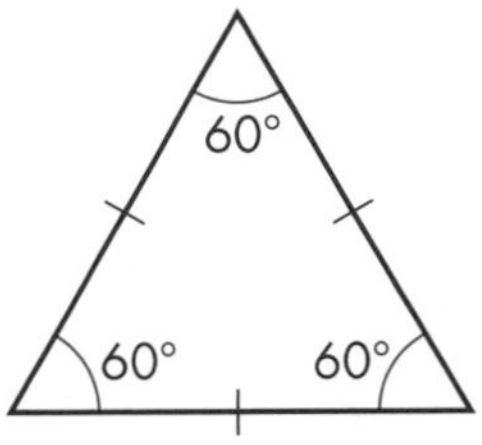

- A triangle that is not one of these special ones is called a scalene triangle.
- The angles in a triangle add to up 180°.

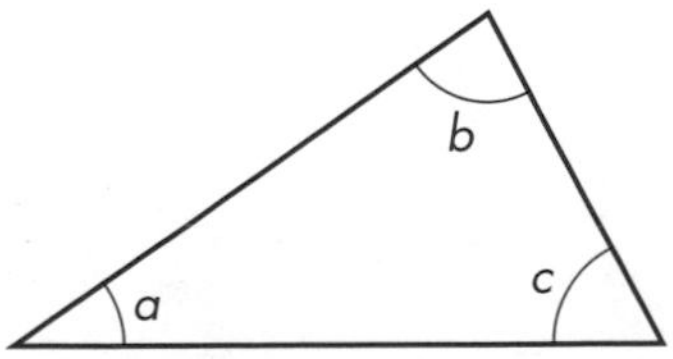

$a + b + c = 180°$

Test Yourself 1

Work out the angles marked with letters in these diagrams.

Give reasons for your answers.

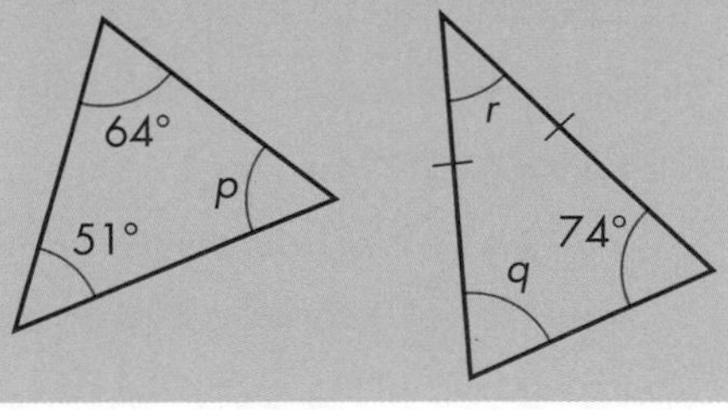

Solutions

Test Yourself 1

$p = 65°$ Angles in a triangle add up to 180°.

$q = 74°$ Base angles in an isosceles triangle are equal.

$r = 32°$ Angles in a triangle add up to 180°.

Quadrilaterals

Revised

- Quadrilaterals have four sides.
- You need to know the properties of the special quadrilaterals.
- Square
  - All angles 90°.
  - All sides equal.
  - Opposite sides parallel.
  - Diagonals equal and bisect at 90°.
  - Four lines of symmetry.
  - Rotation symmetry order 4.

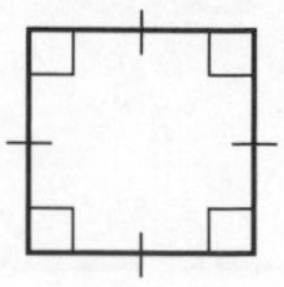

- Rectangle
  - All angles 90°.
  - Opposite sides equal and parallel.
  - Diagonals equal and bisect but not at 90°.
  - Two lines of symmetry.
  - Rotation symmetry order 2.

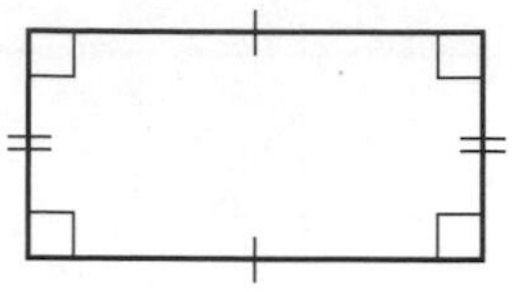

- Parallelogram
  - Opposite angles equal.
  - Opposite sides equal and parallel.
  - Diagonals not equal but bisect, though not at 90°.
  - No line symmetry.
  - Rotation symmetry order 2.

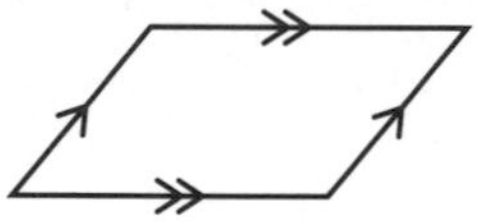

- Rhombus
  - Opposite angles equal.
  - All four sides equal.
  - Opposite sides parallel.
  - Diagonals not equal length but bisect at 90°.
  - Two lines of symmetry.
  - Rotation symmetry order 2.

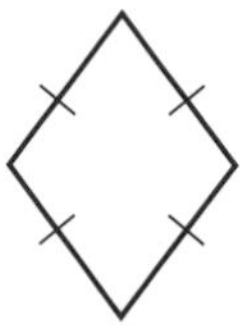

- Trapezium
  - One pair of opposite sides parallel.

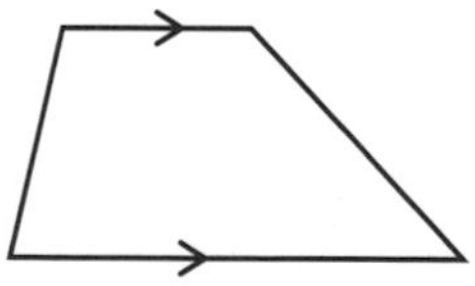

- Isosceles trapezium
  - Two pairs of adjacent angles equal.
  - One pair of opposite sides equal.
  - Other pair of sides parallel.
  - Diagonals equal but do not bisect or cross at 90°.
  - One line of symmetry.
  - No rotation symmetry.

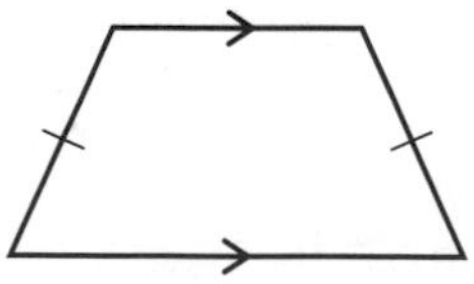

- Kite
  - One pair of opposite angles equal.
  - Two pairs of adjacent sides equal but none parallel.
  - One diagonal bisected at 90°.
  - One line of symmetry.
  - No rotation symmetry.

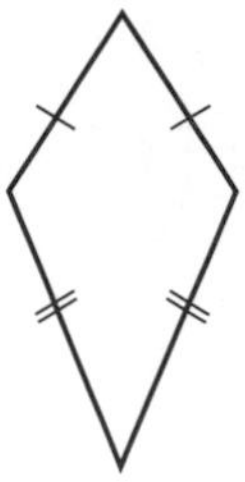

Chief Examiner says

Remember what each shape is called and what it looks like. You can then use a sketch and symmetry to help you see which angles are equal, and so on.

Test Yourself 2

a A quadrilateral has both pairs of opposite sides parallel.
What type of quadrilateral can it be?

b Draw two quadrilaterals which have only one line of symmetry.

Solutions

Test Yourself 2

a It can be a square, a rectangle, a parallelogram or a rhombus.

b

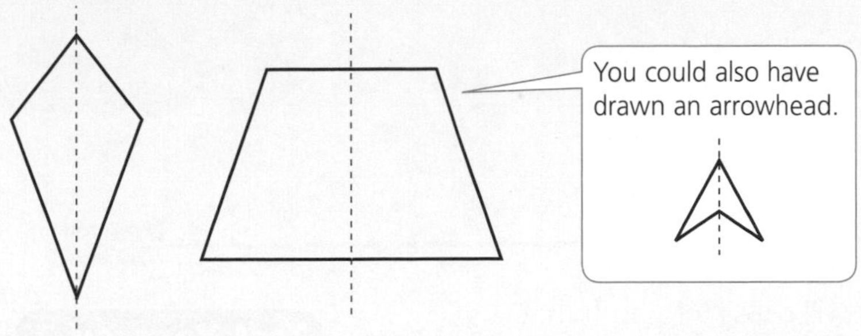

You could also have drawn an arrowhead.

3 Fractions

Equivalent fractions

Revised

- To make equivalent fractions, multiply or divide the numerator and the denominator by the same number.

Test Yourself 1

Fill in the missing numbers in this set of equivalent fractions.

$\frac{2}{5} = \frac{4}{} = \frac{}{25} = \frac{16}{}$

Solution

Test Yourself 1

$\frac{2}{5} = \frac{4}{10} = \frac{10}{25} = \frac{16}{40}$ — Multiply 5 by 2, 2 by 5, and 5 by 8.

Expressing a fraction in its lowest terms

Revised

- If a fraction is in its lowest terms, no number will divide into both the numerator and the denominator.
- Writing a fraction in its lowest terms may be called cancelling, simplifying or writing it in its simplest form.

Test Yourself 2

Write each of these fractions in its lowest terms.

a $\frac{4}{8}$

b $\frac{3}{15}$

c $\frac{12}{20}$

Solutions

Test Yourself 2

a $\frac{1}{2}$ — Divide the numerator and denominator by 4.

b $\frac{1}{5}$ — Divide the numerator and denominator by 3.

c $\frac{3}{5}$ — Divide the numerator and denominator by 4.

Ordering fractions

Revised

- To put fractions in order of size
  - change to equivalent fractions with the same denominator
  - put in order by the numerators.

Test Yourself 3

Put these fractions in order of size, smallest first.

$\frac{1}{2}, \frac{3}{4}, \frac{1}{6}, \frac{2}{3}$

Solution

Test Yourself 3

$\frac{1}{2} = \frac{6}{12}, \frac{3}{4} = \frac{9}{12}, \frac{1}{6} = \frac{2}{12}, \frac{2}{3} = \frac{8}{12}$ — Change each fraction to an equivalent fraction with a denominator of 12.

Order is

$\frac{2}{12}, \frac{6}{12}, \frac{8}{12}, \frac{9}{12} = \frac{1}{6}, \frac{1}{2}, \frac{2}{3}, \frac{3}{4}$

Finding a fraction of a quantity

Revised

- To find a fraction of a quantity, divide the amount by the denominator and multiply by the numerator.

Chief Examiner says

'Of' means multiply.

Test Yourself 4

Find $\frac{3}{4}$ of 24.

Solution

Test Yourself 4

$24 \div 4 = 6$

$6 \times 3 = 18$

$\frac{3}{4}$ of $24 = 18$

Expressing one number as a fraction of another

Revised

- To write one number as a fraction of another, write the first number as the numerator and the second number as the denominator. Write the fraction in its lowest terms, if necessary.

Test Yourself 5

What fraction is 15 of 75?

Solution

Test Yourself 5

$\frac{15}{75} = \frac{1}{5}$

Adding and subtracting fractions

Revised

- To add or subtract fractions, change the fractions to equivalent fractions with the same denominator, and add or subtract the numerators.

Test Yourself 6

Work out these.

a $\frac{1}{6} + \frac{3}{4}$

b $\frac{4}{5} - \frac{2}{3}$

Solutions

Test Yourself 6

a $\frac{1}{6} + \frac{3}{4} = \frac{2}{12} + \frac{9}{12}$ — Change each fraction to an equivalent fraction with a denominator of 12.

$= \frac{11}{12}$ — Then add the numerators.

b $\frac{4}{5} - \frac{2}{3} = \frac{12}{15} - \frac{10}{15}$ — Change each fraction to an equivalent fraction with a denominator of 15.

$= \frac{2}{15}$ — Then subtract the numerators.

Converting a fraction to a decimal

Revised

- To convert a fraction to a decimal, divide the numerator by the denominator. For example, $\frac{4}{5} = 4 \div 5 = 0.8$.

Test Yourself 7

Convert $\frac{3}{20}$ to a decimal.

Solution

Test Yourself 7

$3 \div 20 = 0.15$

Unit B

4 Solving problems

- Some problems need breaking down into steps first.
- Read the question carefully and ask yourself:
  - What do I know?
  - What do I have to find?
  - What methods can I apply?
- Look back when you have finished and ask yourself: 'Have I answered the question?'
- In money problems, check whether you are working in pounds or pence and give the answer to the nearest penny unless told otherwise.

Chief Examiner says

In money questions, if the answer in pounds has only 1 decimal place, remember to write a 0 in the second place. For example, write 3.4 as £3.40.

Problems involving time

Revised

- When dealing with time, remember that there are 60 minutes in an hour and 60 seconds in a minute.
- Times can be given in the 24-hour clock or as a.m. or p.m. For example, 8:30 a.m. is 08:30 and 8.30 p.m. is 20:30.

Test Yourself 1

A film lasted from 13:45 until 15:25. How long was the film?

Solution

Test Yourself 1

From 13:45 until 14:00 is 15 minutes. (60 – 45 = 15)

From 14:00 until 15:25 is 1 hour and 25 minutes.

The total time is 1 hour 25 minutes + 15 minutes = 1 hour and 40 minutes

Problems involving units

Revised

- See Unit A, Chapter 10 for converting between metric units and converting between metric and imperial units.

Test Yourself 2

a A driver fills her car with 36 litres of diesel. How many gallons is this?

A gallon is about 4.5 litres.

b A weather forecast says that 12 inches of snow is expected. How many centimetres is that?

An inch is about 2.5 cm.

Solutions

Test Yourself 2

a $36 \div 4.5 = 8$ gallons

b $12 \times 2.5 = 30$ cm

Reading tables

Revised

- You need to be able to extract information from tables.

Test Yourself 3

This is part of the train timetable between Derby and Crewe.

Derby	1438	1538	1638	1738	1839	1941	2040
Tutbury	1452	1552	1652	1755	1856	1955	2054
Uttoxeter	1503	1603	1703	1806	1907	2006	2105
Blythe Bridge	1517	1617	1717	1820	1921	2020	2119
Stoke-on-Trent	1531	1630	1731	1833	1935	2031	2136
Crewe	1603	1658	1757	1901	2001	2105	2205

a What time does the last train leave Uttoxeter?

b At what time does the 1552 from Tutbury reach Stoke-on-Trent?

c Which is the fastest train from Derby to Crewe?

Solutions

Test Yourself 3

a 2105

b 1630

c The 1638 from Derby takes 1 hour 19 minutes.

5 Angles

Angle facts

Revised

- The sum of angles on a straight line is 180°.

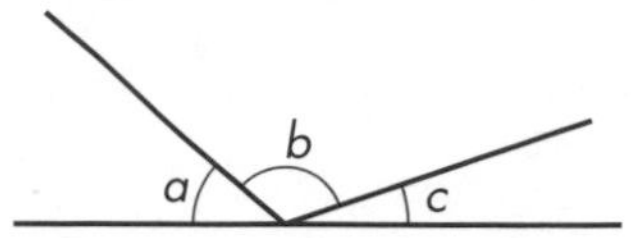

$a + b + c = 180°$

- The sum of the angles around a point is 360°.

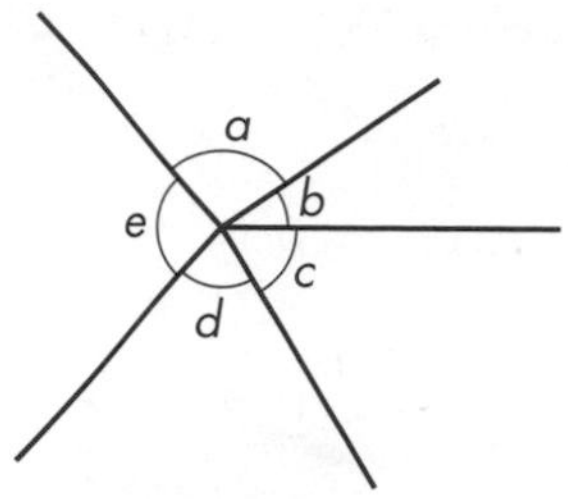

$a + b + c + d + e = 360°$

- When two lines cross, the opposite angles are equal. This is written as 'vertically opposite angles are equal'.

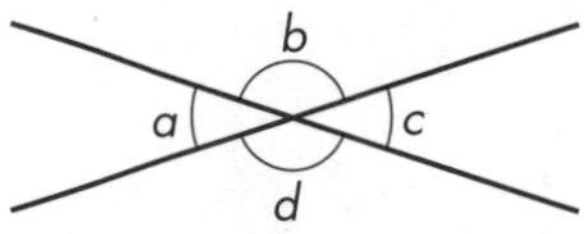

$a = c$ and $b = d$

Chief Examiner says

Sometimes you will be asked to give reasons for your answers. If you fail to do so, you will lose marks.

Test Yourself 1

Work out the angles marked with letters in these diagrams.

Give reasons for your answers.

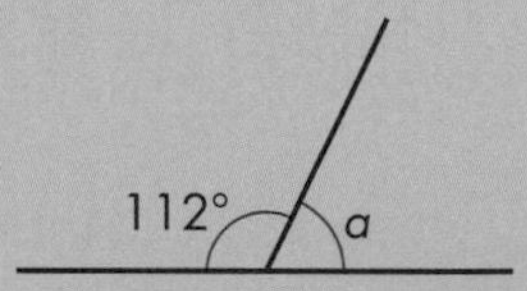

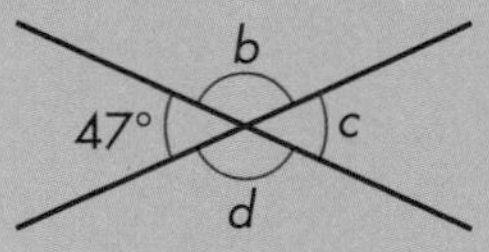

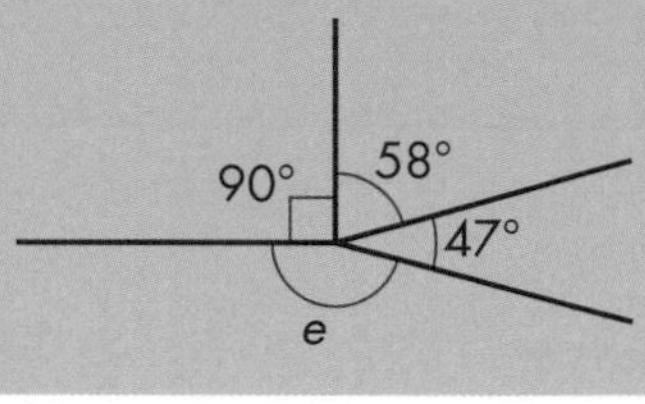

Solution

Test Yourself 1

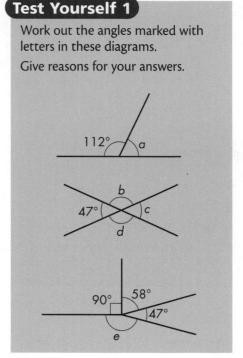

$a = 68°$ Angles on a straight line add up to 180°.

$b = 133°$ Angles on a straight line add up to 180°.

$c = 47°$ Vertically opposite angles are equal or Angles on a straight line add up to 180°.

$d = 133°$ Vertically opposite angles are equal or Angles on a straight line add up to 180°.

$e = 165°$ Angles round a point add up to 360°.

Chief Examiner says

In some cases, more than one reason is possible. Either reason would do for angles *c* and *d* here.

Angles made with parallel lines

Revised

- Two lines that meet at a right angle are called perpendicular.

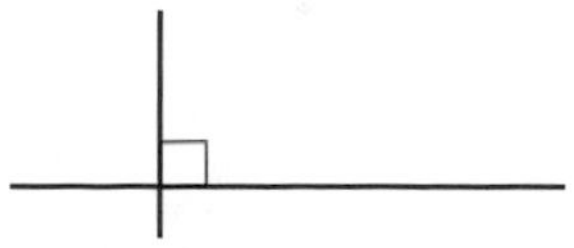

- Two lines that could go on for ever and never meet are called parallel. The lines may be marked with arrows to show that they are parallel.

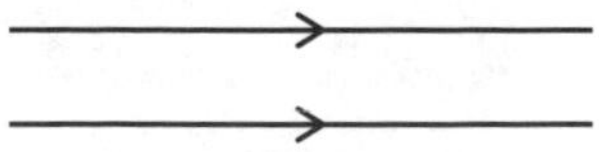

- *a* and *b* are called alternate angles. They are on opposite sides of the transversal.

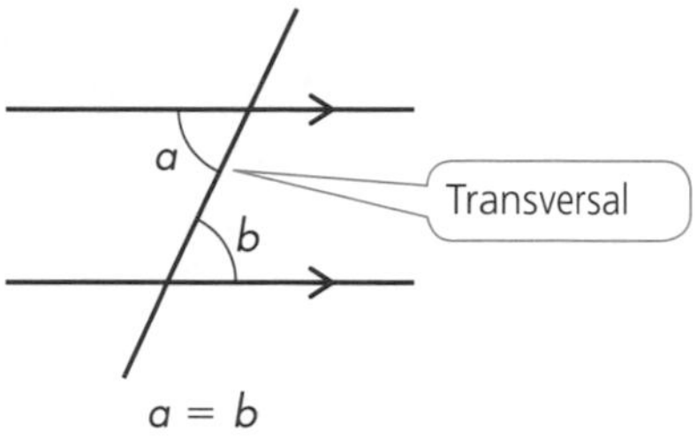

- *c* and *d* are called corresponding angles. They are in the same position between the transversal and the parallel lines.

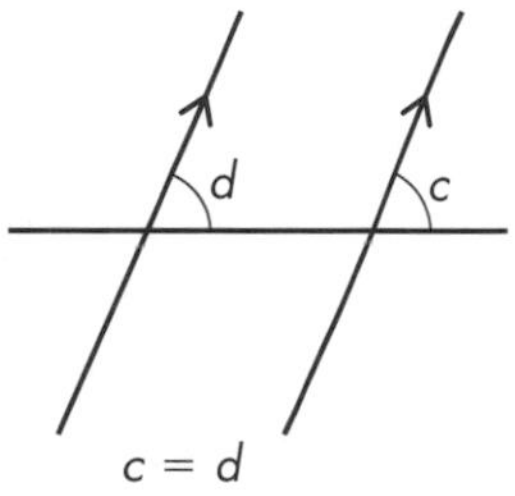

- *e* and *f* are called allied angles. They are the same side of the transversal between the parallel lines.

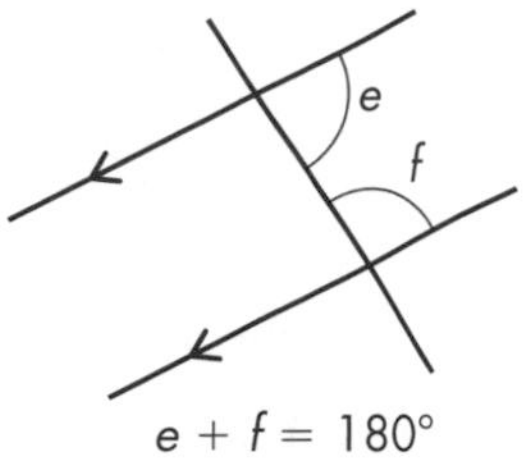

Test Yourself 2

Work out the angles marked with letters in these diagrams.

Give reasons for your answers.

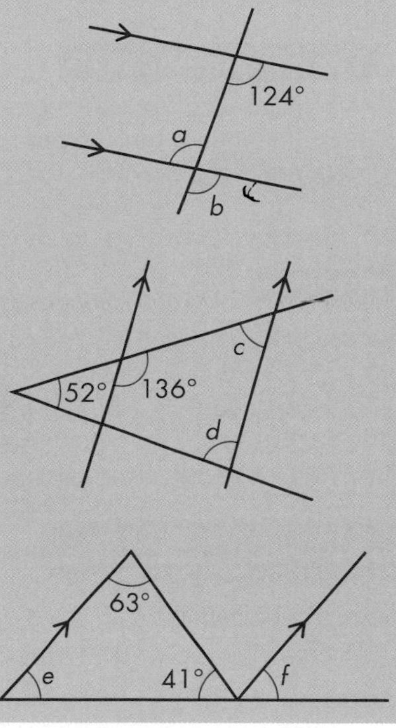

Solution

Test Yourself 2

$a = 124°$	Alternate angles are equal.
$b = 124°$	Corresponding angles are equal or Vertically opposite angles are equal.
$c = 44°$	Allied angles add up to 180°.
$d = 84°$	Angles in a triangle add up to 180°.
$e = 76°$	Angles in a triangle add up to 180°.
$f = 76°$	Corresponding angles are equal.

6 Fractions and mixed numbers

Mixed numbers

Revised

- An improper fraction is a fraction with the numerator larger than the denominator.
- To change an improper fraction to a mixed number, divide the denominator into the numerator and write the remainder over the denominator as a fraction.
- To change a mixed number to an improper fraction, multiply the whole number by the denominator and add on the numerator. Then write this number over the denominator.

Chief Examiner says

When changing from an improper fraction to a mixed number, the most common error is to put the remainder over the numerator rather than the denominator.

Test Yourself 1

a Change $\frac{14}{5}$ to a mixed number.

b Change $3\frac{5}{8}$ to an improper fraction.

Solutions

Test Yourself 1

a $2\frac{4}{5}$ — $14 \div 5 = 2 \text{ r } 4$

b $\frac{29}{8}$ — $3 \times 8 + 5 = 29$

Multiplying fractions

Revised

- When multiplying a fraction by a whole number, multiply the numerator by the whole number and then simplify.
- When multiplying fractions, multiply the numerators, multiply the denominators and then simplify.

Chief Examiner says

Remember, $\frac{1}{2} \times \frac{1}{3} = \frac{1}{6}$. A common error is to multiply 1 × 1 and get 2.

Test Yourself 2

Work out these, giving the answers as simply as possible.

a $\frac{5}{6} \times 9$

b $\frac{4}{5} \times \frac{5}{9}$

Solutions

Test Yourself 2

a $\frac{5}{6} \times 9 = \frac{45}{6} = \frac{15}{2} = 7\frac{1}{2}$ OR $\frac{5}{6} \times 9 = \frac{5}{2} \times 3 = \frac{15}{2} = 7\frac{1}{2}$

You can simplify either before or after mulitplying.

b $\frac{4}{5} \times \frac{5}{9} = \frac{20}{45} = \frac{4}{9}$ OR $\frac{4}{5} \times \frac{5}{9} = \frac{4}{1} \times \frac{1}{9} = \frac{4}{9}$

Dividing fractions

Revised

- When dividing fractions, turn the second fraction upside down and multiply.

Test Yourself 3

Work out these, giving the answers as simply as possible.

a $\frac{3}{4} \div 6$

b $\frac{3}{5} \div \frac{7}{10}$

Solutions

Test Yourself 3

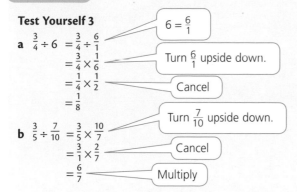

a $\frac{3}{4} \div 6 = \frac{3}{4} \div \frac{6}{1}$ — $6 = \frac{6}{1}$

$= \frac{3}{4} \times \frac{1}{6}$ — Turn $\frac{6}{1}$ upside down.

$= \frac{1}{4} \times \frac{1}{2}$ — Cancel

$= \frac{1}{8}$

b $\frac{3}{5} \div \frac{7}{10} = \frac{3}{5} \times \frac{10}{7}$ — Turn $\frac{7}{10}$ upside down.

$= \frac{3}{1} \times \frac{2}{7}$ — Cancel

$= \frac{6}{7}$ — Multiply

Multiplying and dividing mixed numbers

Revised

- When multiplying and dividing with mixed numbers, change the mixed numbers to improper fractions first.

Test Yourself 4

Work out these.

a $1\frac{2}{3} \times 2\frac{1}{2}$

b $3\frac{3}{4} \div 1\frac{2}{5}$

Solutions

Test Yourself 4

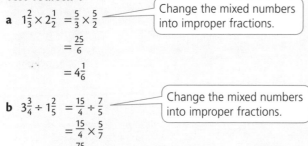

a $1\frac{2}{3} \times 2\frac{1}{2} = \frac{5}{3} \times \frac{5}{2}$ — Change the mixed numbers into improper fractions.

$= \frac{25}{6}$

$= 4\frac{1}{6}$

b $3\frac{3}{4} \div 1\frac{2}{5} = \frac{15}{4} \div \frac{7}{5}$ — Change the mixed numbers into improper fractions.

$= \frac{15}{4} \times \frac{5}{7}$

$= \frac{75}{28}$

$= 2\frac{19}{28}$

Adding and subtracting mixed numbers

Revised

- See Unit B, Chapter 3 for more on adding and subtracting fractions.
- When adding or subtracting mixed numbers there are two methods you can use.
  - Either deal with the whole numbers first and then deal with the fractions.
  - Or change the mixed numbers to improper fractions.

Test Yourself 5

a $2\frac{2}{3} + 1\frac{3}{8}$

b $3\frac{1}{4} - 1\frac{2}{5}$

Solutions

Test Yourself 5

a

Method 1

$2\frac{2}{3} + 1\frac{3}{8} = 3 + \frac{2}{3} + \frac{3}{8}$ — First add the whole numbers.

$= 3 + \frac{16}{24} + \frac{9}{24}$ — Change each fraction to an equivalent fraction with a denominator of 24.

$= 3 + \frac{25}{24}$ — Add the numerators.

$= 4\frac{1}{24}$ — Change the improper fraction to a mixed number and add the whole numbers.

Method 2

$2\frac{2}{3} + 1\frac{3}{8} = \frac{8}{3} + \frac{11}{8}$ — Change to improper fractions.

$= \frac{64}{24} + \frac{33}{24}$ — Change to equivalent fractions with a denominator of 24.

$= \frac{97}{24}$ — Add the numerators.

$= 4\frac{1}{24}$ — Change to a mixed number.

b

Method 1

$3\frac{1}{4} - 1\frac{2}{5} = 2 + \frac{1}{4} - \frac{2}{5}$ — Subtract the whole numbers.

$= 2 + \frac{5}{20} - \frac{8}{20}$ — Change each fraction to an equivalent fraction with a denominator of 20.

$= 1 + \frac{20}{20} + \frac{5}{20} - \frac{8}{20}$ — Change one of the whole numbers to a fraction.

$= 1\frac{17}{20}$ — Collect the fractions.

Method 2

$3\frac{1}{4} - 1\frac{2}{5} = \frac{13}{4} - \frac{7}{5}$ — Change to improper fractions.

$= \frac{65}{20} - \frac{28}{20}$ — Change to equivalent fractions with a denominator of 20.

$= \frac{37}{20}$ — Subtract the numerators.

$= 1\frac{17}{20}$ — Change to a mixed number.

7 Circles and polygons

Circles

Revised

- All the points on a circle are the same distance from its centre.
- You need to know these terms.

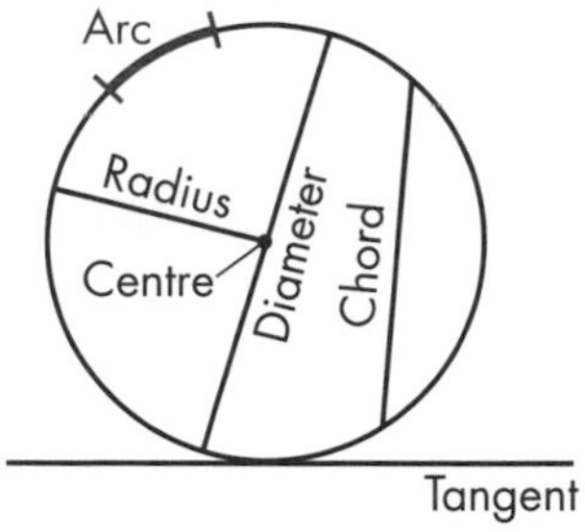

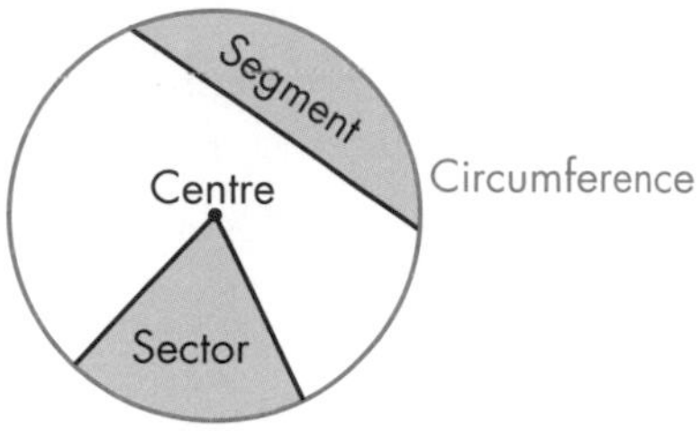

Chief Examiner says

Learn these terms and what they mean.

Test Yourself 1

Complete these sentences.

a A line from the centre of a circle to its circumference is a ....

b A line that touches a circle is a ....

Solutions

Test Yourself 1

a radius

b tangent

Polygons

Revised

- A polygon is a closed shape made from straight lines.
- See Unit B, Chapter 2 for more about triangles and quadrilaterals.
- Pentagons have five sides.

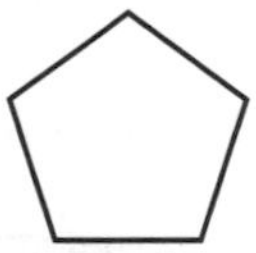

- Hexagons have six sides.

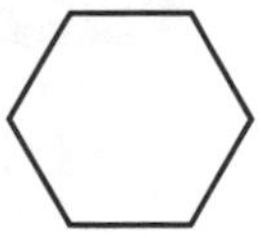

- Octagons have eight sides.

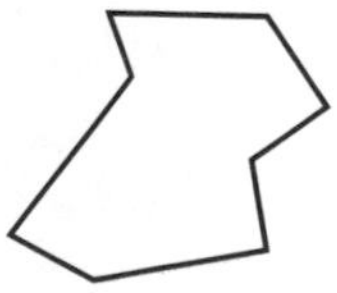

- Decagons have ten sides.

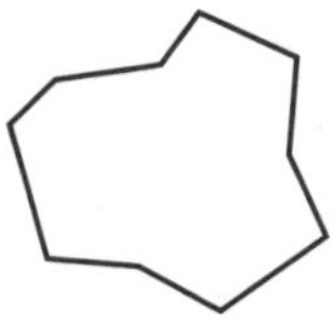

- The sides of a regular polygon are equal in length and the angles are equal in size.

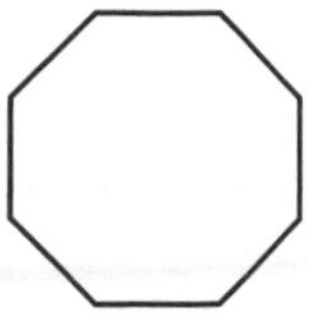

- To construct a regular polygon in a circle.
  - First draw a circle.
  - Draw a radius as a starting line for measuring the angles.
  - Divide 360° by the number of sides to work out the angle you need at the centre of the circle. For example, for a regular pentagon, $360 \div 5 = 72°$.
  - Measure this angle and draw the next radius.
  - Continue round the circle, measuring the same angle and drawing the radius for each angle.
  - Join the points on the circumference to form the regular polygon.

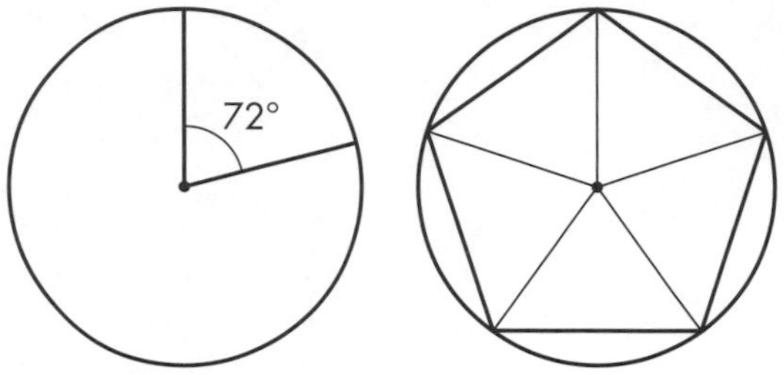

Test Yourself 2

a Complete these sentences.

i A polygon with five sides is

a ....

ii A polygon with four sides is

a ....

b Construct a regular octagon (8 sides).

Solutions

Test Yourself 2

a **i** pentagon

ii quadrilateral

b $360 \div 8 = 45°$

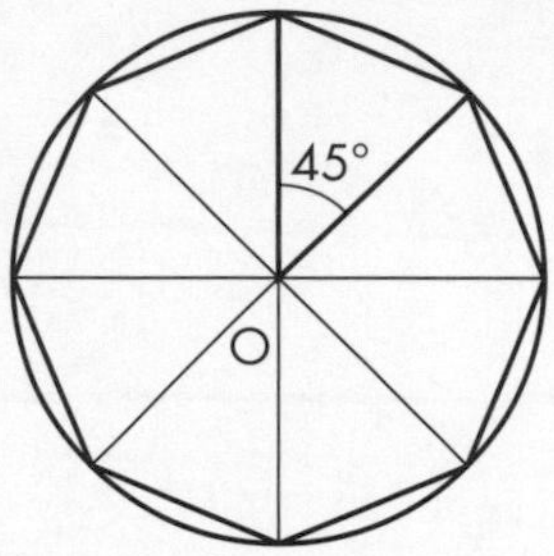

The angles in a triangle

Revised

- See Unit B, Chapter 2 for the angle sum of a triangle.
- If one side of a triangle is extended, the angle formed outside the triangle is called an exterior angle.
- The exterior angle of any triangle is equal to the sum of the opposite interior angles.

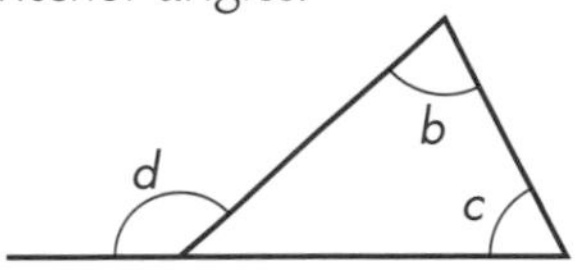

In the diagram, d is the exterior angle. So $d = b + c$

Test Yourself 3

Work out the size of the angle marked t. Give a reason for your answer.

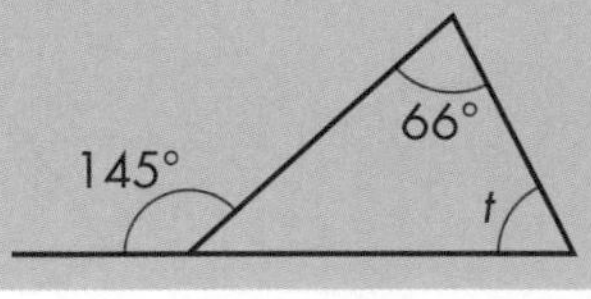

Solutions

Test Yourself 3

$t = 79°$ Exterior angle of triangle equals sum of interior opposite angles.

The angles in a quadrilateral and The angles in a polygon

Revised

- The sum of the interior angles of a quadrilateral is 360°.
- The sum of the interior angles of a pentagon (five sides) is 540°.
- The sum of the interior angles of a hexagon (six sides) is 720°.
- At any vertex of a polygon, the interior and exterior angles make a straight line and add up to 180°.
- The sum of the exterior angles of any polygon is 360°.
- The angle at the centre of a regular polygon = 360° ÷ number of sides.

Test Yourself 4

A regular polygon has 12 sides.

a Work out the size of each exterior angle.

b Work out the size of each interior angle.

c Find the sum of the interior angles.

Solutions

Test Yourself 4

a Each exterior angle $= \dfrac{360}{12}$

$= 30°$

b Each interior angle angle $= 180° - 30°$

$= 150°$

c Sum of the interior angles $= 150° \times 12$

$= 1800°$

Unit B

8 Powers and indices

- See Unit A, Chapters 1, 12 and 14 for more on squares, square roots, cubes, cube roots and powers.

The rules of indices

Revised

- The following rules of indices are used to manipulate expressions involving letters and numbers.
  - $a^m \times a^n = a^{m+n}$
  - $a^m \div a^n = a^{m-n}$
  - $a^1 = a$
  - $a^0 = 1$

Test Yourself 1

Simplify these.

a $2 \times a \times a$

b $a^2b \times ab^3$

c $a^3b^4 \div ab^3$

d $\dfrac{a^3b^2 \times ab^3}{a^2b}$

Solutions

Test Yourself 1

a $2a^2$

b a^3b^4

c a^2b

d a^2b^4

The indices are added.

The indices are subtracted.

For a, $3 + 1 - 2 = 2$

For b, $2 + 3 - 1 = 4$

9 Decimals and fractions

Ordering decimals

Revised

- See Unit B, Chapter 1 for ordering integers.
- See Unit A, Chapter 4 for more on decimals.
- For decimals less than 1, the largest number has its first non-zero digit nearest to the decimal point.

Test Yourself 1

Write these decimals in order, smallest first.

0.007, 0.065, 0.0075, 0.65, 0.0008

Solution

Test Yourself 1

0.0008, 0.007, 0.0075, 0.065, 0.65

Changing a decimal into a fraction

Revised

- See Unit B, Chapter 3 for changing a fraction into a decimal.
- In a decimal number, the places after the decimal point are $\frac{1}{10}$, $\frac{1}{100}$, $\frac{1}{1000}$, and so on.
- You can use place value to change decimal into a fraction.

Test Yourself 2

Change these decimals into fractions.

a 0.75
b 0.09
c 1.02
d 0.632

Solutions

Test Yourself 2

a $\frac{75}{100} = \frac{3}{4}$ **b** $\frac{9}{100}$ **c** $1\frac{2}{100} = 1\frac{1}{50}$ **d** $\frac{632}{1000} = \frac{79}{125}$

Recurring decimals

Revised

- All fractions are equal to either recurring or terminating decimals.
- The fractions equal to terminating decimals have denominators whose only prime factors are 2 and/or 5.
- To convert a fraction to a decimal, divide the numerator by the denominator.
- You can use dot notation to write recurring decimals. For example, $\frac{1}{3} = 0.\dot{3}$.
- If more than one digit recurs, you put a dot over the first and last digit of the group, or period. For example, 0.012 612 6 = $0.0\dot{1}2\dot{6}$.

Test Yourself 3

Write these fractions as decimals.

a $\frac{1}{8}$
b $\frac{1}{6}$
c $\frac{13}{20}$
d $\frac{7}{25}$
e $\frac{3}{7}$

Solutions

Test Yourself 3

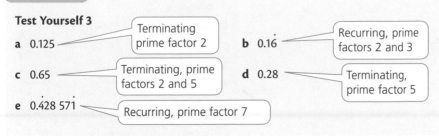

a 0.125 — Terminating prime factor 2

b $0.1\dot{6}$ — Recurring, prime factors 2 and 3

c 0.65 — Terminating, prime factors 2 and 5

d 0.28 — Terminating, prime factor 5

e $0.\dot{4}28\,57\dot{1}$ — Recurring, prime factor 7

10 Real-life graphs

Conversion graphs

Revised

- When dealing with real-life graphs, look at the labels on the axes, to find out what the graph is about.
- When reading off graphs,
  - decide whether you are going from the horizontal axis to the vertical axis or from the vertical axis to the horizontal axis.
  - draw lines from the starting axis to the graph and then to the other axis.
  - ensure you know the value of each small division on the axes.

Chief Examiner says

Notice that each division on the *y*-axis is €1, but there are two divisions for £1 on the *x*-axis.

Test Yourself 1

This graph can be used to change pounds into euros.

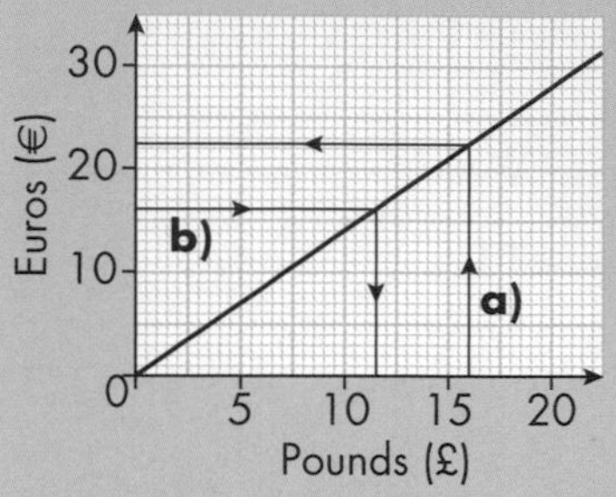

Use the graph to change

a £16 to euros.

b €16 to pounds.

Solutions

Test Yourself 1

a About €22.40 — Read up from the Pounds axis and along to the Euros axis.

b About £11.50 — Read along from the Euros axis and down to the Pounds axis.

Travel graphs

Revised

- The steeper the line, the greater the speed.
- You can find speed from the relationship: Speed = Distance ÷ Time.
- A horizontal line indicates that the object is not moving.

Test Yourself 2

Asif walked to the bus stop, waited for the bus, then travelled on to school. The graph is a distance–time graph for Asif's journey.

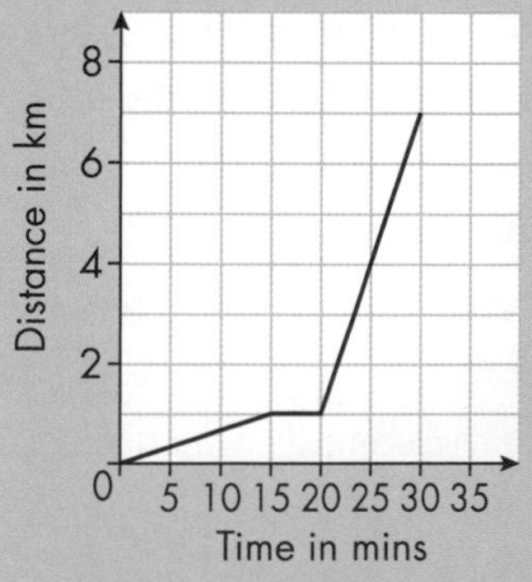

a How long did Asif wait at the bus stop?

b How far did Asif travel

i on foot? **ii** by bus?

c How fast did Asif walk?

d What was the average speed of the bus?

e Why are the sections of the graph, in reality, unlikely to be straight?

Solutions

Test Yourself 2

a 5 mins

b **i** 1 km **ii** 6 km

c $\frac{1}{15}$ km/min or 4 km/h

d $\frac{6}{10}$ km/min or 36 km/h

e Stops and starts are likely to be gradual, not sudden. Speed unlikely to be constant.

Chief Examiner says

Remember to find the rate of change for each part of the graph. If it is zero, say how long this lasts.

11 Reflection

Reflection symmetry

Revised

- A shape has reflection symmetry if it fits onto itself when reflected in a mirror line, or folded along the mirror line.
- In two dimensions, the mirror is the line of symmetry. In three dimensions, the mirror is the plane of symmetry.

Test Yourself 1

Find the number of lines of symmetry of each of these shapes.

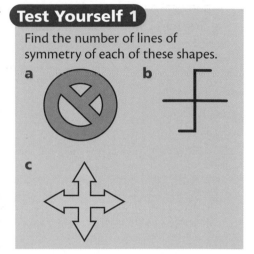

a

b

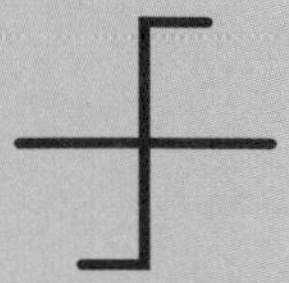

c

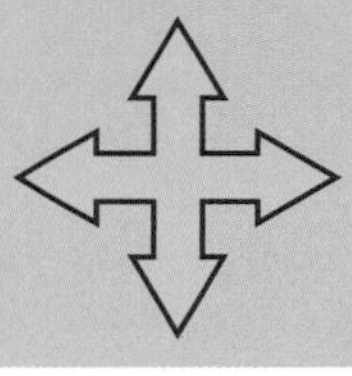

Solutions

Test Yourself 1

a One

b None

c Four

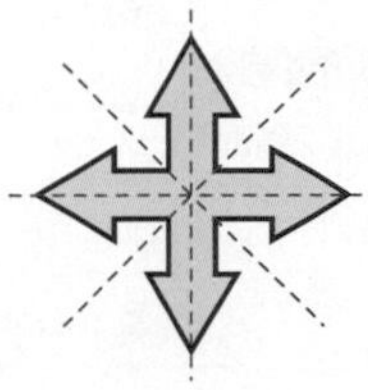

Reflections

Revised

- The distance between each point on the image and the mirror line is the same as the distance between the mirror line and the corresponding point on the object.
- The image is the same size and shape as the object, but is reversed. The object and its image are congruent.
- When describing a reflection, you must state
  - that it is a reflection
  - the mirror line.

Chief Examiner says

You can use tracing paper to check reflections. The complete diagram can be folded along the mirror line and the image and object will fit onto each other.

Test Yourself 2

a Draw the reflection of this triangle in the mirror line.

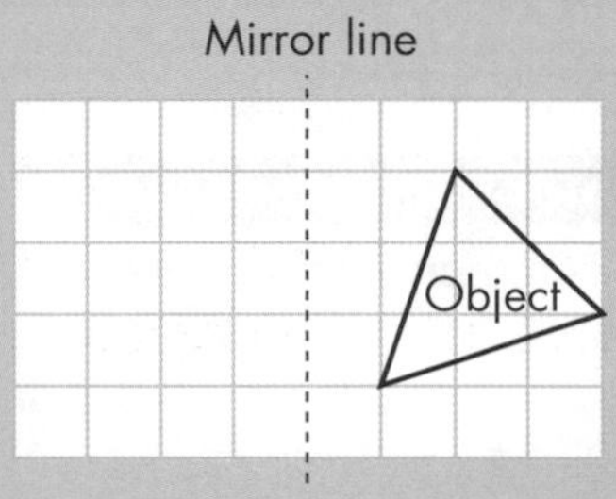

b Describe fully the transformation that maps the object on to the image in this diagram.

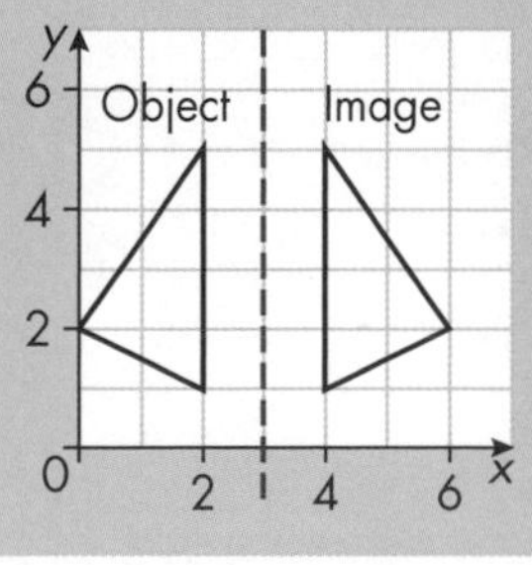

Solutions

Test Yourself 2

a

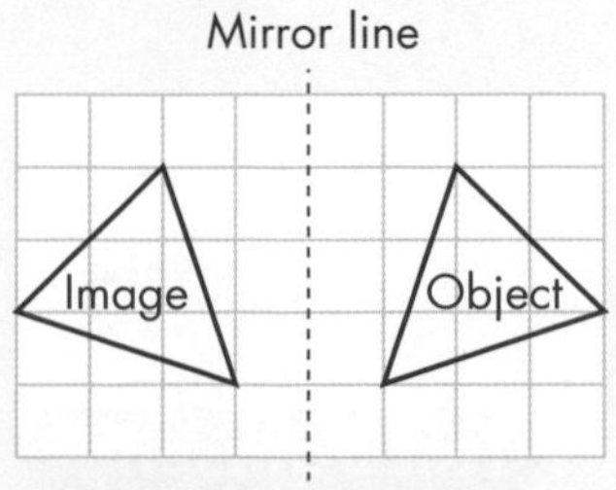

b A reflection in the line $x = 3$.

12 Percentages

The % symbol

Revised

- A percentage is a part of 100. For example, 43 out of 100 is written as $\frac{43}{100}$ as a fraction or 43% as a percentage.

Test Yourself 1

In a school, 37 out of 100 students have broadband.

What percentage

a have broadband?

b do not have broadband?

Solutions

Test Yourself 1

a 37%

b 63% (37 + 63 = 100)

Fractions, decimals and percentages

Revised

- To change a percentage to a fraction, write the percentage over 100 and cancel. For example, $35\% = \frac{35}{100} = \frac{7}{20}$. (Divide top and bottom by 5.)
- To change a percentage to a decimal, divide by 100. For example, $35\% = 35 \div 100 = 0.35$.
- To change a decimal to a percentage, multiply by 100. For example, $0.8 = 0.8 \times 100 = 80\%$.
- To change a fraction to a percentage, first change the fraction to a decimal and then multiply by 100. For example, $\frac{3}{5} = 3 \div 5 = 0.6$; $0.6 \times 100 = 60\%$.
- When ordering fractions, percentages and decimals, it is best to change them all to decimals or percentages and put these in order.

Chief Examiner says

A common error is to write 5% as 0.5 rather than 0.05, for example.

Test Yourself 2

a Change $\frac{3}{10}$ to

i a decimal.

ii a percentage.

b Change 22% to

i a decimal.

ii a fraction.

c Put these numbers in order, smallest first.

0.45, 25%, $\frac{2}{5}$, 0.31, 30%

Solutions

Test Yourself 2

a i 0.3 ($3 \div 10 = 0.3$) **ii** 30% ($0.3 \times 100 = 30$)

b i 0.22 ($22 \div 100 = 0.22$) **ii** $\frac{22}{100} = \frac{11}{50}$ (Cancel by 2.)

c 0.45, 0.25, 0.4, 0.31, 0.3 (Changed to decimals.)

Order is 0.25, 0.3, 0.31, 0.4, 0.45

That is 25%, 30%, 0.31, $\frac{2}{5}$, 0.45

Finding a percentage of a quantity

Revised

- There are two methods to find a percentage of a quantity,
  - either change the percentage to a fraction and find the fraction of the quantity
  - or change the percentage to a decimal and multiply.

Test Yourself 3

Find 4% of £84.

- See Unit B, Chapter 3 for finding a fraction of a quantity.
- See Unit A, Chapter 4 and Unit B, Chapter 1 for multiplying decimals.

Chief Examiner says

If you are allowed to use a calculator, use it to multiply the decimal by the amount.

Solution

Test Yourself 3

Method 1

$4\% = \frac{4}{100}$

$\frac{4}{100}$ of £84 $= 84 \div 100 \times 4$

$= 0.84 \times 4$

$= £3.36$

Method 2

4% of £84 $= 0.04 \times 84$

$= £3.36$

$4 \times 84 = 336$ and there are two figures after the decimal point.

Percentage increase and decrease

Revised

- To calculate a percentage increase or decrease
  - first find the increase or decrease,
  - then for an increase, add it to the original amount
  - or for a decrease, subtract it from the original amount.

Test Yourself 4

a Sally earned £400 a week. She was given a 5% rise. How much was she paid each week after her pay rise?

b A shop reduces all its prices by 15%. How much would a pair of shoes cost which were £140 before the sale?

Solutions

Test Yourself 4

a 10% of £400 = £40 so 5% is £20.

$400 + 20 = 420$

Sally earns £420 after her pay rise.

b 10% of £140 is £14 so 5% is £7 and 15% is £21.

$140 - 21 = 119$

The shoes cost £119 in the sale.

Calculating one quantity as a percentage of another

Revised

- To work out A as a percentage of B, first write A as a fraction of B, then change to a decimal and multiply by 100.
- To find an increase or decrease as a percentage, divide the increase or decrease by the original value and multiply by 100.
- See Unit B, Chapter 3 for writing one number as a fraction of another.

Chief Examiner says

Make sure the units are the same.

Chief Examiner says

If you are allowed to use a calculator, use it, at least to check, even if you feel you can do it in your head.

Test Yourself 5

a Express £30 as a percentage of £80.

b David's wage increased from £160 to £180 a week.

What percentage increase was this?

Solutions

Test Yourself 5

a $\frac{30}{80} = 0.375$

Percentage $= 0.375 \times 100$

$= 37.5\%$

b Increase $= £20$

$\frac{20}{160} = 0.125$

Percentage $= 0.125 \times 100$

$= 12.5\%$

Divide the increase by the original.

13 Rotation

Rotation symmetry

Revised

- A shape has rotation symmetry if it fits on to itself more than once in a complete turn.
- The number of times it fits on to itself is called the order of rotation.

Test Yourself 1

Find the order of rotation symmetry of each of these shapes.

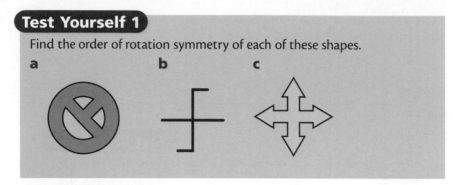

a

b

c

Solutions

Test Yourself 1

a 1 — This is the same as saying that the shape has no rotation symmetry.

b 2

c 4

Completing shapes

Revised

- You can complete shapes so they have rotation symmetry.

Test Yourself 2

Shade more squares so that the pattern has rotation symmetry of order 2.

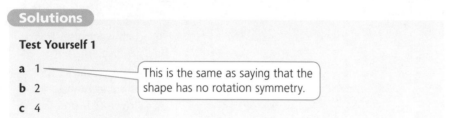

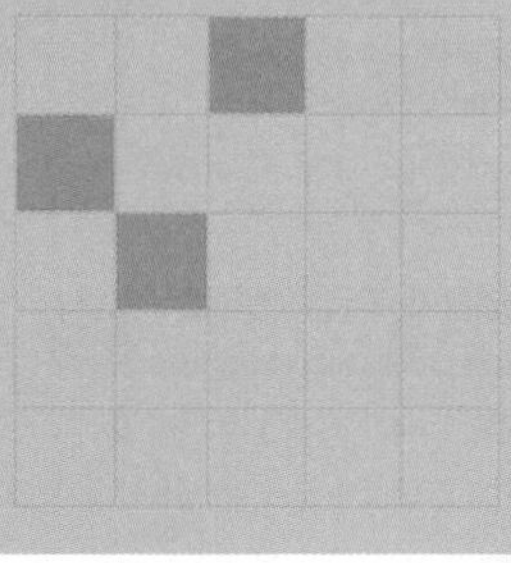

Solution

Test Yourself 2

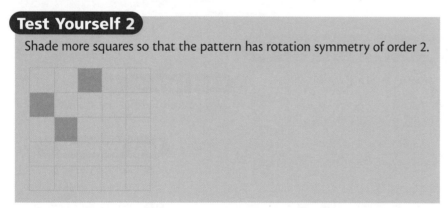

Drawing rotations

Revised

- An object can be rotated about a point, called the centre of rotation.
- The rotation can be clockwise or anticlockwise through an angle which can be a fraction of a turn or a number of degrees.
- Corresponding points on the object and image are the same distance from the centre of rotation.
- The image and the object are congruent.
- Rotations are anticlockwise unless stated otherwise.

Chief Examiner says

Remember to ask for tracing paper in an exam. It as an optional extra. Use it for transformation questions.

Solution

Test Yourself 3

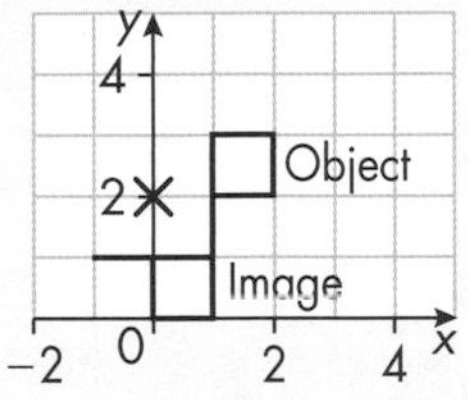

Test Yourself 3

Rotate this flag through 90° clockwise about (0, 2).

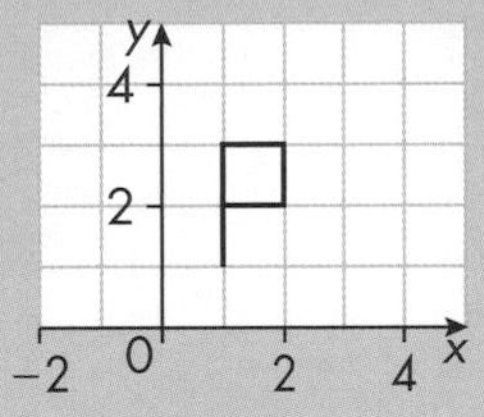

Recognising and describing rotations

Revised

- To describe a rotation, you must state
  - that it is a rotation
  - the centre of rotation
  - the angle of rotation
  - the direction – clockwise or anticlockwise.

Test Yourself 4

Describe fully the single transformation that maps flag A on to flag B.

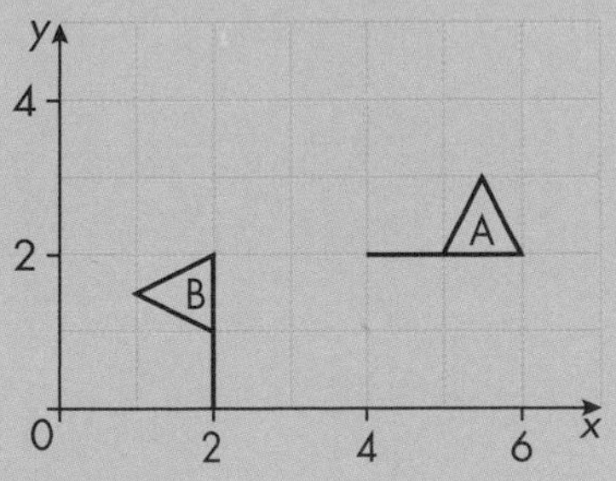

Solution

Test Yourself 4

A rotation of 90° anticlockwise about (4, 0)

14 Estimation

Rounding to 1 significant figure

Revised

- See Unit A, Chapter 12 for rounding to 1 significant figure.
- To estimate answers to problems, round each number to 1 significant figure and then carry out the calculation without a calculator.

Chief Examiner says

Round each number to 1 significant figure. If the answer does not work out exactly, give the answer correct to 1 or 2 significant figures. '≈' means 'approximately equals'.

Test Yourself 1

Estimate the answer to each of these calculations.

a 47.5×12.6

b $628 \div 43$

c $\frac{24 \times 6.99}{3.4}$

Solutions

Test Yourself 1

a $50 \times 10 = 500$

b $600 \div 40 = 15$

c $\frac{20 \times 7}{3} = \frac{140}{3}$

$= 46.666 \ldots$

≈ 50

Checking answers

- As well as rounding the numbers to obtain an estimate to check the result of a calculation, you can also use
  - common sense – is it about the right size; is it possible
  - number facts – multiplying by a number between 0 and 1 will give a smaller answer
  - inverse operations – if you multiplied, divide your answer by one of the numbers

Test Yourself 2

Which of these answers might be correct and which are definitely wrong? Show how you decided.

a $437.8 \times 0.765 = 3327$

b $0.326 \div 53.8 = 0.00606$

c The volume of a bottle of lemonade $= 3.14 \times 50^2 \times 200 = 1\,570\,796$ litres

Solutions

Test Yourself 2

a Wrong: the answer should be smaller than 437.8 as it is multiplied by a number between 0 and 1.

b Could be correct: rounding the numbers and using inverse operations, $0.006 \times 50 = 0.3$.

c Wrong: it would be a big bottle of lemonade! The answer is enough for a swimming pool.

15 Enlargement

Scale factor and Centre of enlargement

Revised

- The image is the same shape as the object but each length on the image is the corresponding length on the object multiplied by the scale factor. This is the only transformation you meet at GCSE where the object and the image are not congruent. When two things are the same shape but a different size like this, they are called similar shapes.
- The distance of each point on the object from the centre of enlargement is multiplied by the scale factor to find the distance from the centre to the corresponding points on the image.
- To find the centre of enlargement, join corresponding points on the object and image and extend the lines until they meet.
- When describing an enlargement, state
  - that it is an enlargement
  - the centre of enlargement
  - the scale factor.

Test Yourself 1

a Enlarge this flag with centre (0, 3) and scale factor 2.

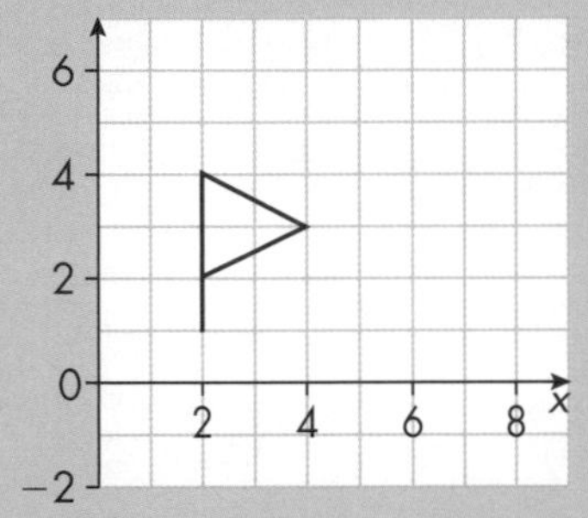

b Describe the transformation that maps rectangle A on to rectangle B.

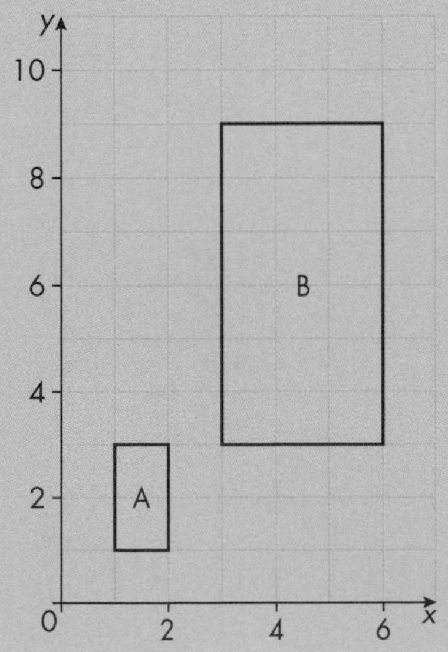

Solutions

Test Yourself 1

a

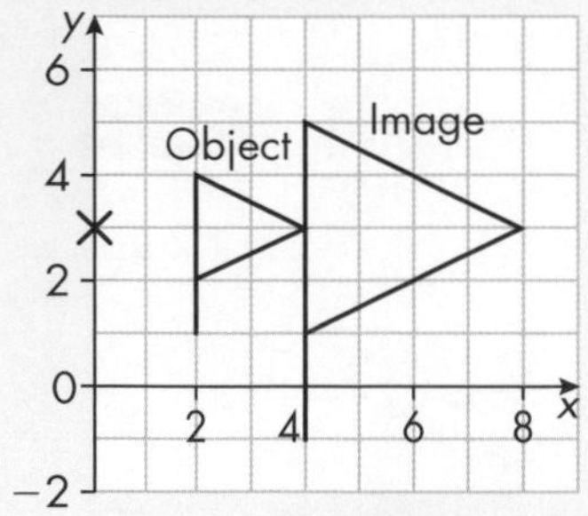

b Enlargement scale factor 3, centre (0, 0)

Fractional scale factors

Revised

- If the scale factor is less than 1 but greater than 0, the image will be smaller than the object. The transformation is still called an enlargement, however.

Test Yourself 2

Enlarge this flag with centre (8, 0) and scale factor $\frac{1}{2}$.

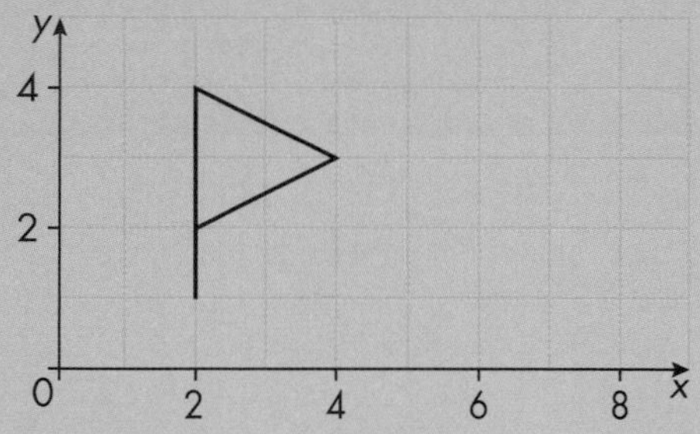

Solution

Test Yourself 2

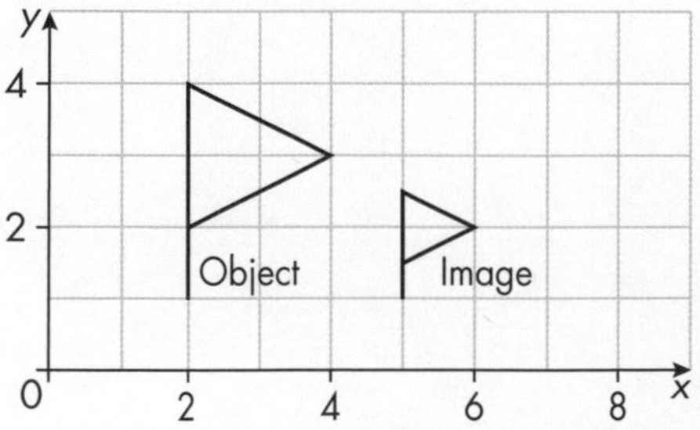

16 Scatter diagrams and time series

Scatter diagrams

Revised

- Scatter diagrams (or graphs) are drawn to investigate any possible link between two variables. Values of the two variables are plotted as points on a graph. If the points lie approximately in a straight line, then there is a correlation between the two variables. The closer the points are to a straight line, the stronger the correlation.
- If y increases as x increases (the higher the value of x, the higher the value of y), the correlation is positive.
- If y decreases as x increases (the higher the value of x, the lower the value of y), the correlation is negative.
- If there is a correlation, then a line of best fit can be drawn. It should reflect the slope of the points and have approximately the same number of points on either side.
- The line of best fit can be used to estimate a value of y from a given value of x (or vice versa). It should not be used to estimate too far outside the range of data.

Test Yourself 1

The table below shows the amount of time spent, and marks gained, on a piece of work.

Time (*h*)	5	8	3	6	6	7	4	10	8	7
Mark	12	15	9	14	11	13	10	19	16	14

a Plot a scatter diagram for this information.
b What conclusions can be drawn?
c Draw a line of best fit.
d Use your line of best fit to estimate the mark of a student who spent 9 hours on the work.

Solutions

Test Yourself 1

a c

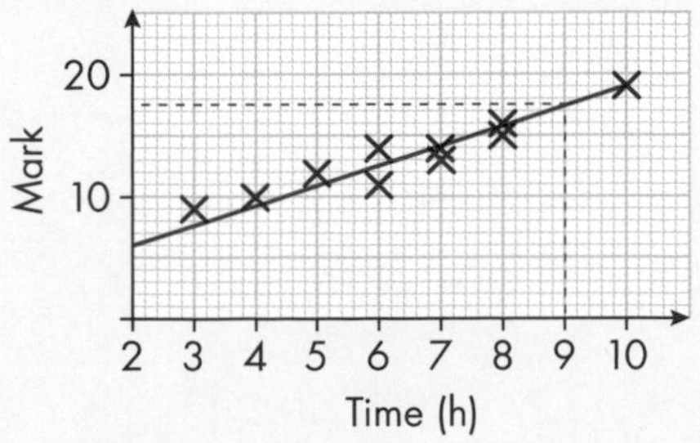

b Fairly strong positive correlation
d 17 or 18

Time series

Revised

- A time series is a graph where the x-axis is time and the y-axis is any quantity which varies with time. For example, quarterly sales of a company.
- A time series graph may have a cyclical pattern.
- A time series graph may show a long-term trend.

Test Yourself 2

The table gives the sales figures in £millions for a company.

Quarter	1st	2nd	3rd	4th
1998	4.2	5.6	7.2	4.9
1999	3.9	5.5	6.8	4.7
2000	3.8	5.2	6.5	4.6

a Plot a time series graph.

b Describe the long-term trend.

Solutions

Test Yourself 2

a

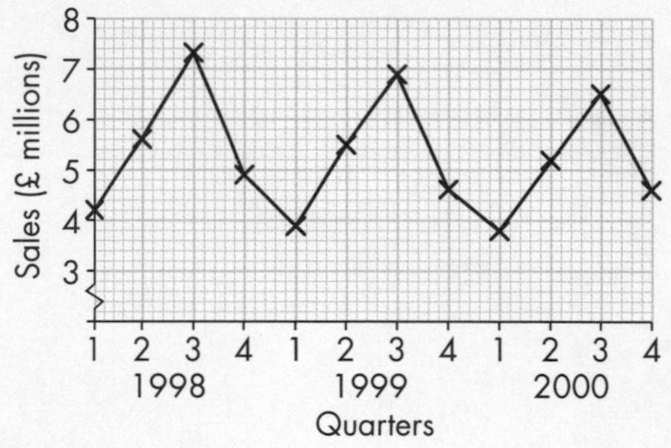

b The sales are falling.

17 Straight lines and inequalities

Drawing straight-line graphs

Revised

- See Unit A, Chapter 7 for more on horizontal and vertical lines.
- See Unit A, Chapter 5 for substituting values into an algebraic expression.
- There are two main types of equation linked to straight line graphs.
  - The type $y = 2x + 1$.
  - The type $3x + 2y = 6$.
- To draw the first type, follow these steps.
  - Draw up a table of values using at least three x values.
  - Substitute these into the formula to find the corresponding y values.
  - Plot the coordinate pairs – they should lie in a straight line.
- To draw the second type, follow these steps.
  - Draw up a table of values, using $x = 0$ and $y = 0$.
  - Substitute these into the formula to find the other values.
  - Plot the coordinate pairs.
- When plotting coordinates, remember that the first coordinate is across, the second coordinate is up (or down).

Test Yourself 1

a Draw the line $y = 2x + 1$.
b Draw the line $3x + 2y = 6$.

Solutions

Test Yourself 1

a

x	0	1	2
y	1	3	5

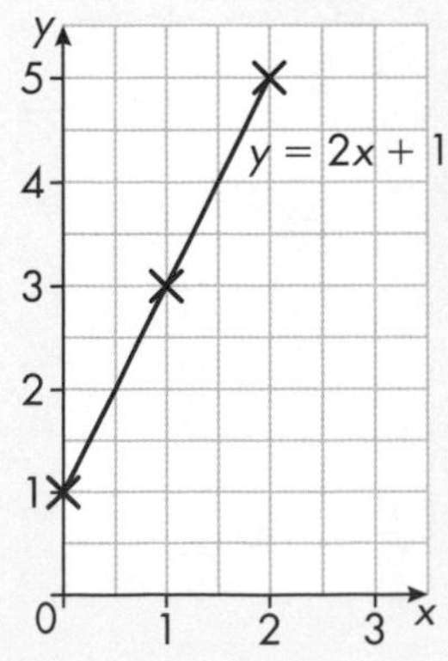

b

x	0	2
y	3	0

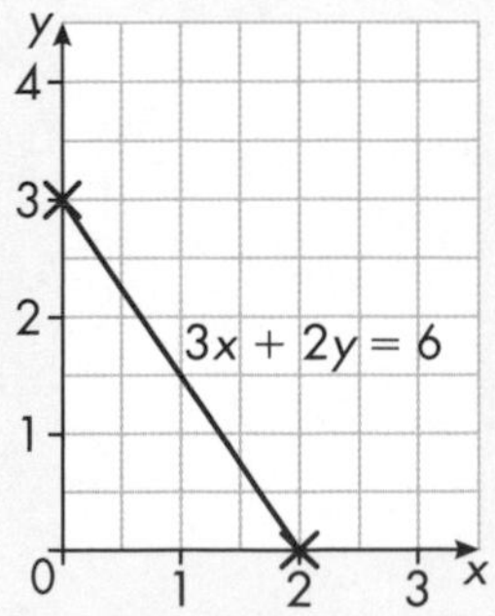

The graphical solution of simultaneous equations

Revised

- Make a table of values for each equation and plot the graphs on the same pair of axes.
- Write down the coordinates of the point where the graphs cross.

Test Yourself 2

Solve graphically
$y = 4x - 1$ and
$x + y = 4$.

Solution

Test Yourself 2

$y = 4x - 1$

x	0	1	2
y	−1	3	7

$x + y = 4$

x	0	4	1
y	4	0	3

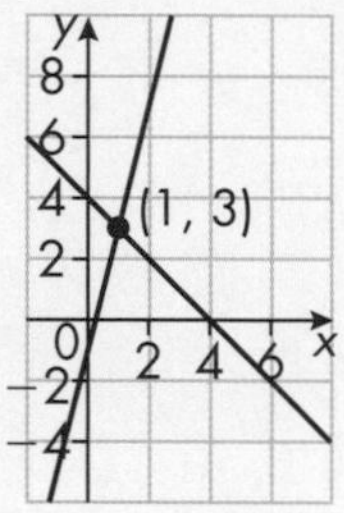

Answer: $x = 1$, $y = 3$

The equation of a line

Revised

- The gradient of a line is the number indicating how steep it is. The larger the number, the steeper the line.
- Lines with positive gradients slope forwards / , lines with negative gradients slope backwards \.
- Gradient $= \dfrac{\text{increase in } y}{\text{increase in } x}$
- The y-intercept is the y-value where the line crosses the y-axis.
- If the equation of a line is written in the form $y = mx + c$, m represents the gradient and c represents the y-intercept.
- Lines with the same gradient are parallel.

Test Yourself 3

a Find the gradient and *y*-intercept of each of these lines.

i

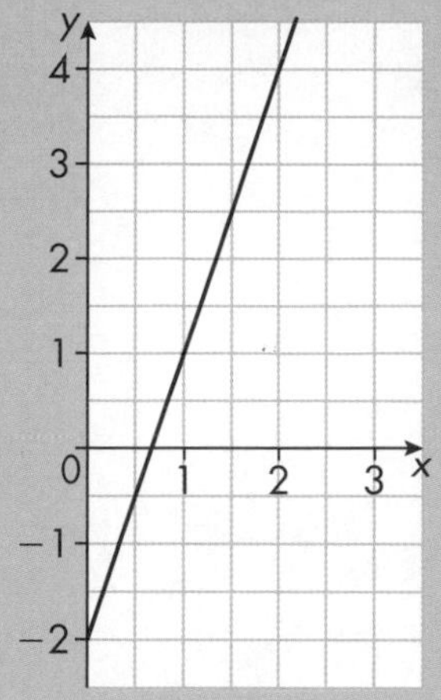

ii

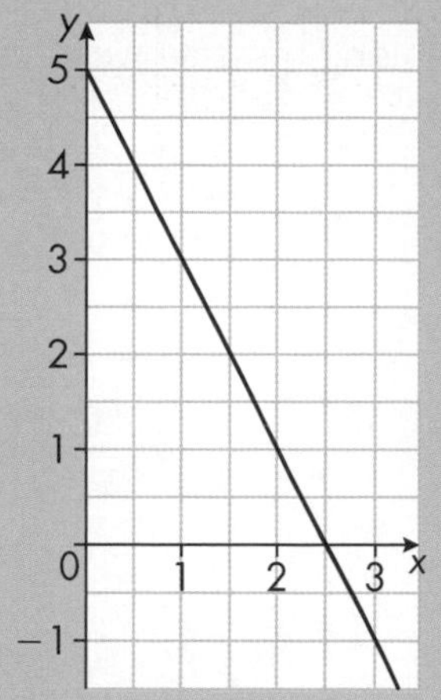

b Find the gradient and *y*-intercept of each of these lines.

i $y = x + 4$ **ii** $2y = 6x - 3$

iii $5x - 2y = 12$

c Write down the equation of the line parallel to $y = 2x - 5$ and passing through the point (0, 4).

Solutions

Test Yourself 3

a i Gradient $= \frac{6}{2} = 3$

y-intercept $= -2$

ii Gradient $= -\frac{4}{2} = -2$

y-intercept $= 5$

b i $y = 1x + 4$

Gradient $(m) = 1$, *y*-intercept $(c) = 4$

ii $y = 3x - 1\frac{1}{2}$

Gradient $(m) = 3$, *y*-intercept $(c) = -1\frac{1}{2}$

iii $-2y = -5x + 12$

$y = 2\frac{1}{2}x - 6$

Gradient $(m) = 2\frac{1}{2}$, *y*-intercept $(c) = -6$

c From $y = 2x - 5$, $m = 2$

From (0, 4), $c = 4$

The equation is $y = 2x + 4$.

Inequalities

Revised

- You need to know the inequality symbols.
  - $>$ means greater than
  - $<$ means less than
  - $\geqslant$ means greater than or equal to
  - $\leqslant$ means less than or equal to
- Inequalities are generally solved using the same rules as for solving equations.

- The exception is when multiplying and dividing by a negative number. In this case the inequality sign is reversed. This problem is best avoided. You do this by moving the unknown to the side where it is positive.
- Inequalities can be shown on a number line using these conventions:

 when 'equals' is not included

 when 'equals' is included

Test Yourself 4

a Solve the inequality $3x - 1 \geqslant 11$. Show the answer on number line.

b Solve the inequality $4x < 6x + 2$.

c Solve $-10 < 2x + 1 \leqslant 15$.

Solutions

Test Yourself 4

a $3x - 1 \geqslant 11$

$3x \geqslant 12$

$x \geqslant 4$

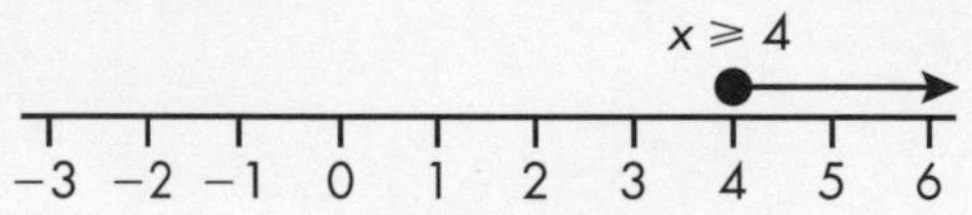

b $4x < 6x + 2$

$4x - 2 < 6x$ — Subtract 2 from both sides.

$-2 < 2x$ — Subtract $4x$ from both sides.

$-1 < x$ — Divide both sides by 2.

$x > -1$ — Swap sides so x is on the left. Remember to turn the inequality sign round as well.

c $-10 < 2x + 1 \leqslant 15$

$-11 < 2x \leqslant 14$ — Subtract 1 from each section.

$-5.5 < x \leqslant 7$ — Divide each section by 2.

18 Congruence and transformations

Congruence

Revised

- Two shapes are congruent if they have the same lengths and angles as each other.
- If one were traced, the tracing would fit on the other shape, although the tracing might need to be turned round or turned over.

Chief Examiner says

You can use tracing paper to check if two shapes are congruent.

Test Yourself 1

Match the pairs of congruent rectangles.

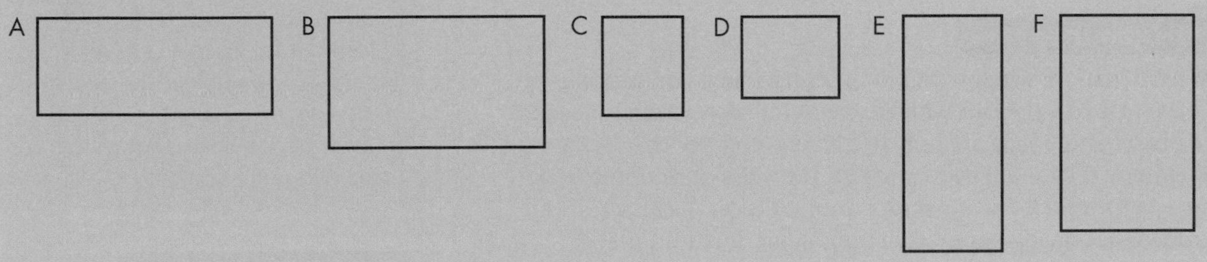

Solution

Test Yourself 1

A and E, B and F, C and D

Translations

Revised

- Each point on the image has moved the same distance, in the same direction, from the corresponding point on the object.
- The image is the same size and shape as the object and is the same way up.
- The object and the image are congruent.
- To describe a translations, state
  - that it is a translation
  - the column vector or how many units the shape has moved in each direction.

Solution

Test Yourself 2

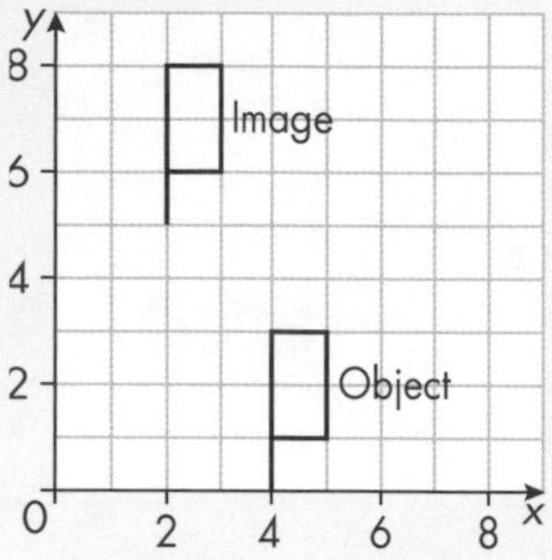

Translate by the vector $\begin{pmatrix} -2 \\ 5 \end{pmatrix}$ means move 2 units across to the left and 5 units up.

Test Yourself 2

Translate this flag by $\begin{pmatrix} -2 \\ 5 \end{pmatrix}$

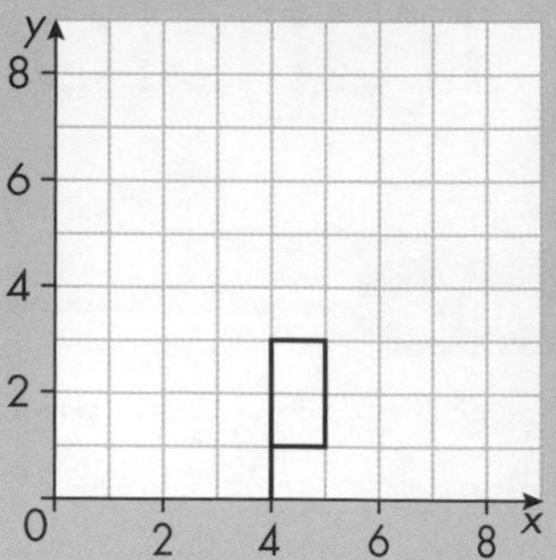

Combining transformations

Revised

- Perform the transformations in the order given.
- Compare the object and the final image to find the equivalent single transformation.

Chief Examiner says

In an examination, when asked to describe a single transformation, you have first to work out which type of transformation is needed. If the object and image are not the same size, check that it is an enlargement. If they are the same size, draw the object on tracing paper and move the tracing paper until it fits on the image. If you just move the tracing paper in a straight line, it is a translation. If you need to turn the tracing paper round, it is a rotation. If you turn the tracing paper over, it is a reflection.

Test Yourself 3

Draw axes from −8 to 6 for x and −8 to 4 for y. Plot the points (4, 2), (4, 3), (4, 4) and (5, 3) and join them to form a flag. Reflect the flag in the line $x = 1$. Then reflect the image in the line $y = -2$. Find the single transformation that is equivalent to these two reflections.

Chief Examiner says

Don't forget to give all the information needed to define the transformation.

Solution

Test Yourself 3

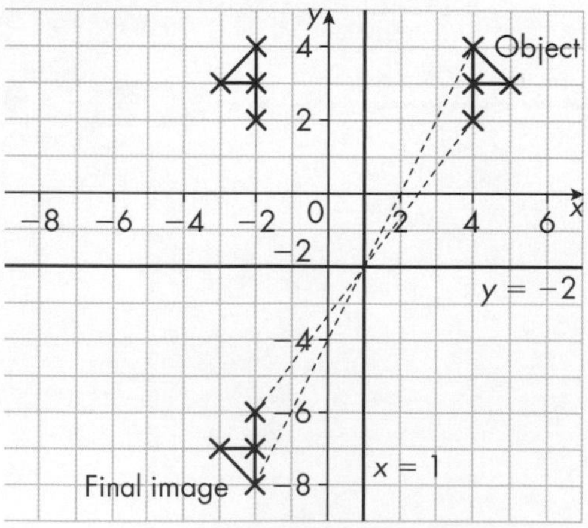

The transformation is a rotation of 180° about a centre (1, −2).

1 Two-dimensional representation of solids

Recognising nets

Revised

- The net of a solid is the two-dimensional (flat) shape that can be folded to make the three-dimensional (3-D) solid.

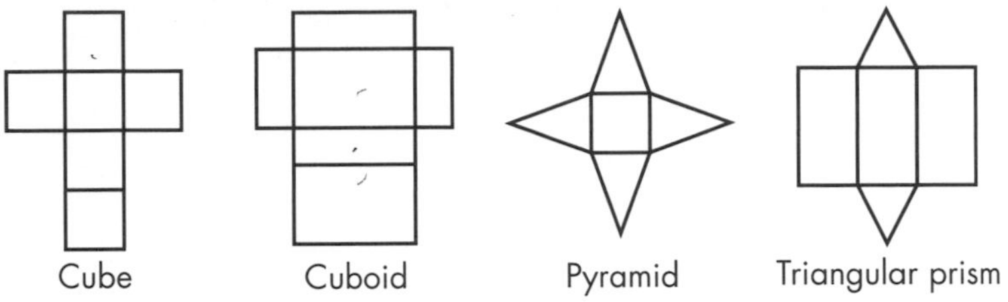

Test Yourself 1

Which of these could be the net of a cube?

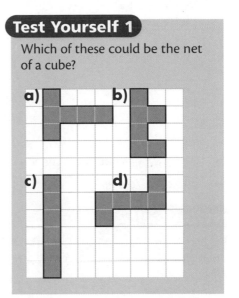

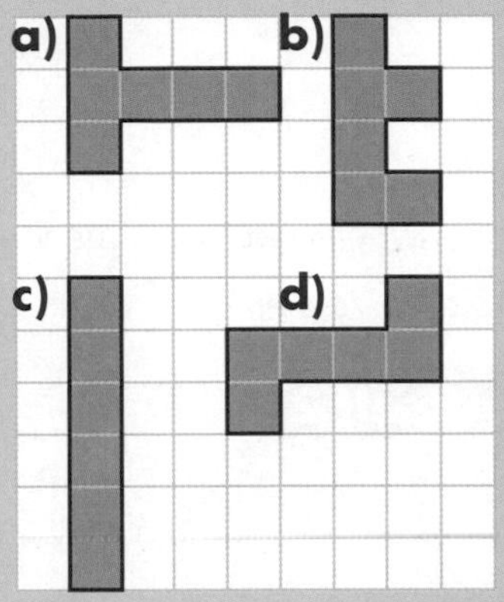

Solution

Test Yourself 1

a) and d)

Drawing nets

Revised

- You may need to draw accurate nets for 3-D shapes. For example, here are some possible nets for a cube.

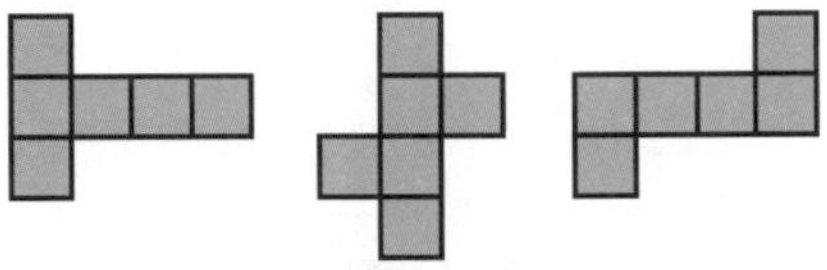

Chief Examiner says

There is more than one way of drawing nets for three-dimensional shapes. If you have difficulty imagining how nets make the shapes, you can copy them, cut them out and fold them to make the three-dimensional shapes to check you are correct.

- There are seven main solid (three-dimensional) shapes.

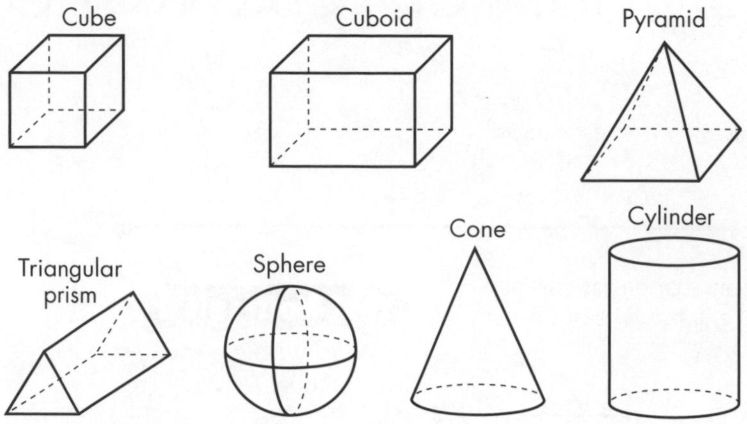

- You also need to know these three terms:
  - face – a side of a solid shape
  - edge – where two faces meet
  - vertex – a corner

Test Yourself 2

a Draw accurately on squared paper the net of this cuboid.

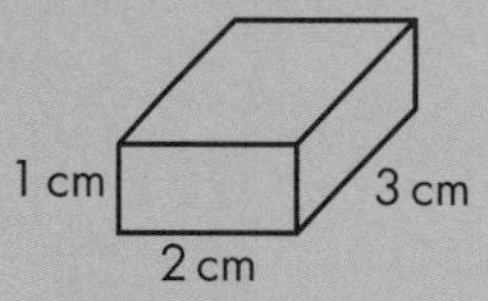

b Write down the number of faces, edges and vertices of a triangular prism.

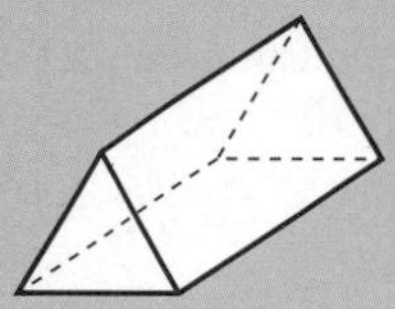

Solutions

Test Yourself 2

a

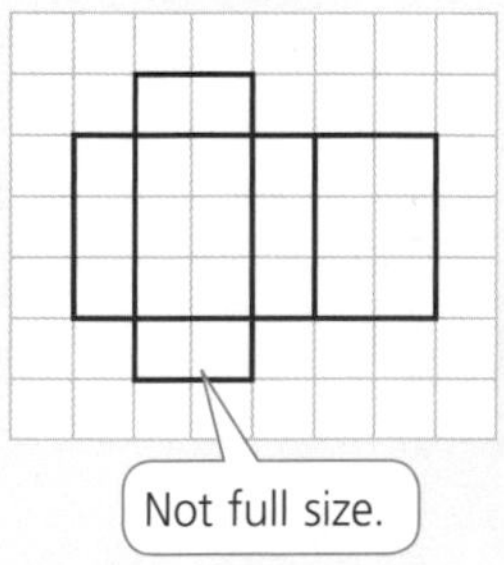

b Faces: 5
Edges: 9
Vertices: 6

Isometric drawings

Revised

- 3-D shapes can be represented on isometric paper.

Chief Examiner says

Right angles appear as 60° or 120° when drawn on isometric paper.

Solution

Test Yourself 3

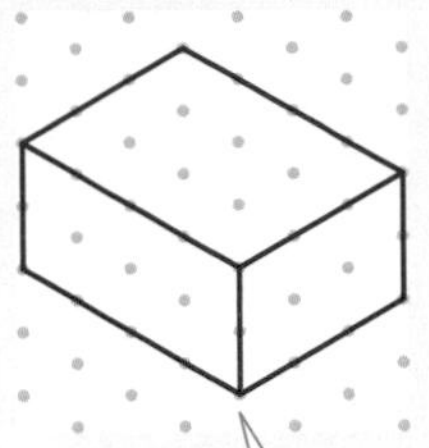

Not full size.

Test Yourself 3

Make a drawing on isometric paper of a cuboid measuring 3 cm by 4 cm by 2 cm.

Plans and elevations

Revised

- The plan view of an object is the view seen directly from above.
- The front elevation is the view seen directly from the front.
- The side elevation is the view seen directly from one side (there are two possible side elevations).

Test Yourself 4

Sketch the plan (P), the front elevation (F) and side elevations (S_1 and S_2) of this shape.

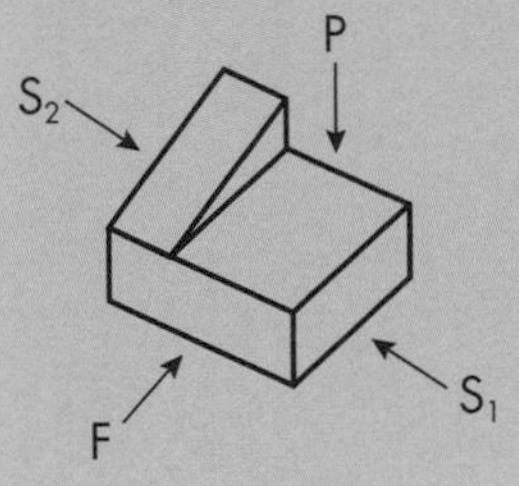

Chief Examiner says

Remember that hidden edges are shown as dotted lines and right angles should be right angles.

Solution

Test Yourself 4

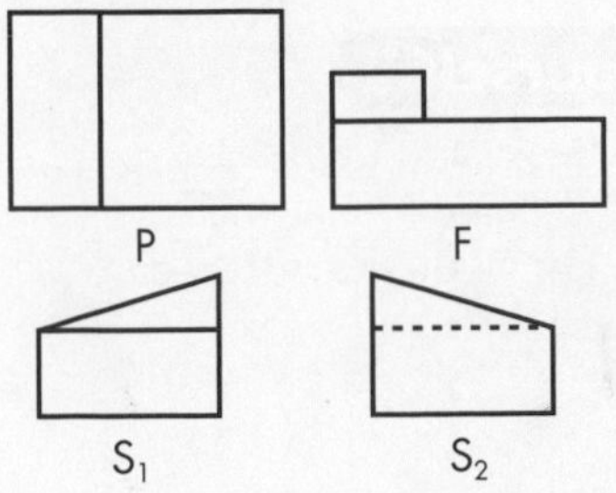

2 Probability 1

The language of probability and the probability scale

Revised

- The words *certain, likely, evens, unlikely* and *impossible* can be used to describe how likely it is for an event to happen.
- Probabilities can be expressed as fractions or decimals. All probabilities are between 0 and 1 inclusive.

  - 0 is the probability that an event cannot happen.
  - 1 is the probability that an event is certain to happen.

Calculating probabilities

Revised

- P(A) is a useful shorthand for the probability that A happens.
- For equally likely outcomes,

$$P(A) = \frac{\text{number of ways A can happen}}{\text{total possible number of outcomes}}$$

Chief Examiner says

Never write probabilities as '1 in 5' or as a ratio '1 to 5' or 1 : 5. You will lose marks if you do. Instead, write $\frac{1}{5}$ or 0.2.

Test Yourself 1

A bag contains five red, three green and four white balls (and no others). One is drawn out at random.

Work out these probabilities.

a P(red)

b P(green)

c P(white)

d P(black)

Solutions

Test Yourself 1

a $\frac{5}{12}$ — There are 5 red balls. There are 12 balls in the bag in total.

b $\frac{1}{4}$ — $\frac{3}{12} = \frac{1}{4}$ You should cancel fractions wherever possible.

c $\frac{1}{3}$ — $\frac{4}{12} = \frac{1}{3}$

d 0 — There are no black balls in the bag.

The probability of two events

Revised

Equally likely outcomes may be

- listed in a table.
- shown on a grid.

Chief Examiner says

Be systematic to make sure you don't miss out any possibilities.

Test Yourself 2

Arusha, Becky and Carol have seats H8, H9 and H10 at the cinema. List all the ways they can sit in these seats.

Solution

Test Yourself 2

H8	A	A	B	B	C	C
H9	B	C	A	C	A	B
H10	C	B	C	A	B	A

Experimental probability

Revised

- If outcomes are not equally likely you can use experimental or other evidence to estimate the probability of an event.
- Experimental probability $= \dfrac{\text{the number of times an event happens}}{\text{the total number of trials}}$
- You need to carry out a large number of trials to get a good estimate.

Test Yourself 3

A biased coin is tossed. It shows heads 54 times and tails 26 times.
What is the experimental probability that the coin will show heads?

Solution

Test Yourself 3

$\frac{54}{80} = \frac{27}{40}$ or 0.675

Unit C

3 Perimeter, area and volume 1

Perimeter and Area

Revised

- The perimeter is the distance round the outside of a shape.
- The area is the amount covered by a shape.

Chief Examiner says

Since perimeter is a length, its units will be centimetres (cm), metres (m) and so on.

The units of area are square centimetres (cm^2), square metres (m^2) and so on.

Test Yourself 1

a Find the perimeter of this shape.

b Find the area of this shape.

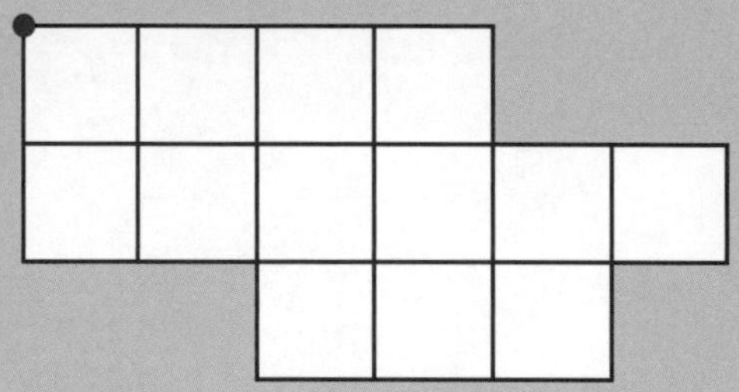

Solutions

Test Yourself 1

a Start at the dot and work round the shape.

Perimeter = 4 + 1 + 2 + 1 + 1 + 1 + 3 + 1 + 2 + 2

= 18 cm

b Count the squares.

Area = 13 cm^2

The area of a rectangle

Revised

- Area of a rectangle = length × width

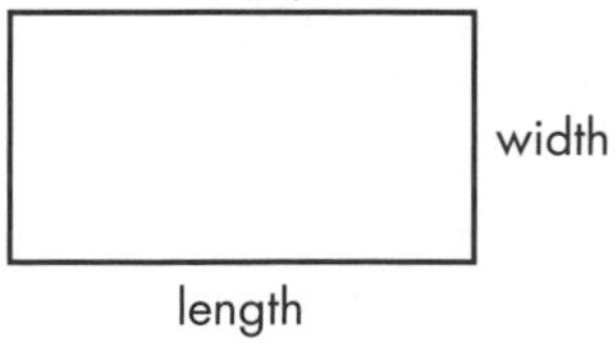

	… employment for less than 16 hours per week	
	Self-employed for 16 hours or more per week	
	Self-employed for less than 16 hours per week	
Not in Paid Employment	Not in paid employment, looking for work and available to start work	
	Not in paid employment, not looking for work and/or not available to start work (including retired)	
Voluntary work	Voluntary work	
Gap year	Gap year before starting HE	
In Education	Traineeship	
	Apprenticeship	
	Supported Internship	
	Full-time education	
	Part-time education	
	Higher Education	
Other	Unable to contact learner	
	Other – Please state	
Date that the outcome data was collected from the learner		

Staff Name (Print Name)			
Staff Signature		**Date**	
LSM Signature		**Date**	

CIS/PIF use only

Date received		Processed by		Date processed	

1 2 3 4/5 6 7 8/9 10 11 12/13 14 15

| 16/ 17

129.75

+

19
+23
42

4

534
-476

adele ______

Jones- ______

5

10

29
+29
58

28
+28

£15.

11111

129.75

10

25
25
50

Solution

Test Yourself 2

Area = length × width

= 3 × 8

= 24 cm²

Test Yourself 2

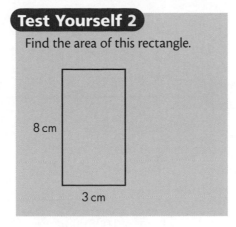

Find the area of this rectangle.

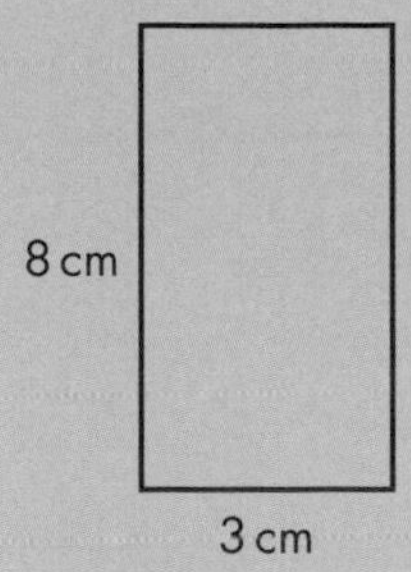

The volume of a cuboid

Revised

- The volume of a cuboid = length × width × height

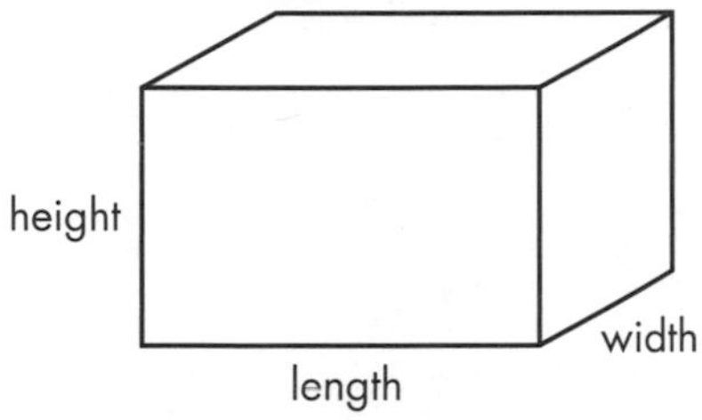

Chief Examiner says

The units of volume are cubic centimetres (cm^3), cubic metres (m^3) and so on.

Test Yourself 3

Find the volume of this cuboid.

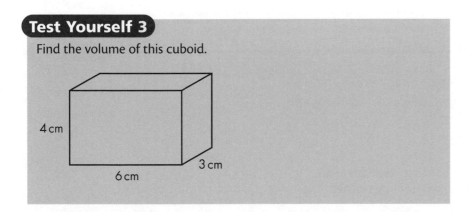

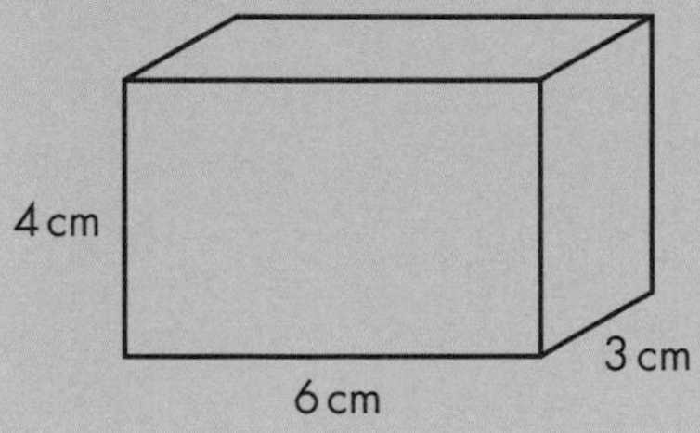

Solution

Test Yourself 3

Volume = length × width × height

= 6 × 3 × 4

= 72 cm³

4 Measures

Converting between measures

Revised

- See Unit A, Chapter for converting between linear metric units.
- As well as converting between linear metric units, you need to know how to convert area and volume units.

Length: $1\,\text{cm} = 10\,\text{mm}$ $\quad 1\,\text{m} = 100\,\text{cm}$

Area: $1\,\text{cm}^2 = 10^2\,\text{mm}^2 = 100\,\text{mm}^2$ $\quad 1\,\text{m}^2 = 100^2\,\text{cm}^2 = 10\,000\,\text{cm}^2$

Volume: $1\,\text{cm}^3 = 10^3\,\text{mm}^3 = 1000\,\text{mm}^3$ $\quad 1\,\text{m}^3 = 100^3\,\text{cm}^3 = 1\,000\,000\,\text{cm}^3$

Chief Examiner says

If you are asked to change the units of area or volume, it is often easiest to change the lengths you are given to the new units and to work out the area or volume using those. If you are not given the lengths, you need to use the information in the list above.

Test Yourself 1

Change these units.

a $10\,500\,\text{cm}^2$ to m^2

b $4.2\,\text{cm}^3$ to mm^3

Solutions

Test Yourself 1

a $10\,000\,\text{cm}^2 = 1\,\text{m}^2$

so $10\,500\,\text{cm}^2 = 10\,500 \div 10\,000$

$= 1.05\,\text{m}^2$

b $1\,\text{cm}^3 = 1000\,\text{mm}^3$

so $4.2\,\text{cm}^3 = 4.2 \times 1000$

$= 4200\,\text{mm}^3$

Accuracy in measurement

Revised

- A length measured as 45 cm to the nearest centimetre lies between 44.5 cm and 45.5 cm. So the lower bound is 44.5 cm and the upper bound is 45.5 cm.

Chief Examiner says

A common error is to give the upper bound as 45.49 cm in an example like this, since the upper bound cannot be reached. The correct bound, however, is 45.5 cm.

Test Yourself 2

Give the bounds of these measurements.

a 86 mm to the nearest millimetre

b 48 g to the nearest gram

c 52 litres to the nearest litre

d 80 cm to the nearest centimetre

Solutions

Test Yourself 2

a 85.5 mm and 86.5 mm

b 47.5 g and 48.5 g

c 51.5 litres and 52.5 litres

d 79.5 cm and 80.5 cm

Working to a sensible degree of accuracy

Revised

- Measurements should not be given too accurately for their purpose.
- The accuracy of the measures in the question give an idea of the accuracy required in the answer.

Compound measures

Revised

- The three compound measures you are most likely to meet are:
  - speed
  - density
  - population density

Chief Examiner says

The units tell you which way to divide. Density measured in g/cm^3 means grams (mass) divided by cm^3 (volume).

- You can use these triangles to help you solve problems relating to compound measures.
- $\text{Speed} = \dfrac{\text{Distance}}{\text{Time}}$
- $\text{Distance} = \text{Speed} \times \text{Time}$
- $\text{Time} = \dfrac{\text{Distance}}{\text{Speed}}$.

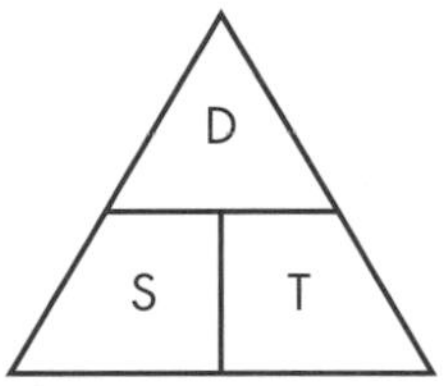

- $\text{Density} = \dfrac{\text{Mass}}{\text{Volume}}$
- $\text{Mass} = \text{Density} \times \text{Volume}$
- $\text{Volume} = \dfrac{\text{Mass}}{\text{Density}}$.

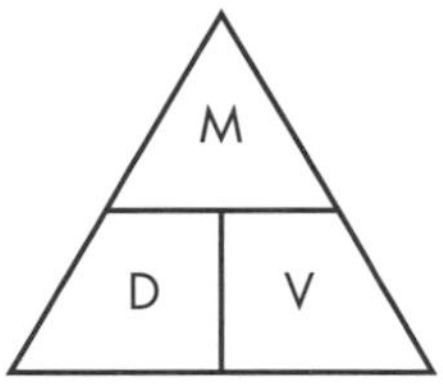

- $\text{Population density} = \dfrac{\text{Population}}{\text{Area}}$
- $\text{Population} = \text{Population density} \times \text{Area}$
- $\text{Area} = \dfrac{\text{Population}}{\text{Population density}}$.

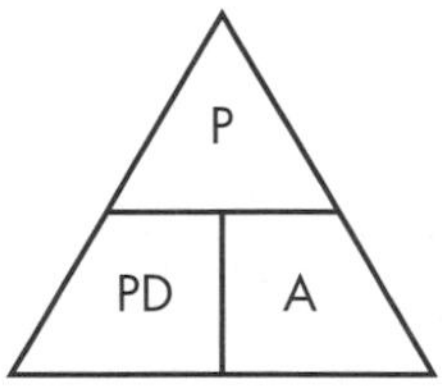

Test Yourself 3

a Jane drives for 2 hours at 70 mph and then for 30 minutes at 40 mph.

i Find the total distance for the journey.

ii Calculate her average speed for the journey.

Chief Examiner says

Don't be tempted to find the average of the two speeds – the times are different.

b The area of San Marino is 61 km² and its population is given as 24 000. What is its population density? Give your answer to a sensible degree of accuracy.

Solutions

Test Yourself 3

a **i** Distance = Speed × Time

At 70 mph she travels $2 \times 70 = 140$ miles.

At 40 mph she travels $0.5 \times 40 = 20$ miles

Total distance = $140 + 20$

$= 160$ miles

30 minutes = 0.5 hours

ii Total time = 2.5 hours

$$\text{Average speed} = \frac{\text{Total distance}}{\text{Total time}}$$

$$= \frac{160}{2.5}$$

$$= 64 \text{ mph}$$

b $$\text{Population density} = \frac{\text{Population}}{\text{Area}}$$

$$= 24\,000 \div 61$$

$$= 393.44\ldots$$

$$= 390 \text{ or } 400 \text{ people/km}^2$$

5 The area of triangles and parallelograms

The area of a triangle

Revised

- Area of a triangle

  $A = \frac{b \times h}{2}$

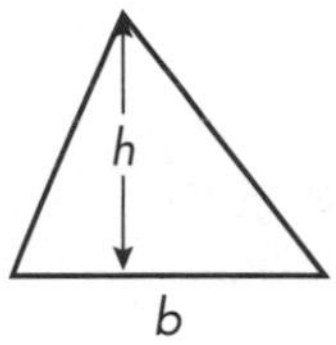

Test Yourself 1

The vertices of a triangle are at (2, 2), (2, −3) and (14, −3).

Draw axes and plot the triangle.

Find its area.

Solution

Test Yourself 1

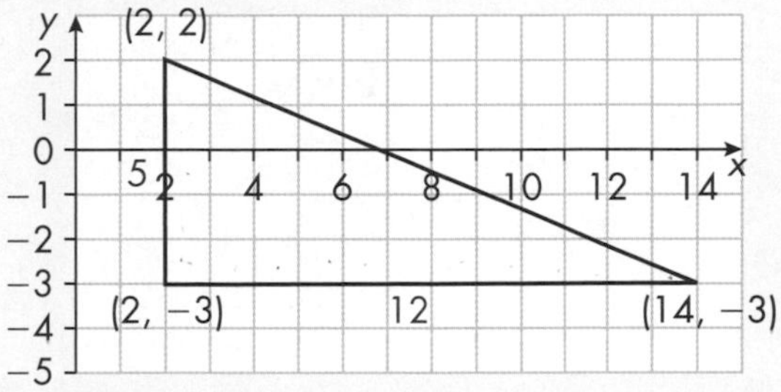

$A = \frac{12 \times 5}{2} = 30 \text{ units}^2$

The area of a parallelogram

Revised

- Area of a parallelogram

  $A = b \times h$

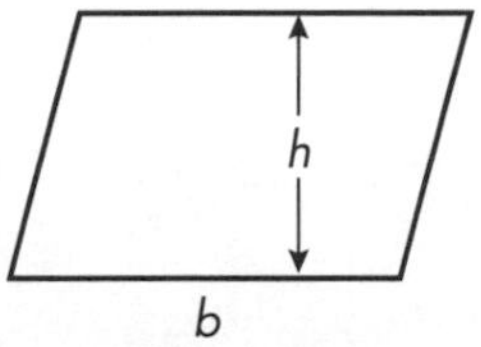

Solution

Test Yourself 2

Area = $6 \times 3.2 = 19.2 \text{ cm}^2$

Test Yourself 2

Find the area of this parallelogram.

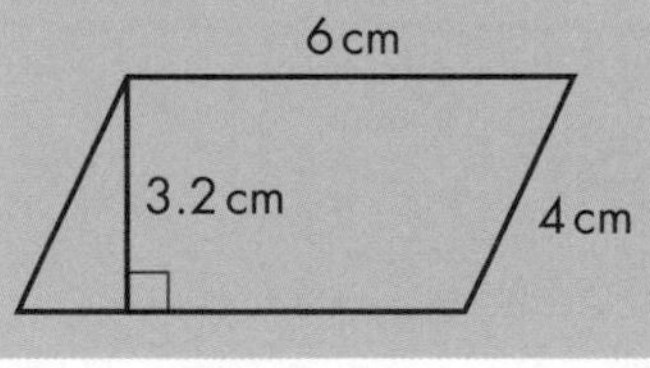

Chief Examiner says

Don't forget you need the perpendicular height not the slant height.

6 Probability 2

- See Unit C, Chapter 2 for more on probability.

The probability of an outcome not happening and Probability involving a given number of different outcomes

Revised

- P(A does not happen) = 1 − P(A), where P(A) means 'the probability that A happens'.
- Mutually exclusive outcomes are those which cannot happen together. If A, B and C are mutually exclusive outcomes, covering all possibilities, then P(A) + P(B) + P(C) = 1.

Test Yourself 1

A bag contains red, green and white balls and no others. One ball is drawn at random.

If P(red) = 0.5 and P(green) = 0.3, work out

a P(white)

b P(Not white)

Solutions

Test Yourself 1

a P(white) = 1 − (P(red) + P(green))
= 1 − (0.5 + 0.3)
= 0.2

b P(Not white) = 1 − P(white)
= 1 − 0.2
= 0.8

Expected frequency

Revised

- Expected frequency = Probability × Number of trials

Test Yourself 2

The probability that Amin's school bus is late is 0.2.

How many times would you expect it to be late in a school year of 195 days?

Solution

Test Yourself 2

Expected frequency = 0.2 × 195
= 39

Relative frequency

Revised

- $\text{Relative frequency} = \dfrac{\text{number of times event occurs}}{\text{total number of trials}}$
- When theoretical probabilities are not known, relative frequency can be used to estimate probability.
- The greater the number of trials, the better the estimate. The graph of relative frequency against the number of trials may vary greatly at first, but later 'settles down'.
- Relative frequency experiments may be used to test for bias. For example, you could carry out an experiment to see whether a dice is fair.

Test Yourself 3

Sarah has a biased dice. This graph shows the relative frequency of throwing a 6 when Sarah threw the dice 1000 times.

Use the graph to answer these questions.

a What is the approximate probability of scoring a 6 with Sarah's dice?

b If Sarah threw this dice 5000 times, how many times would she be likely to score a 6?

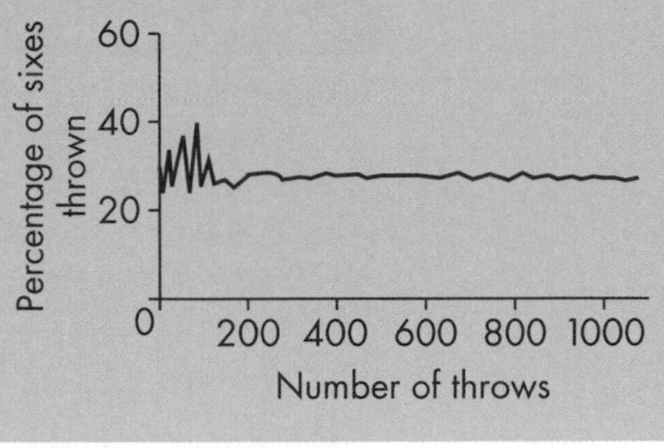

Solutions

Test Yourself 3

a P(6) = 30% — The graph 'settles down' at about 30%.

b $5000 \times 30\% = 1500$ times

7 Perimeter, area and volume 2

- See Unit C, Chapters 3 and 5 for more on perimeter, area and volume.

The circumference of a circle and The area of a circle

Revised

- Circumference of a circle
  $C = \pi d$

'Circumference' is just another name for the perimeter of a circle.

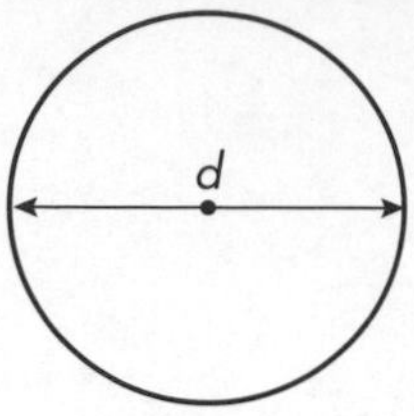

- Area of a circle
  $A = \pi r^2$

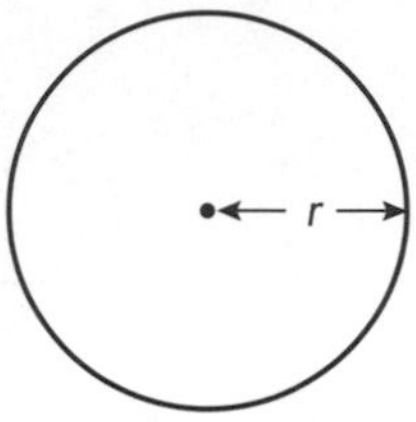

- You may be asked to find an exact value for the circumference or area of a circle. This means leave π in your answer.

Test Yourself 1

a A circular flowerbed has a diameter of 8 m. Find the perimeter of the flowerbed in terms of π.

b A circular pond has an area of 40 m². Calculate the radius of the pond.

Solutions

Test Yourself 1

a Circumference of circle $= \pi d$

$= \pi \times 8 = 8\pi$

Do not substitute the numerical value of π.

Perimeter of the flowerbed $= 8\pi$ m

b $\pi r^2 = 40$

$r^2 = \dfrac{40}{\pi} = 12.732$

$r = \sqrt{12.732}$

$= 3.57$ m (correct to 2 d.p.)

The area of complex shapes

Revised

- To find the area of a complex shape, divide it into shapes that you can find the area of, such as rectangles and triangles.
- You can split up the shape or enclose it and take off the remainder.

Test Yourself 2

Find the area of this shape.

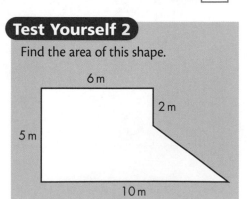

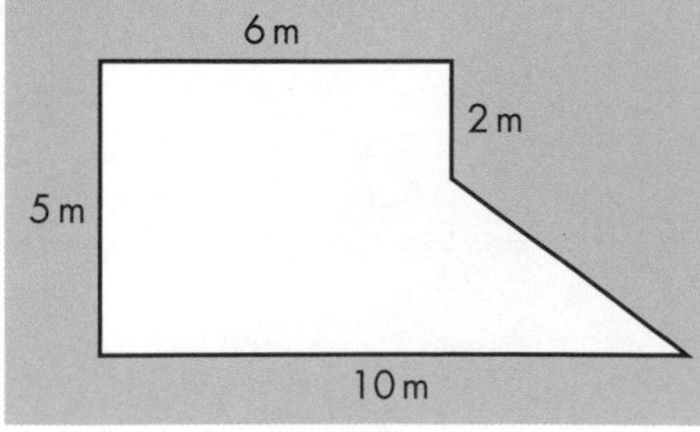

Solution

Test Yourself 2

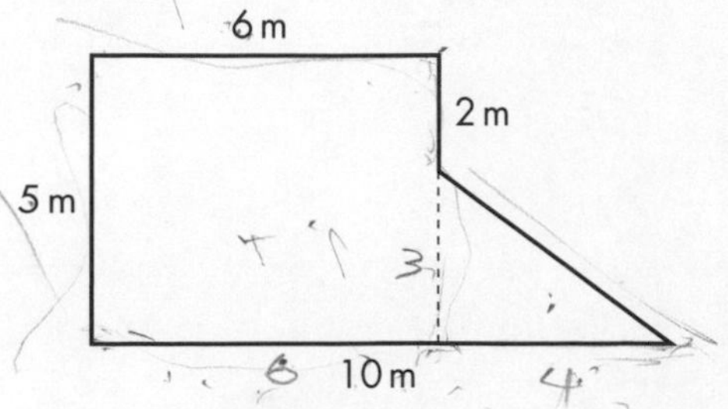

Area of rectangle $= 5 \times 6 = 30$

Area of triangle $= \frac{1}{2} \times 4 \times 3 = 6$

Base = 10 – 6 = 4 and height = 5 – 2 = 3

Total area = 36 m²

The volume of complex shapes

Revised

- To find the volume of a complex shape, divide it into shapes that you can find the volume of, such as cuboids.

Solution

Test Yourself 3

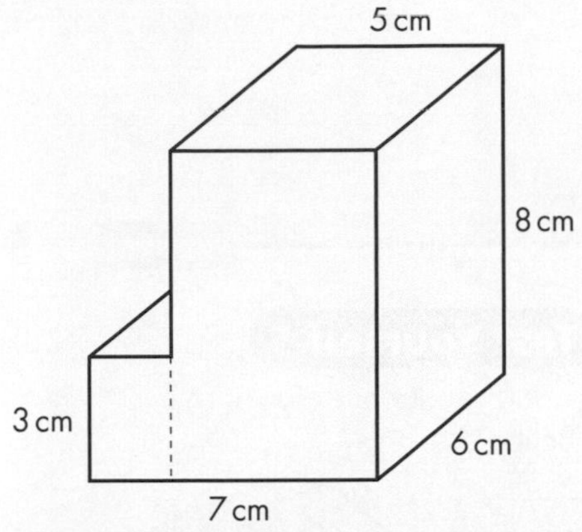

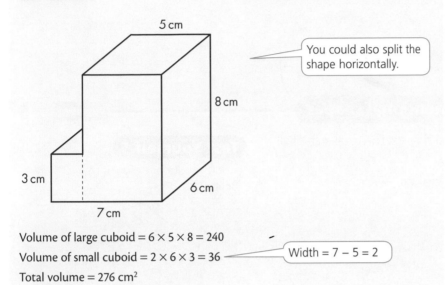

You could also split the shape horizontally.

Volume of large cuboid = 6 × 5 × 8 = 240

Volume of small cuboid = 2 × 6 × 3 = 36 (Width = 7 − 5 = 2)

Total volume = 276 cm²

Test Yourself 3

Find the volume of this shape.

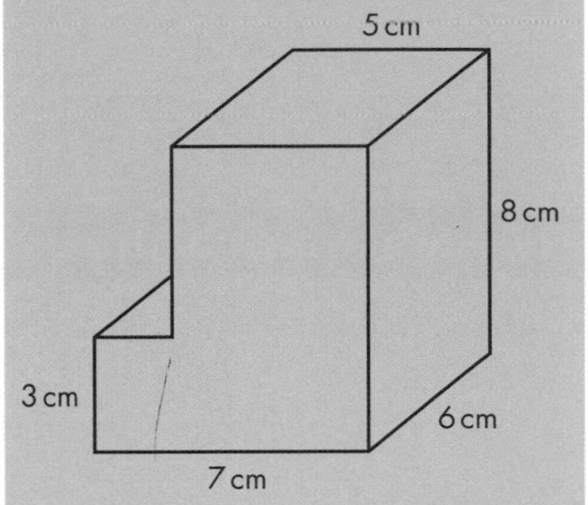

The volume of a prism

Revised

- A prism is a three-dimensional shape with a constant cross-section.
- These are some examples of prisms.

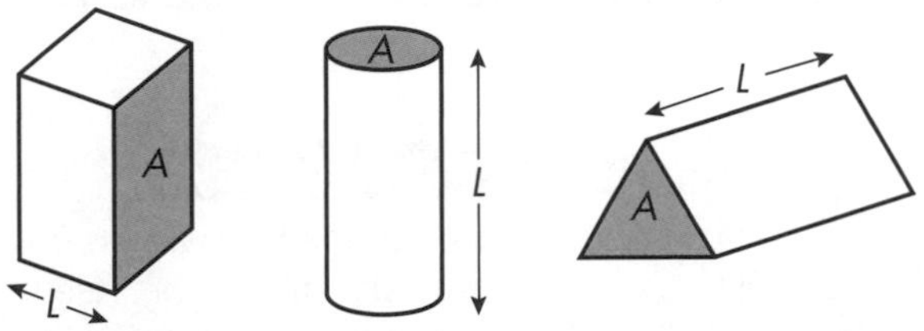

Cuboid Cylinder Triangular prism

- For all prisms, Volume = Area of cross-section × length, or $V = A \times L$.

Chief Examiner says

Don't forget to include the units in your answer.

Test Yourself 4

Find the volume of this shape.

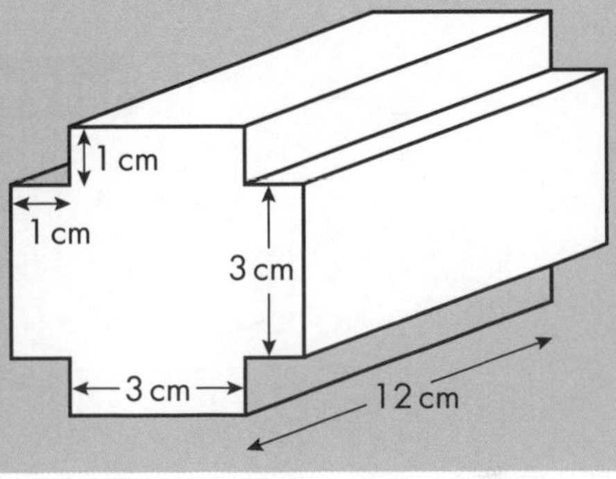

Solution

Test Yourself 4

Area of cross-section $= 5 \times 5 - 4 \times 1 \times 1$

$= 25 - 4$

$= 21\ \text{cm}^2$

Volume of prism = Area of cross-section × length

$= 21 \times 12$

$= 252\ \text{cm}^3$

The surface area of three-dimensional shapes

Revised

- The surface area of a three-dimensional shape is the total area of all its faces.
- You can draw the net of the solid to help you.

Test Yourself 5

Find the surface area of this cuboid.

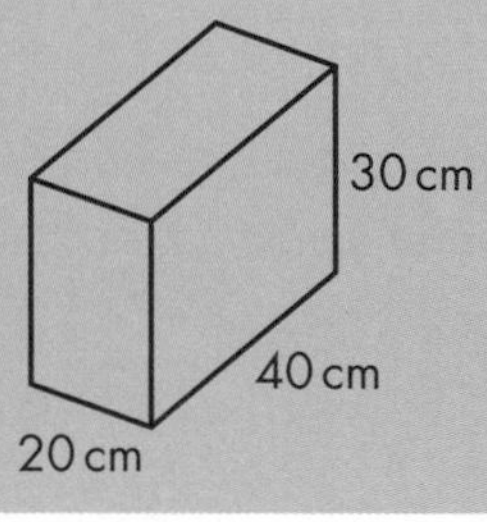

Solution

Test Yourself 5

Surface Area $= 2 \times \text{top} + 2 \times \text{side} + 2 \times \text{front}$

$= 2(20 \times 40) + 2(40 \times 30) + 2(20 \times 30)$

$= 1600 + 2400 + 1200$

$= 5200\ \text{cm}^2$

The volume of a cylinder and The surface area of a cylinder

Revised

- A cylinder is a special type of prism with a circle as its cross-section.
- Volume of a cylinder $V = \pi r^2 h$
- Curved surface area of a cylinder $= 2\pi rh$
- Total surface area of a cylinder $= 2\pi rh + 2\pi r^2$
- You may be asked to find an exact value for the volume or surface area of a cylinder. This means leave π in your answer.

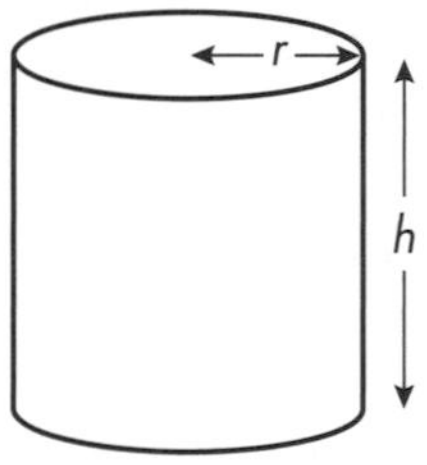

Chief Examiner says

Don't use rounded answers in the middle of a calculation. Keep all the figures on your calculator (e.g. use the answer function) and just round at the end. Give your answer to a sensible degree of accuracy if no specific accuracy is stated.

Test Yourself 6

Find the volume and surface area of this cylinder.

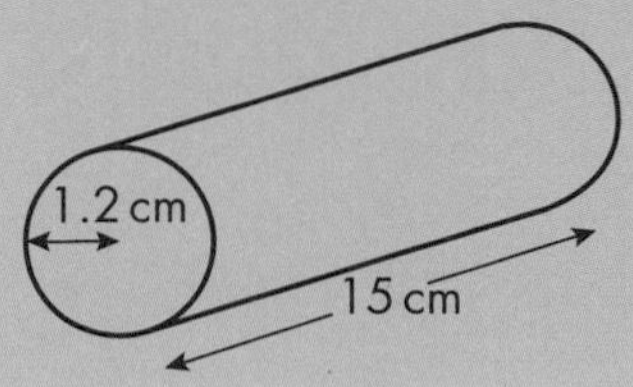

Solution

Test Yourself 6

Volume $= \pi r^2 h$

$= \pi \times 1.2^2 \times 15$

$= 67.9\ \text{cm}^3$ (to 1 d.p.)

Total surface area $= 2\pi rh + 2\pi r^2$

$= 2 \times \pi \times 1.2 \times 15 + 2 \times \pi \times 1.2^2$

$= 122.1\ \text{cm}^2$ (to 1 d.p.)

8 Using a calculator

- Calculators vary. The position and symbols used on the keys differ, depending on the make and model of calculator. The order in which the keys have to be pressed can also vary. Make sure you know how your calculator works. Don't borrow a different calculator or change your calculator just before an exam. If you are unsure, ask your teacher.
- For order of operations, see Unit A Chapter 12.

Fractions on your calculator

Revised

- To key a fraction into your calculator, use the [$a\frac{b}{c}$] button. For example, to input the fraction $\frac{3}{4}$, key in [3] [$a\frac{b}{c}$] [4].
- To convert a fraction to a decimal, key it in, then press [=] [$a\frac{b}{c}$].

Test Yourself 1

a Change $\frac{3}{8}$ to a decimal.

b Find $\frac{3}{5}$ of £8.

c Write $\frac{25}{100}$ as a fraction in its simplest form.

d Work out $1\frac{2}{3} + \frac{3}{4}$.

Solutions

Test Yourself 1

Or you could input [3] [÷] [8] [=]

a [3] [$a\frac{b}{c}$] [8] [=] [$a\frac{b}{c}$] = 0.375

b [3] [$a\frac{b}{c}$] [5] [×] [8] [=] [$a\frac{b}{c}$] = 4.8

= £4.80

c [2] [5] [$a\frac{b}{c}$] [1] [0] [0] [=] 1 ⌟ 4

$= \frac{1}{4}$

d [1] [$a\frac{b}{c}$] [2] [$a\frac{b}{c}$] [3] [+] [3] [$a\frac{b}{c}$] [4] [=]

= 2 ⌟ 5 ⌟ 12

$= 2\frac{5}{12}$

Chief Examiner says

The display 4 ⌟ 4 ⌟ 5 means $4\frac{4}{5}$. Press [$a\frac{b}{c}$] again and the answer will change to decimal form. Make sure you interpret the display correctly. Here the question is in pounds, so the answer should have two figures after the decimal point.

Rounding to a given number of significant figures

Revised

- See Unit A, Chapter 12 for rounding to 1 significant figure.
- In any number, the first digit from the left which is not 0 is the first significant figure.
- When rounding to a given number of significant figures,
  - if the first digit not required is 4 or less, then just ignore it and, if necessary, include the correct number of zeros to show the size of the number. For example, 0.3719 to 2 significant figures is 0.37 and 3719 to 2 significant figures is 3700.
  - if the first digit not required is 5 or more, add 1 to the last significant figure required and, if necessary, include the correct number of zeros to show the size of the number. For example, 0.062 85 to 2 significant figures is 0.063 and 6285 to 2 significant figures is 6300.

Test Yourself 2

Write the following correct to 3 significant figures.

a 43 287

b 0.003 454 9

c 6 036 456

Chief Examiner says

The number 0.997 correct to 2 significant figures is 1.0 but correct to 1 significant figure it is 1. Extra zeros are used only to show the size of a number, as in 200, for example.

Solutions

Test Yourself 2

a 43 300

b 0.003 45

Chief Examiner says

Just look at the fourth significant figure. Don't start at the right-hand end and round each digit in turn.

c 6 040 000

9 Trial and improvement

Solving equations by trial and improvement

Revised

- Some equations cannot be solved by algebraic methods. To solve them you need to use a trial and improvement procedure.
- To start trial and improvement you need a first estimate. This could come from a graph, but in examinations you are usually given a hint to the first estimate.
- Start with two values, one which gives too big a result and the other too small. The true solution will be between them.
- Try in between (usually half way).
- Continue the process, finding two values one of which is too big and the other too small until you have an answer to the required accuracy.

Test Yourself 1

A solution of the equation
$x^3 + 4x - 8 = 0$
lies between 1 and 2.

Find the solution correct to 1 decimal place.

Chief Examiner says

Don't forget to write down the outcome of each trial. There is no need to keep more than three decimal places.

Solution

Test Yourself 1

Chief Examiner says

Remember that it is the solution (for x) that is required to 1 decimal place, not the outcome of the trial.

$x = 1$	$1^3 + 4 \times 1 - 8 = -3$	Too small.
$x = 2$	$2^3 + 4 \times 2 - 8 = 8$	Too big. Try between 1 and 2.
$x = 1.5$	$1.5^3 + 4 \times 1.5 - 8 = 1.375$	Too big. Try between 1 and 1.5.
$x = 1.2$	$1.2^3 + 4 \times 1.2 - 8 = -1.472$	Too small. Try between 1.2 and 1.5.
$x = 1.3$	$1.3^3 + 4 \times 1.3 - 8 = -0.603$	Too small. Try between 1.3 and 1.5.
$x = 1.4$	$1.4^3 + 4 \times 1.4 - 8 = 0.344$	Too big.

The answer lies between 1.3 and 1.4, so the answer, to 1 decimal place, is either 1.3 or 1.4.

To check which is the correct one try halfway between.

$x = 1.35$	$1.35^3 + 4 \times 1.35 - 8 = -0.139625$	Too small.

So the answer is between 1.35 and 1.4.

$x = 1.4$ (to 1 d.p.)

10 Enlargement

The scale factor of enlargement

Revised

- When one shape is an enlargement of another, the two shapes are similar.
- If two shapes are similar all the corresponding lengths have the same scale factor.
- Scale factor $= \dfrac{\text{length of image}}{\text{lenth of object}} = \dfrac{PQ}{AB} = \dfrac{PR}{AC} = \dfrac{QR}{BC}$

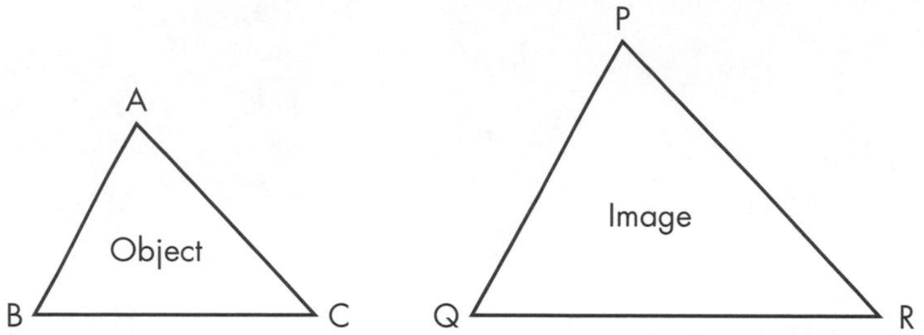

- You can use this triangle to help you.
  - Image length = Scale factor × Object length
  - Object length $= \dfrac{\text{Image length}}{\text{Scale factor}}$
  - Scale factor $= \dfrac{\text{Image length}}{\text{Object length}}$

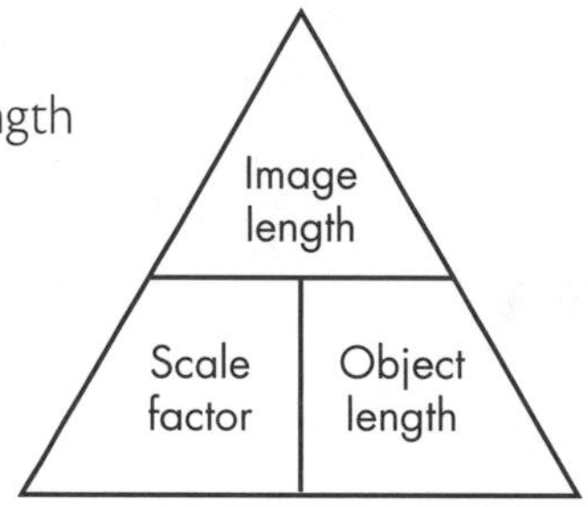

Chief Examiner says

Make sure you use corresponding sides.
If ABC is similar to PQR then AB corresponds to PQ, BC corresponds to QR and AC corresponds to PR.

Test Yourself 1

Triangles ABC and PQR are similar.
Calculate the lengths of PR and BC.

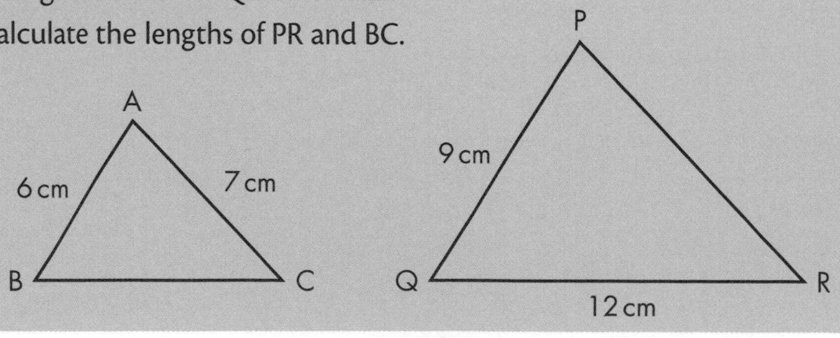

Solution

Test Yourself 1

Scale factor $= \dfrac{\text{Image length}}{\text{Object length}} = \dfrac{9}{6} = 1.5$

PR = Scale factor × Object length = 1.5 × 7 = 10.5 cm

BC $= \dfrac{\text{Image length}}{\text{Scale factor}} = \dfrac{12}{1.5} = 8$ cm

The area and volume of similar shapes

Revised

- For similar shapes, the area scale factor is the square of the linear scale factor.
- For similar shapes, the volume scale factor is the cube of the linear scale factor.

Test Yourself 2

An enlargement is made of this rectangle with scale factor 3.

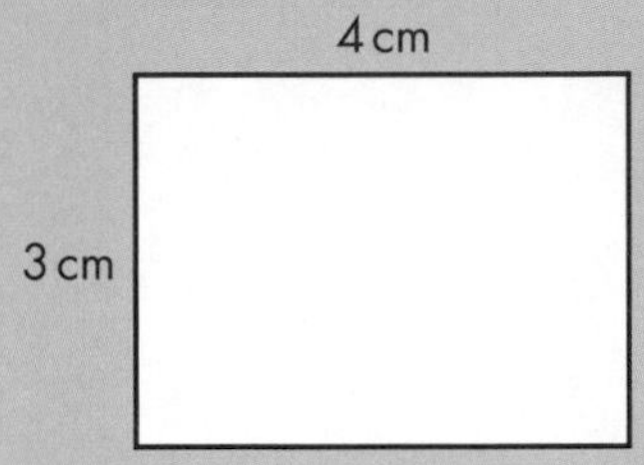

a Find the dimensions of the new rectangle.

b How many times bigger than the area of the original rectangle is the area of the new rectangle?

Solutions

Test Yourself 2

a 12 cm by 9 cm

b Area of original rectangle $= 4 \times 3 = 12\,\text{cm}^2$

Area of new rectangle $= 12 \times 9 = 108\,\text{cm}^2$

Number of times bigger $= \frac{108}{12} = 9$

9 is 3^2 and is the length scale factor squared.

11 Graphs

Distance–time graphs

Revised

- See Unit B, Chapter 10 for travel graphs.
- Travel graphs can also be called distance–time graphs.

Other real-life graphs

Revised

- Look at the labels on the axes – they tell you what the graph is about.
- Check whether the graph is a straight line or a curve.
- Look at the slope of the graph – this gives you the rate of change.

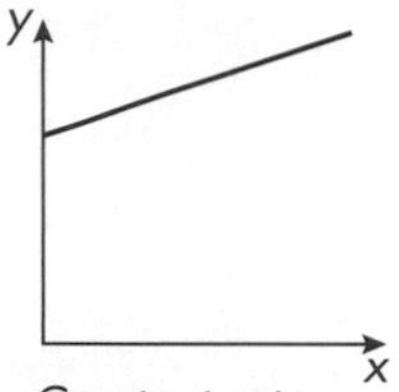

Constant rate of change

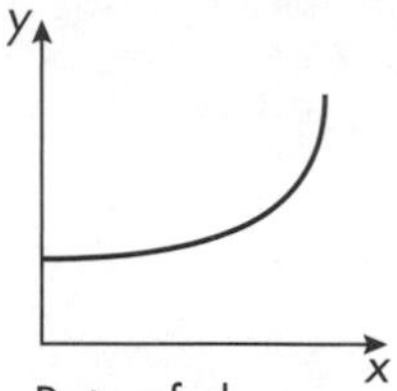

Rate of change increasing

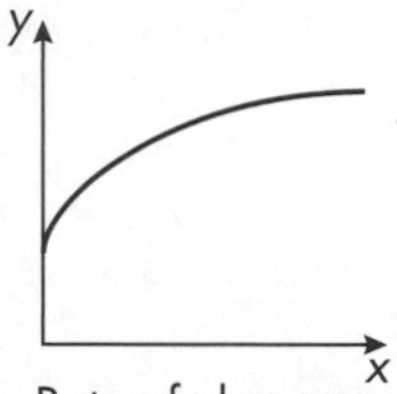

Rate of change decreasing

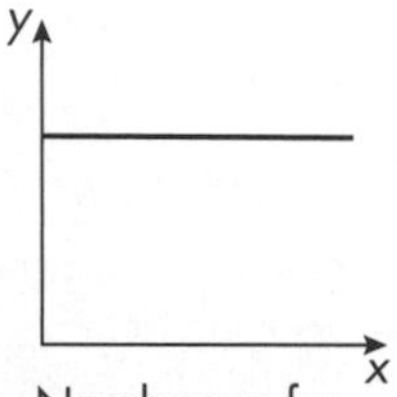

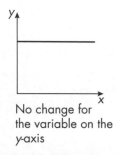

No change for the variable on the y-axis

Solution

Test Yourself 1

Since the radius is gradually decreasing, the rate of change will increase until it overflows.

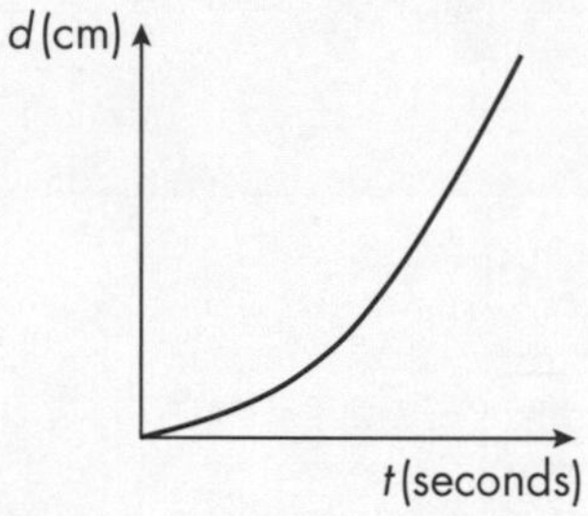

Test Yourself 1

Water is poured into this vessel at a constant rate. Sketch a graph of depth of water (d cm) against time (t seconds).

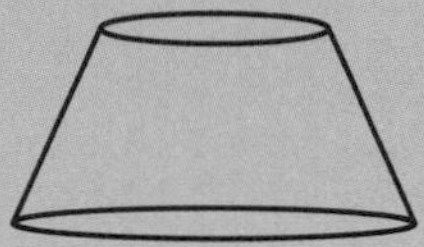

Quadratic graphs

Revised

- Graphs of equations of the form $y = ax^2 + bx + c$ are parabolas.
- They look like this.

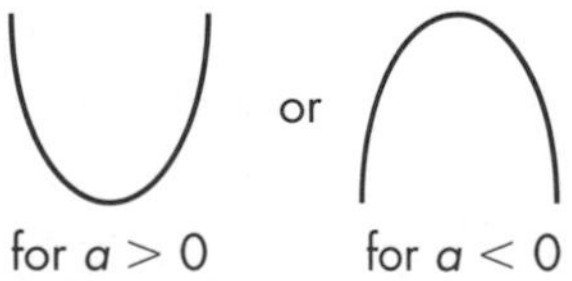

- All parabolas are symmetrical. This symmetry can also be seen in the table of values.
- The solutions of $ax^2 + bx + c = k$ are the values of x where the graph of $y = ax^2 + bx + c$ crosses the line $y = k$.

Chief Examiner says

When drawing an accurate graph, use a table to work out the points, even if you are not asked to do so.

Chief Examiner says

As well as doing it by hand, can you also use a spreadsheet to work out the values and draw these graphs?

Test Yourself 2

a Complete this table for $y = x^2 - 4x + 3$ and draw the graph for $-1 \leqslant x \leqslant 5$.

x	−1	0	1	2	3	4	5
x^2	1	0	1	4	9	16	25
$-4x$	4	0	−4	−8	−12	−16	−20
3	3	3	3	3	3	3	3
y							

b Use the graph to solve these equations.

i $x^2 - 4x + 3 = 0$ **ii** $x^2 - 4x + 3 = 6$

Solutions

Test Yourself 2

a

x	−1	0	1	2	3	4	5
x^2	1	0	1	4	9	16	25
$-4x$	4	0	−4	−8	−12	−16	−20
3	3	3	3	3	3	3	3
y	8	3	0	−1	0	3	8

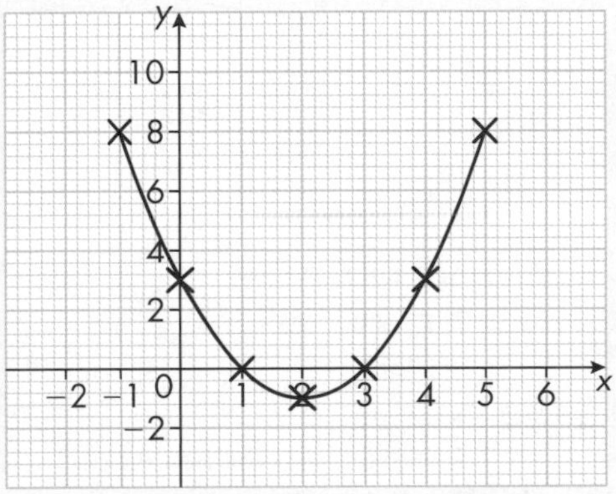

b **i** $x = 1$ or $x = 3$ — Look where the graph crosses $y = 0$, the x-axis.

ii $x = -0.6$ or 4.6 — Look where the graph crosses $y = 6$.

Three-dimensional coordinates

Revised

- To describe a point in three dimensions there are three coordinates, x, y and z.

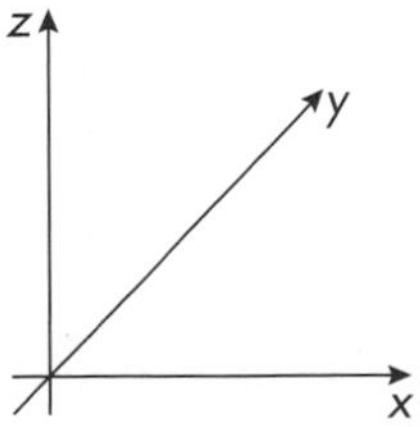

- The x and y-axes lie flat with the z-axis vertical.
- The midpoint of the line segment joining the points (a, b, c) and (d, e, f) is $\left(\frac{a+d}{2}, \frac{b+e}{2}, \frac{c+f}{2}\right)$.

Test Yourself 3

ABCDEFGH is a cuboid. Write down the coordinates of the following points.

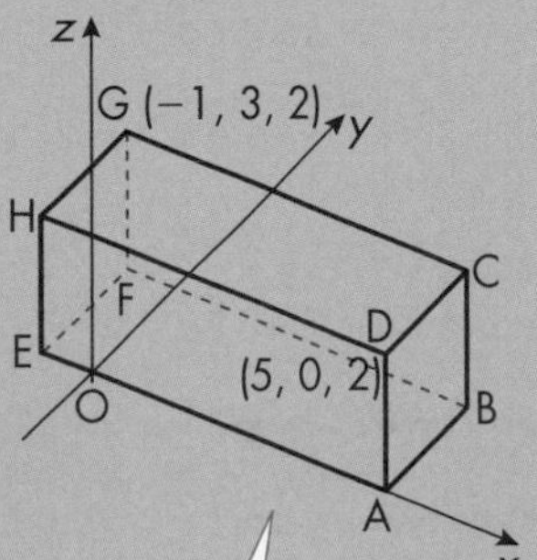

a C
b H
c F

Solutions

Test Yourself 3

a (5, 3, 2)
b (−1, 0, 2)
c (−1, 3, 0)

12 Percentages

Percentage increase and decrease

Revised

- See Unit B, Chapter 12 for one method of calculating a percentage increase or decrease.
- This is an alternative method which is quicker when you have to calculate repeated percentage change.
  - Add or subtract the percentage to or from 100.
  - Change the result to a decimal. (This is the multiplier.) For example, to increase by 6% the multiplier is 1.06; to decrease by 12% the multiplier is 0.88.
  - Then multiply.
  - For repeated change, use the multiplier for each repeat. For example, to increase by 6% five times, multiply by $(1.06)^5$.
  - See Unit A, Chapter 12 for using your calculator to work out powers.

Test Yourself 1

a Sheila invests £6000 at 4% compound interest. How much will the investment be worth after 10 years?

b A car depreciates in value by 12% per year. It cost £12 500 when new. How much will it be worth after

i 2 years?

ii 5 years?

Chief Examiner says

Compound interest is repeated percentage increase.

Solutions

Test Yourself 1

a Value $= 6000 \times (1.04)^{10}$
$= £8881.47$ (to the nearest penny)

b i Value after 2 years $= 12\,500 \times 0.88^2$
$= £9680$

ii Value after 5 years $= 12\,500 \times 0.55^5$
$= £6596.65$ (to the nearest penny)

Solving problems

Revised

- See Unit B, Chapter 4.

Index numbers

Revised

- Index numbers are a measure of annual increase in things like the cost of living or average earnings.
- The Retail Price Index (RPI) was fixed at 100 in 1987. So if in a certain year it was 218 this means that retail prices have increased by 118% or, in other words, have been multiplied by 2.18 since 1987.

Test Yourself 2

a In 1987 the cost of a loaf of bread was 56p.

How much would you expect a loaf of bread to have cost in 2009 when the RPI was 214.

b In 2003 the Average Earnings Index in an industry was 113.5.

In 2008 the Average Earnings Index was 137.7.

By what percentage did average earnings increase from 2003 to 2008?

Solutions

Test Yourself 2

a $0.56 \times 2.14 = £1.20$ (to the nearest penny)

b Increase $= 137.7 - 113.5 = 24.2$

Percentage increase $= \dfrac{24.2}{113.5} \times 100 = 21.3\%$ (to 1 d.p.)